Nora Chadwick

THE CELTS

WITH AN

INTRODUCTORY CHAPTER

BY J. X. W. P. CORCORAN

PENGUIN BOOKS

PENGUIN BOOKS

Published by the Penguin Group
Penguin Books Ltd, 27 Wrights Lane, London W8 5TZ, England
Penguin Books USA Inc., 375 Hudson Street, New York, New York 10014, USA
Penguin Books Australia Ltd, Ringwood, Victoria, Australia
Penguin Books Canada Ltd, 10 Alcorn Avenue, Toronto, Ontario, Canada M4V 3B2
Penguin Books (NZ) Ltd, 182–190 Wairau Road, Auckland 10, New Zealand

Penguin Books Ltd, Registered Offices: Harmondsworth, Middlesex, England

First published by Pelican Books 1971
Reprinted in Penguin Books 1991
3 5 7 9 10 8 6 4 2

Printed in England by Clays Ltd, St Ives plc
Set in Monotype Bembo

Contents

List of Plates

Preface

THE Celts may be taken as a starting-point for a study of the long series of peoples whose arrival and settlement in Britain have contributed to its history. They provide a link between the prehistoric period – at the end of which they had emerged as the product of much cultural evolution – and the early historic period. The Celts in the prehistoric period had no writing, and so were unable to leave written records of themselves. We know of them from place-names, from the reports of classical writers – often their enemies – and from archaeology. For centuries they have been relegated to the remote parts of our islands, beautiful but somewhat inaccessible, and commercially and politically of little importance. In consequence their part in our history has been neglected. More recently, however, intensified archaeological research has begun to remedy this. A new appreciation of the Celtic peoples, both on the Continent and in the British Isles, has been gained through excavation and other archaeological techniques and has allowed a more accurate assessment of this ancient people, older than the classical Roman world, older than the history of Britain. In so doing it has given an added dimension to the distant past. It has emphasized that the art of writing was a relatively late acquisition as far as the contemporary recording of the history of early Europe and the British Isles is concerned.

We have been in the habit of thinking of the Celts as they were left by their Saxon and Norman conquerors, a somewhat backward and relatively thin population in the less accessible mountain highlands of Scotland and Wales. But this is only the end of the story which stretches much further back into the centuries before Christ. Earlier than this the Celtic peoples occupied at least the greater part of the British Isles. At the time of their greatest power and extent the political divisions of the land were Celtic, their rulers had Celtic names, their laws and institutions and their economy and way of life were all Celtic, from Scotland to Kent, and from the Aran Islands to the North Sea. Indeed, the Celtic peoples of the British Isles formed a part of the great Celtic peoples who occupied and ruled a large part of Europe before their conquest by the Romans.

It is with the origins and development of these Celtic peoples in Britain, their art and their religion – first heathen and then Christian – and their unique and individual contribution to European society that this book is mainly concerned, up to the time of the gradual transformation of their culture in parts of Britain, first under the Romans and later by the Saxons. The Celts of Britain and Ireland are not the earliest we know, nor are they the Celts of widest distribution. They are, however, the Celtic peoples about whom we know most, for they have left us the most complete picture of their civilization, having enjoyed freedom from foreign, especially Roman, conquest longer than their continental neighbours – and in parts escaped it altogether – and thus preserved their own culture in a purer form. Wherever relevant, however, some discussion of the whole background of the Celtic world is included.

I am greatly indebted to Dr John X. W. P. Corcoran, who read the manuscript in its final stages and made many valuable suggestions, as well as contributing the preliminary chapter on the archaeological evidence for Celtic origins, and additional material in chapters 5 and 6.

MAPS

0
50
100
Roman Miles.
Coloniae or Municipia
Civitas capitals
Other towns
Fortresses
Civitas boundaries are approximate only
Inchtuthil
CALEDONIAN CONFEDERACY
Carpow
Antonine Wall
VOTADINI
DAMNONII
SELGOVAE
NOVANTAE
Hadrian's Wall
Carlisle
CARVETII
BRIGANTES
PARISI
York
Brough
SETANTII
Anglesey
DECI ANGLI
Deva
ORDOVICES
CORNOVII
CORITANI
Caister
Burgh Cas.
ICENI
Godmanchester
DEMETAE
DOBUNNI
CATUVELLAUNI
TRINOVANTES
Camulodunum
Carmarthen
Glevum
Corinium
Londinium
Isca
Venta Silurum
ATREBATES
CANTIACI
Bath
BELGAE
DUROTRIGES
REGNENSES
DUMNONII
Dorchester
Isle of Wight
-H.A.S-

Monastery
Royal site
Other sites
Eremitic monasteries
Regions of England occupied by the Jutes, Angles and Saxons
Hadrian's Wall
Iona
Fahan
Dooey
Aileach
Derry
Bann
Lough Ravel
Lisnacroghera
ULSTER
Inismurray
Devenish
Emain
Armagh
Lough Gara
CONNAUGHT
Cruachan
MEATH
Ardakillan
Fore
Kells
Boyne
Roscommon
Uisneach
Tara
Ballinderry
Clonard
Lagore
Clonmacnois
Finglas
Clonfert
Rahan
Durrow
Liffey
Kildare
Tallaght
Aran
Lorrha
Cahercommaun
Terryglass
Dunailinn
Inis Cealtra
Clonenagh
Glendalough
LEINSTER
Shannon
Cashel
Barrow
Carraig Aille
MUNSTER
Suir
Blackwater
Lismore
Garryduff
Garranes
St David's
0
50
100 Miles
0
50
100
150 Km.
-H.A.S-

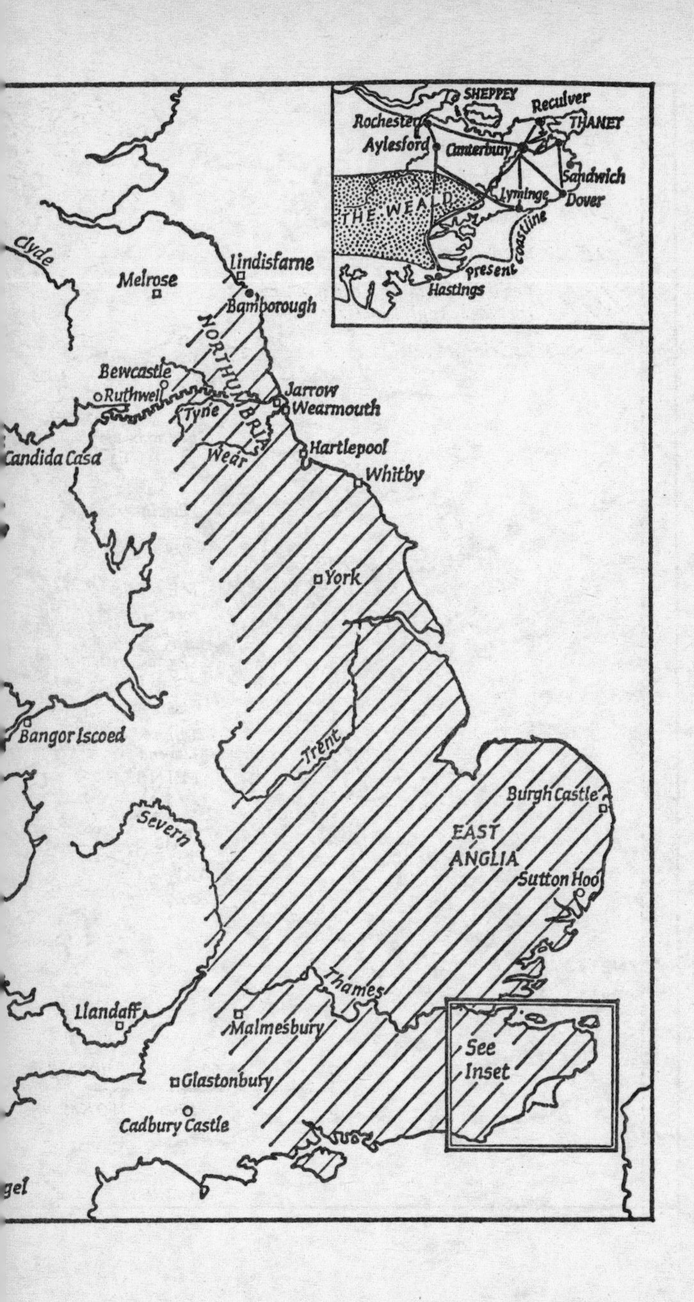
SHEPPEY
Reculver
Rochester
THANET
Aylesford
Canterbury
Sandwich
THE WEALD
Lyminge
Dover
coastline
present
Hastings
Clyde
Melrose
Lindisfarne
Bamborough
NORTHUMBRIA
Bewcastle
Ruthwell
Tyne
Jarrow
Wearmouth
Wear
Candida Casa
Hartlepool
Whitby
York
Trent
Bangor Iscoed
Severn
Burgh Castle
EAST ANGLIA
Sutton Hoo
Thames
Llandaff
Malmesbury
See Inset
Glastonbury
Cadbury Castle
gel

21
BELGAE
Rhine
SUEVI
TREVERI
9
27
35
BELLOVACI
PARISI
4
28
13
32
12
OSISMI
REDONES
CORIOSOLITAE
15
Armorica
Seine
CARNUTES
23
VENETI
19
BITURIGES
25
NAMNETES
34
SEQUANI
18
16
HELVETII
3
AEDUI
ARVERNI
Rhône
26
AQUITANI
VOLCAE TECTOSAGES
31
ALLOBRIGES
8
SALUVII
29
7
20
LIGURIANS
17
IBERIANS
CYNETES

1 Ambracia
2 Aquileia
3 Augustodunum
4 Basse-Yutz (Niederjutz)
5 Delphi
6 Drunemeton
7 Entremont
8 Glanum
9 Goloring
10 Gundestrup
11 Hallstatt
12 Heuneburg
13 Hirschlanden
14 Holzgerlingen
15 Kermaria
16 La Tène
17 Lerins
18 Luxeuil
19 Marmoutier
20 Massilia
21 Medionemeton
22 Miletus
23 Montbouy
24 Mšecke Žehrovice
25 Neuvy-en-Sullias
26 Nemetobriga
27 Pfalzfeld
28 Reinheim
29 Roquepertuse
30 Rome
31 Tolosa
32 Trichtingen
33 Únětice
34 Vix
35 Waldalgesheim
GALATAE - Names of tribes and peoples
0 500 Miles
0 500 Km.
NES
Elbe
24.
33
BOII
Pannonia
SCYTHIANS
Illyria
Danube
6
GALATAE
1
5.
22

CHAPTER I

The Origins of the Celts: The Archaeological Evidence

J. X. W. P. Corcoran

IT is difficult to pin-point the origins of a people either in space or in time, for throughout the story of man there are certain threads of continuity. These threads reach backwards through millennia of the pre-literate past in such a manner that significant transitions are rarely perceptible, and then only after those transitions have been accomplished. It is also difficult to define concisely what is meant by Celt or Celtic. To the Greek and Latin writers of the second half of the first millennium B.C. the Celts were recognizable as a cultural entity occupying part of Europe. The words *Keltoi* or *Galli* (Gauls), the name used by the Romans, presumably required no explanation. In more recent times expressions such as the 'Celtic Fringe' have been used freely without the necessity of explaining that the term applies to the Celts of Brittany, Britain and Ireland. These latter are the Celts, something of whose culture, languages, law and social institutions has survived into modern times. They would seem to be the inheritors of a Celtic way of life which originated in the prehistoric past.

If, for the present, this premise may be accepted, that the origins of the Celts belong to the prehistoric past, the corollary must follow that there can be no literary evidence to document their origins and formative phases. There appears to be no historically acceptable remnant of any possible oral tradition which might have been incorporated at a later time in the earliest surviving literature of the Celts. It is necessary therefore to examine archaeological evidence. This may, and does, provide data of value, but they are concerned essentially with the material aspects of life. Occasionally some archaeological evidence allows hypotheses relevant to intangibles, such as social organization and religious beliefs, to be offered. But these must remain no more than hypotheses.

Classical references to the Celts are of value in that they provide literary evidence for the existence of a people in temperate Europe, the material remains of whom may be identified in the archaeological record. From this starting-point further examination of archaeological material offers a means of interpreting the tangible remains of the peoples who preceded them. In this way something may be seen of the movements of people and ideas into temperate Europe, for a recurrent characteristic of Europe from the sixth millennium B.C. onwards was a lack of social and cultural equilibrium. It was during this period that the basis was laid of what might be regarded as a distinctively European, as opposed to Oriental, civilization in early historical times. In this context the Celts emerge as one of the important peoples of Europe during the first millennium B.C. During the preceding millennia, however, Europe was influenced considerably by what was happening in the Middle East. Before returning to the situation in temperate Europe in the first millennium B.C., it is necessary to examine some of these formative external influences, and something of the manner in which they were absorbed into the life of the prehistoric Europeans. Although Europe was in varying degrees dependent on the East, the continent did not become a mere colony of the higher civilizations. The Europeans adopted some, but not all, ideas and techniques. They also adapted them to serve their own needs.

To anticipate, it may be accepted that the Celts had emerged by 500 B.C. as a recognizable people in Central Europe. This region may be taken for the purposes of this book to comprise part or whole of the modern states of Czechoslovakia, Hungary, Austria, Switzerland and the neighbouring areas of southern Germany. The region is open to movement of peoples and ideas from many quarters, including the vigour of the north, the civilization of the south, and a frequent and distinctive contribution from the east. Many formative developments in the learning and the arts of modern Europe took place here. Archaeological evidence suggests that in the prehistoric period the contribution of this region to what was to become a distinctively European culture was no less seminal.

One of the most important, and perhaps the most far-reaching, advances ever achieved by man was that represented by the acquisition of control of his food supply. In place of a largely parasitic and often uncertain economy based on hunting, fishing and collecting, one was developed which depended increasingly on the cultivation of plants and the domestication of animals. Present evidence suggests that farming, involving both domestication and cultivation of hitherto wild congeners, developed in the Middle East between 10,000 and 7,000 B.C. By the latter date at latest a number of factors, probably including climatic change, perhaps exhaustion of the soil, and certainly an increase of population, impelled a spread of farming communities into environments other than those in which the transition to a farming economy had been accomplished. An additional contributory factor was undoubtedly the adoption of farming by hitherto hunting communities living on the periphery of the areas occupied by agriculturalists. By 6,000 B.C. knowledge of farming appears to have reached south-eastern Europe. In this area crucial adjustments, including the important ones which allowed the cultivation of crops in an environment intermediate between that of the Middle East and temperate Europe, were made.

Knowledge of farming was brought into Central Europe by immigrants, and during the fifth millennium B.C. appears to have spread widely and rapidly. This spread was facilitated by the presence of discontinuous but extensive areas of loess, a light soil which was worked easily and successfully by the fairly simple techniques and equipment of the first farmers in Central

Europe. Access to this desirable soil was made easy by the probable use of routes along natural waterways, notably the middle and upper Danube and the Rhine and their tributaries. In this manner was founded the basis of a peasant farming economy successfully adjusted to the environment of temperate Europe. Without this adjustment there would have been little opportunity for further advance, either in technology or in social organization.

The earliest farmers brought with them not only knowledge of agriculture but also some of the ancillary crafts and skills which had been developed in the Middle East. These included such techniques as the making of pottery and polished stone tools, and the building of houses and farm buildings. The advance from a hunting to a farming economy was important, not only in the context of food-winning, but equally in that the farming year offered temporary respite from the continual quest for food which a hunting and collecting economy normally demanded. But the material culture of Central Europe at this time was not a mere copy of that of the Middle East. One example may be cited. Flat-roofed houses with a superstructure of sun-dried mud brick or adobe served adequately in the dry climate of the Middle East and parts of the Mediterranean. The moist climate of temperate Europe demanded something more substantial, and there is plentiful evidence from Czechoslovakia to the Low Countries of strong, timber-framed houses with sturdy, probably ridged, roofs. The long houses of Central Europe differ from those of the Middle East not only in construction, but also in size and in plan and in their arrangement within settlements. The shape and decoration of the pottery are also distinctive of Europe at this time.

Of equal importance is the evidence which might be interpreted as relevant to social organization and cult-practices. There is little evidence, for example, of remains of buildings which might be regarded as the house of a chieftain, a shrine or a temple. The size of the settlements, some of which may have contained a population of several hundreds, and the regular arrangement of houses suggest that there must have been some form of social organization. Whatever this may have been, it does not appear to have conferred on any 'leader' material or spiritual benefits above those of the mass of the people. This is suggested further by the apparent absence of burials distinguished either by any elaboration of structure or by grave goods additional to the norm. One explanation for these contrasts between Central Europe and certain parts of the Middle East at a comparable level of development is that in the former area there would have been little opportunity of amassing an excess of food above that essential for individual communities. In certain areas of the Middle East, however, and particularly along the Tigris, Euphrates and the Nile, it was possible to produce a food surplus, even with simple farming tools. This in turn encouraged the development of specialization within society, a specialization which eventually was to extend beyond workers and craftsmen to priests and kings. In time this sometimes led to a certain rigidity within a hierarchical social structure which tended to have an adverse effect on technological and material advance.

Central Europe might be considered fortunate in the long run in avoiding this rigidity, despite the contemporary absence in that part of the continent of true civilization. During the period in which the East continued to advance, however, Europe's technological advance was linked indirectly but significantly to it. This may be understood by reference to the complex nature of metal-working, more especially that of copper and bronze. The complexities are inherent in the sequence which involves the location, identification and extraction of raw materials, through the processes of smelting and associated techniques, to the casting and finishing of the tool or weapon. It is improbable that the entire sequence could have been achieved by other than specialists. It has been shown that the stone-using peasant farmers are unlikely to have been able to produce a surplus of food sufficiently adequate to support specialists. Without some form of external stimulus it is improbable that Europe by itself could have progressed as rapidly as it did towards a bronze-using economy. This stimulus was provided, and it arrived at an opportune moment.

In the course of time the widespread and homogeneous culture of the first farmers in Central Europe began to fragment into more localized groups. The arrival of later groups of immigrants may have contributed to this development, but the adoption of farming by native hunting and gathering communities may also have been significant. The importance of these latter peoples should not be underestimated in any account of prehistoric Europe. They were the descendants of later Upper Palaeolithic (Old Stone Age) groups who, at a period broadly contemporary with the first experiments at farming in the Middle East, had begun to adjust their economy to the temperate environment which gradually encroached on Central Europe after the end of the last Ice Age. In so doing they had acquired a useful body of skills and a knowledge of the natural potential of that environment which, in due course, they came to share by acculturation with immigrant farmers.

These later Neolithic (New Stone Age) cultures largely appear to have possessed a social organization comparable with that of the earlier farming communities. There is some evidence, however, of change. The amount of land available for cultivation by primitive techniques was limited. One reason was the nature of cultivation which, in the apparent absence of knowledge of fertilizing the soil, involved the periodic abandonment of land until it could regain its fertility by natural means. Another reason was the increase of population. This may have led towards competition for land, and the growth of enmity between neighbouring groups. Some evidence for this is suggested by the construction of defences around some later Neolithic settlements. This may further have led in time towards the emergence of local leaders to organize defence, particularly as at this time there is also some evidence for the increasing importance given to livestock, perhaps a contribution made by the descendants of native hunters.

But at least one stimulus towards the emergence of an embryonic warrior aristocracy was to come from beyond Central Europe, as was the stimulus towards metal-working. These two stimuli were approximately contemporary and were in part related. Two new groups of people, one certainly immigrant, appear to have been particularly influential, and each may be distinguished archaeologically by a characteristic artifact commonly found in their respective graves. One was a Bell Beaker or drinking vessel, and this was sometimes accompanied by archer's equipment, including flint-tipped arrows, a stone arm-bracer to withstand the rebound of the bow-string and, more significantly, an occasional small metal tanged-dagger. There remains some doubt as to the origins of the Beaker folk. Many authorities argue for a beginning during the latter part of the third millennium B.C. in Iberia, where their characteristic artifacts are found, as they are elsewhere in Europe. An alternative homeland has been suggested in Central Europe itself.

The second group is characterized by a perforated battle-axe of stone, some few of which might also be accompanied by a metal dagger and personal ornaments. The common form of burial is that of an individual, accompanied by his grave goods, often under a circular barrow or earthen mound, and sometimes enclosed within a timber mortuary-house. All evidence points towards an origin for this burial practice, and some of the associated artifacts, in the steppe-lands of southern Russia, between the Caucasus and the Carpathian mountains. The stone battle-axe is of particular interest, for its shape may have been influenced by shaft-hole axe-heads of copper of Middle Eastern derivation. Closely comparable axe-heads, possibly cast from local metal deposits in the Carpathians, are known from eastern Europe and from Slovakia, and date from the latter part of the third millennium B.C. The initial spread of Battle-Axe people, however, apparently outpaced any widespread use of metal in Central Europe, and any local exploitation of raw materials. The spread of the Beaker folk was similarly rapid, and there is evidence to suggest that they may have been involved more directly than were the Battle-Axe folk in the extraction of metal and the production of metal artifacts. In Central Europe the two groups fused.

The significance of this influx of new peoples was twofold. They provided a nucleus from which were to grow warrior aristocratic elements, and introduced into Central Europe a knowledge of, and a demand for, the use of metal. In doing so they brought to an end the simple self-sufficiency of Neolithic economy and society. At this time, that is at the close of the third millennium B.C., the foundations of the Celtic culture contemporary with the classical civilizations were laid, although there was to be more development before the full achievement was realized.

The movement of the Battle-Axe people has an additional significance, and not only for the origins of the Celts. Some reservations must remain in any attempt at identifying the preliterate forerunner of a historically attested language with an archaeological culture, yet there are cogent arguments, based on the study of both philology and archaeology, for suggesting that the initial spread of the Indo-European group of languages may be attributed to the Battle-Axe folk. These peoples not only penetrated Central Europe, but spread over wide areas of the Continent. The Indo-European group of languages embraces most of those current in present-day Europe, including modern Celtic languages, as well as ancient Celtic, Greek and Latin, and ancient languages beyond Europe, such as Hittite and Sanskrit. It is also possible that the basis of a social organization common to a number of barbarian peoples in Europe, and indeed to the progenitors of the Greeks and Romans also, was disseminated by Battle-Axe people at this time.

As far as is known, the arrival of new peoples in Central Europe did not bring about any significant alteration to the basic economy, apart from an increase in the importance of stock-raising, which may already have begun in late Neolithic times. The importance of cattle as a basis of wealth and of prestige is well attested in barbarian societies, including that of the Celts. It also offered an inducement to raiding and warfare, evidence for which increases from this time onwards. Although crop-raising remained important and may have been improved by the introduction of a light traction plough, it is improbable that there was any significant increase in the food surplus, at least until later in the Bronze Age. It is possible, however, that any small surplus which may have been available to individual farming communities was now collected systematically and contributed to the support of metal-workers, although for some time to come this could not compare in extent with that of the Middle East. Some indication of the powers of organization over wide areas may be gauged from the activities of the Beaker folk and their successors in southern Britain, who were responsible respectively for the transport from Pembrokeshire of stones for part of the setting at Stonehenge and the final impressive stage of that monument.

The mere arrival of the Beaker and Battle-Axe peoples in Central Europe would seem to be an inadequate cause for the development of a true European Bronze Age. Europe came into the Bronze Age rapidly and successfully, not simply because of local organization, needs or desires, but because of a shortage of the raw materials of metal-working, particularly of tin, in the higher civilizations of the south-east. Parts of Europe, including Central Europe, had deposits of copper and tin. These were located, exploited and exported, and local groups in control of such assets were enabled to progress materially. In time Central Europe, in common with some areas of Western Europe, such as Brittany and Wessex, produced successful Bronze Age societies which benefited from their contact with the eastern

Mediterranean and beyond, not only in the import from such areas of tools, weapons and ornaments, but also in knowledge of the current techniques of metal-working and other crafts. But the chieftains of the Early Bronze Age in Central Europe developed and controlled a culture which was distinctive of themselves. It was neither an eastern culture nor an eastern way of life translated to temperate Europe. It might be an anachronism, but one might say that already it was a 'European' culture.

From this period onwards the line of continuity which leads directly to the historic Celts may be traced in its essentials from the archaeological evidence. This continuity is identified archaeologically by the successive Únětice, Tumulus and Urnfield cultures of the Central European Bronze Age. The developed Únětice culture, named after the type-site south of Prague, appears to have emerged from the fusion of Battle-Axe and Beaker peoples and their immediate descendants, although elements developed from the former and their south Russian antecedents seem to have been the stronger of the two. Local development towards more clearly marked divisions within society was accelerated. This is shown most clearly in the disparity of grave furniture between the burials of the ordinary people and the aristocratic tombs of warriors and their consorts. There is nothing yet known which might be identified as the 'palace' of a princeling. Yet the wealth of metal-work in weapons and ornaments found in the burials clearly demonstrates the privileged position of these chieftains, as they may justifiably be termed.

There were several reasons for this pre-eminence of the Únětice culture in temperate Europe by the middle of the second millennium B.C. The aristocratic tendencies of immigrant warriors and their possible powers of organization of the native farming peoples have been noted. More significant were the valuable deposits of copper and tin ores, as, for example, in the Tyrol and Czechoslovakia respectively. It was fortunate again that more developed cultures to the south-east were in need of such raw materials. The eastern Mediterranean was developing rapidly, and was learning much from the Middle East, including Anatolia. A large part of the second millennium B.C., following a time of disruption at the close of the third millennium, was a period of expansion for the growing civilizations of Sumer and Egypt. From their beginnings these cultures had been accustomed to search far from their home territories for the raw materials of metal-working, for they possessed no appreciable deposits close at hand. It was probably an extension of this already accustomed search which was to lead prospectors, although not necessarily those of the higher civilizations themselves, into distant territories, and so eventually to Central Europe.

The geographical position of the Únětice culture also appears to have been an important reason for its rapid advance. It was conveniently located to benefit from trade passing between the south-east and more distant parts of Europe. Tin from Cornwall, for example, gold and possibly copper from Ireland, may have been exported to Central Europe and beyond. Amber certainly, and possibly perishables such as skins, were exported from southern Scandinavia to such an extent that, despite a lack of any nearby metal deposits, this remote area was able also to develop a rich, distinctive and early tradition of metal-working. The Únětice culture in fact controlled a nodal point of trade routes within barbarian Europe. Increasingly it was linked by trade with the eastern Mediterranean, notably in its later stages with the Mycenaean culture, with which it probably shared some kinship in antecedents.

The Tumulus culture which followed the Únětice, and from which it derived, dominated Central Europe during much of the second part of the second millennium B.C. During this period trade contacts with the south-east were maintained and probably increased, and this may have contributed to the increased power and prestige of the Tumulus chieftains who appear to have gained control of areas beyond the territory of the ancestral Únětice culture. As the name implies, the Tumulus culture is distinguished by the continued practice of burying the dead beneath burial mounds. The practice of burying weapons and ornaments also continued, and from these burials it is possible to discern not only evidence of trade, but also the development of localized types of bronzes, which in turn were traded. This implies the establishment of local schools of metallurgy to serve local demand.

Taken together, the Únětice and Tumulus cultures provide evidence of a flourishing barbarian society in Central Europe which was allowed to develop without any disruption of local peoples by large-scale immigration. To a certain extent, this apparent stability was conditional on settled conditions beyond Central Europe, for despite the evidence of weapons, it is improbable that any large-scale penetration by determined incomers could have been repulsed. When this external stability was upset, Central Europe was bound to be affected, particularly in matters such as trade and technological knowledge, and perhaps even in the structure of society. Towards the close of the second millennium B.C. there is again evidence of widespread disruption which, as at the close of the third, affected higher civilizations to the south-east, and in the case of the Hittites and the Mycenaeans, reduced them to a fraction of their earlier power and importance.

With the emergence of the Urnfield culture of Central Europe, there appear a people whom some scholars regard as being 'proto-Celtic', in that they may have spoken, as is suggested by the evidence of place-names, an early form of Celtic. Apart from the influence of some immigrants from the east during the early first millennium B.C., there is little to distinguish the Urnfield people from their descendants of the Hallstatt culture, other than the latter's use of iron. Again it would seem that the thread of continuity is strong. As the name suggests, the people of the Urnfield culture cremated their dead and placed the remains in cinerary urns which were buried in flat cemeteries without any covering mound.

This contrasts with the inhumation burials beneath tumuli which characterized the funerary cults of the previous phase. It has sometimes been taken to imply that this resulted from a new influx of people from beyond Central Europe, but it now seems more probable that it stemmed from a largely internal modification of ritual thought associated with the disposal of the dead. The change in funerary ritual, however, forms but a small part of the total archaeological evidence for this most important phase of European prehistory, which began in the last quarter of the second millennium B.C. and continued into the first. The period of the Urnfield culture, like that of the Tumulus culture, was one of expansion, particularly during the first part of the first millennium, and it would seem that Central European warriors now possessed weapons which were not simply for parade, but were intended for war and aggrandizement.

This potential for warfare resulted in part from an increase in the output both of metal ores in Central Europe, and of weapons produced within the area. The standard of local metalworking had improved. For some time it had been influenced by models adopted and adapted from the south-east, but local craftsmen increasingly developed local types until eventually the quality of design and efficiency began to overtake those of some more civilized people to the south. This is shown, for example, in certain articles of beaten bronze, including vessels and parade equipment, such as armour and shields. Of greater importance was the appearance in Central Europe, and in some quantity, of heavy slashing swords. There is even evidence to suggest that Central Europeans armed with these weapons may have contributed to assaults and disturbances in the eastern Mediterranean, whether as mercenaries or as raiders – or as both. If so, it would seem to foreshadow later Celtic assaults on the classical world. A further indication of an increase in warfare is suggested by the construction of strongly fortified settlements, the defences of which were strengthened internally and externally by timber bracing and revetments. Some of the settlements appear to have contained houses which may now confidently be attributed to chieftains. From such fortified sites were to develop the more massive hill-forts of Celtic Europe.

Not all of the output of bronze went into the production of weapons, nor did warfare completely monopolize the activities of the Urnfield people. Reference has been made to vessels of sheet bronze, and their use implies not only an improvement in the quality of cooking, but also some social embellishment of eating and drinking, essential adjuncts of later Celtic society. Personal adornments of bronze were abundant; again this is typical of the Celts. Trade also continued. To support this society, agriculture naturally remained important, as it had done since Neolithic times in Central Europe, although the population of individual settlements appears in general to have been smaller than those of the earlier peasant farmers. The farmers of the Late Bronze Age were undoubtedly more efficient husbandmen. Crop rotation and the use of manure probably helped to produce an increased yield. The plough appears to have been in general use, and some farmers might now hope to acquire metal tools, such as sickles. Carpenters' tools are also more evident, and these and heavy bronze axe-heads would have benefited craftsmen and workers as well as armourers and the builders of defences. The solidity of some of the buildings of the Urnfield culture also suggest an increase of wood-working skills generally. All these things imply a not inconsiderable increase in the standard of living, at least for part of the community.

Whereas the Urnfield people may justifiably be considered to have been proto-Celtic, their descendants in Central Europe, the people of the Hallstatt culture, were certainly fully Celtic. The Hallstatt culture and its successor, that of La Tène, together represent archaeologically the iron-using prehistoric peoples of Central, Western and, temporarily at least, some other parts of Europe. These are the *Keltoi*, the *Galli* and *Galatae* of classical writers. The two cultures are named respectively after sites at which were found during the last and present centuries archaeological artifacts now considered to be representative of a particular stage of each culture. Hallstatt is a village in the Salzkammergut in Austria at which was found an important cemetery: La Tène is situated near the north-eastern end of Lake Neuchâtel in Switzerland. In very general terms the Hallstatt culture in Central Europe existed approximately from 700 to 500 B.C. The La Tène culture in those parts of Europe which subsequently formed part of the Roman Empire ended with the arrival of the Romans. Beyond the Empire influences stemming from this culture continued important until the first centuries A.D., as in Ireland and northern Britain.

A distinction, frequently made in archaeological literature, between the Bronze and Iron Ages tends to obscure the considerable evidence of continuity between the Urnfield and Hallstatt cultures. It cannot be doubted that the mastery of iron-working was an important technological advance. When this knowledge reached Central Europe it allowed a more plentiful output of tools and weapons, cheaper than comparable types made of bronze. This in turn had important economic and military consequences. As far as may be deduced from archaeological evidence, most of the characteristics of the Hallstatt culture were already present in the Urnfield culture. The importance during the Bronze Age of a warrior aristocracy, seen in its nascent form at the beginning of the period, reaches its apogee at its close in the final stages of the Urnfield culture.

There is some justification on archaeological grounds for making a distinction between the Urnfield and Hallstatt cultures, apart from that based on the technological transition from bronze to iron for tools and weapons. At the beginning of the Hallstatt period there was a reversion among the aristocracy to inhumation in timber burial chambers, often beneath tumuli. This might be considered as having resulted simply from a change in emphasis of funerary ritual, as had occurred at the beginning of the Urnfield period – perhaps a return to an older tradition. There is further evidence, however, which strongly suggests that it was prompted, in part at least, by external influences. This evidence consists principally of bronze harness mounts and horse-bits which have been found in Eastern and Central Europe, but also less commonly further west, as in Glamorganshire. Most finds appear to date from the eighth and seventh centuries B.C., and so overlap with the beginnings of the Hallstatt culture. Parallels to this horse-gear may be identified in the steppes of southern Russia, particularly in a culture which may convincingly be identified with that of the Cimmerians who, at a slightly earlier date, appear to have been pushed westwards by the Scythians. Further support for a derivation from southern Russia is provided by the adoption by early Hallstatt chieftains of wagon burial, a practice whose origins may be traced in the steppes during the second millennium B.C. It seems probable that some aristocratic refugees came, either to dominate, or more probably to become absorbed in, certain groups of late Urnfield peoples in Central Europe. The impetus which this provided is documented archaeologically by the beginnings of the Hallstatt Culture. And so the end of the Bronze Age in Central Europe is marked, as it began, by the arrival and absorption of peoples who had moved westwards from their homeland on the steppes of southern Russia.

The immediate ancestors of the Celts known to the Greeks and Romans may therefore be identified as the late Urnfield people of Central Europe. The latter emerge as possessing a compound of traditions matured during the preceding millennia. In this sketch only some of what appear to the writer to be particularly meaningful strands in the thread of continuity have been isolated. To attempt more would involve a consideration of the entire prehistory of Central Europe. Some of the characteristics of Celtic society, shared by other Indo-European groups, may already be identified at the beginning of the Bronze Age. What distinguishes the earlier aristocratically controlled society from that of late Urnfield times is that the survival of the former was affected, perhaps even to a limited extent controlled, by contact with more advanced cultures by way of trade and the exchange of technological expertise. Late Urnfield peoples were much more independent, particularly after the advent of iron-working. Central Europe was no longer dependent on the East. Attention has been directed in this survey to the more aristocratic elements of society, for evidence of their existence, and more particularly of their death, has a better chance of survival in the archaeological record. The ordinary people, descendants of the earliest farmers and native hunters, are less well documented, but their existence must not be overlooked. Without the base which they provided, the pyramid of Celtic society could not have been built.

THE HALLSTATT AND LA TÈNE CULTURES

It has been seen that many characteristics of the Hallstatt culture may be identified in that of the later Urnfield people. These include a settled peasantry living in small communities, and by this time there is some evidence to suggest continuity of settlement, implying competent arable farming. This substratum helped to support a superstructure which included craftsmen and warriors. It may be supposed that, as later, varying degrees of status may have been accorded to members of the latter class, but this is not readily apparent from the archaeological record.

Knowledge of iron-working and the arrival of horsemen from the east together provided stimuli to further development, and contributed to a new wave of expansion, again following the Urnfield precedent, which was eventually to take

Celtic peoples in varying numbers to Italy and Iberia, to Greece and even beyond to Asia Minor, to France, to Britain and to Ireland. There is no overall pattern in this dispersal. Some groups were motivated by warfare, either as raiders or mercenaries; others were more peaceful in intent, although perhaps not initially in action, in that they sought land for settlement. The possession of iron weapons and tools was a powerful aid to both. Weapons comparable in efficiency with the best which could be produced by armourers of the higher civilizations were available cheaply and in quantity to warrior chieftains and their followers in a way impossible earlier, even during the final centuries of the Bronze Age when bronze was relatively plentiful. The availability of iron tools meant that new territory could be cleared for farming, which itself may have become more productive. This in turn may have contributed to an increase of population, always conducive to social instability and aggression. The infusion of a new aristocratic element may have provided the final stimulus. Descendants of late Urnfield chieftains appear to have been receptive to the example of the newcomers, for among later Urnfield burials there is evidence of richly furnished cremation burials, indicative of high status.

The earliest Hallstatt burials, dating from the seventh century B.C., are found in the Upper Danube region, in Upper Austria and Bavaria, and in Bohemia, and it may be supposed that in this area the culture emerged. This therefore may answer the question, implied at the beginning of this chapter, as to when and where the historic Celts originated. The most distinctive burials are those which contained a four-wheeled wagon on which the dead person was placed. Animals were not buried, but harness and functional and decorative fittings, including horse-bits, were. In addition, there were many other grave goods. The whole funerary deposit was enclosed in a wooden burial chamber, which may have been set in the ground, covered by a mound, or both. During the sixth century the centre of power appears to have moved westwards into the

Upper Rhine area, south-western Germany, Switzerland and Burgundy. An outstanding burial from Burgundy is that from Vix, near Châtillon-sur-Seine in the Côte d'Or. The burial was that of a young woman of about thirty, found lying on a bier originally forming part of a four-wheeled wagon or funerary car, the wheels of which had been removed and placed against the eastern wall of the wooden burial chamber. The burial is interesting on two counts. First, it provides archaeological evidence complementary to the literary evidence of the existence of Boudicca in Britain and the legendary Medb (Maeve) of Ireland, which appear to show that women were accorded parity with men in aristocratic society. Second, not only does the rich array of grave furniture confirm this at Vix, but, more important, these artifacts provide evidence of trade. Outstanding among them is a huge bronze *krater*, or wine container, over five feet high, the largest vessel of its kind known to survive from classical antiquity. The vessel is of Greek manufacture and dramatically underlines the importance of trade between Hallstatt Celts and the Graeco-Etruscan world, for which there is abundant evidence from a number of sites.

Although the Greeks regarded the Celts as barbarians, they were not averse to taking advantage of the markets offered in the aristocratic courts of warrior chieftains in temperate Europe, particularly as the Greeks were beginning to suffer from commercial competition elsewhere in the Mediterranean. Trade between the Greek world and that of the Celts passed through Greek colonies on the northern shores of the Mediterranean. An important colony was Massalia (modern Marseilles), founded at about 600 B.C. Archaeological evidence consistently supports the hypothesis that one of the principal exports – if not the principal export – to the Celts was wine. This is shown, for example, in the many finds of characteristic Massaliote *amphorae* (pottery vessels for the transport of wine), found in southern Gaul and as far north as the Upper Danube. With the wine, however, went pottery finer than utilitarian *amphorae*, such as cups and mixing-bowls of fine figured pottery. Bronze flagons and other vessels too associated with wine-drinking, of which the *krater* from Vix is the outstanding example, were also traded to the Celts. Etruscan manufactures from northern Italy similarly reached the Celts.

It is less easy to document archaeologically the content of Celtic trade to the classical world. From the quality of many Greek and Etruscan imports it nevertheless may be inferred that this return trade was both substantial and important. It may be supposed that raw materials formed a large part, and metals such as copper and tin remained important, even if no longer destined for tools and weapons. During the height of the Hallstatt culture and later there is evidence for an increase in the extraction of salt, including actual salt-mines. Salt, therefore, was probably exported, and perhaps salted food-stuffs. Slaves may also have been exported. In addition, the chieftains of the Hallstatt culture, like their predecessors earlier, may have acted as intermediaries in trade passing through Central Europe from the north to the Mediterranean.

Prolonged contact with the classical world through trade undoubtedly stimulated among some Celtic chieftains a taste for certain aspects of civilized living, particularly those associated with feasting and drinking. Yet here again, as often in the past, the Central Europeans asserted their artistic independence by producing a distinctive style of decorative metal-work. This emerged in a developed form during the La Tène period, but some of the stimuli which went into its make-up were being absorbed during the Hallstatt period as an adaptation of classical motives offered as exemplars in imported pottery and bronzes. These were combined with some eastern art-styles, in part transmitted to the Celts through their contact with the Graeco-Etruscan world, and added to the repertoire of native decorative metal-work, the origins of which may be traced at least to Urnfield times. Inspiration from the classical world was not confined to the peaceful pleasures of the table, but also extended to warfare, as may be seen in body armour and helmets. More interesting is the at present unique construction, as far as Central Europe is concerned, employed in the fourth phase of the Heuneburg, a hill-fort on the Upper Danube in southern Germany. The use of mud-brick resting on stone foundations and a line of projecting square bastions appear to indicate Greek military influence. The relatively small size of the hill-fort suggests that this may have been the stronghold of a Celtic chieftain conscious of prestige and display, for the positioning of the bastions was unnecessary and their close spacing tactically superfluous. Elsewhere in the area of the Hallstatt culture more conventional hill-forts were built, their defences strengthened by internal timber bracing, a development from the Urnfield tradition of construction. Hill-forts of this period varied in size. Some of the smaller, like the Heuneburg, may have been the fortified residences of chieftains. The larger may have served as tribal strongholds, refuges in time of war, and from which later they were to evolve into *oppida*, true tribal capitals.

There can be little doubt that warfare, perhaps inter-tribal and almost certainly concerned with cattle-raiding, was common in the world of both the Hallstatt and La Tène Celts. This is shown by the large quantities of weapons which have survived, and more so by the evidence of burning and other destruction found in excavated hill-forts. There may also have been warfare on a larger scale, as is suggested by the archaeological evidence for the territorial expansion of both cultures. Some of the literary evidence for the expansion of the La Tène Celts is discussed in the following chapter, but archaeological evidence suggests that this followed the example set during the Hallstatt period. Although warfare tends to dominate any discussion of the archaeological material relating to the Celts in Europe, there is also evidence for the arts of peace at this time. This is shown in skills such as iron-working, in decorative metal-working, wood-working, pottery and weaving.

There are several reasons for distinguishing archaeologically between the Hallstatt and La Tène cultures, but this need not imply any significant break in overall cultural continuity. One important and distinctive feature of the La Tène culture, already mentioned, is the superb art-style, largely but not exclusively abstract in form, and most typically represented in metal-work. There are also, of course, changes in the style of artifacts, such as pottery, bronze dress-fasteners, tools, weapons and armour. Also indicative of a change which perhaps involved a further shift in the focus of power is the appearance of light two-wheeled war chariots found in graves along the middle Rhine and the Marne. The vehicle had changed, but the burial of a warrior with his weapons and ornaments was a continuation of the Hallstatt funerary tradition. Although it is unnecessary to invoke any new immigration to account for this change, the sudden appearance of a chariot probably resulted from the acceptance, in temperate Europe at least, of new modes of warfare. Trade with the Mediterranean, with the Greeks and Etruscans, and later with the Romans, continued throughout the La Tène period, and afforded the Celts an opportunity of acquiring and adapting new ideas. Although the war chariot in temperate Europe must have been inspired by external prototypes – perhaps again from eastern rather than classical sources – once adopted the design was adapted to Celtic needs. Celtic wheelwrights, carpenters and blacksmiths cooperated in the production of some of the most technologically advanced wheeled vehicles of the ancient world, four-wheeled wagons as well as the lighter war chariots. The skill of the blacksmith is seen also in the weapons of the period, particularly the long swords, and in the decorated fire-dogs which may have graced a chieftain's hearth. In general, the technological level of the La Tène Celts, with very few exceptions, was equal to, and in some matters surpassed, that of the Romans.

It was inevitable, however, that in any conflict between Celts and Romans, the superior powers of organization, sense of discipline and general orderliness of the Roman culture were bound to overcome the volatile and undisciplined Celts whose sense of loyalty, powerful though it might have been, was normally centred on an individual rather than on an institution or on an ideal. But before the Romans were able to conquer the greater part of the Celtic-dominated areas of continental Europe, the Celts during the La Tène period, which began around 500 B.C., were to achieve their most widespread expansion. They spread into and beyond areas previously dominated by their predecessors of the Urnfield and Hallstatt cultures. They burst their way forcibly into Greek and Roman history, sacking, among other centres, Rome in about 390 B.C., and Delphi around 279 B.C. From this time onwards until the final destruction of Celtic culture on the Continent archaeological evidence may increasingly be supplemented by the writings of classical authors, culminating in Caesar's war memoirs of his campaigns against the Celts of Gaul, his *Gallic War*. From the various writings of this period some insight into the Celts' motives for expansion may be gained. In the Balkans, in Greece, and beyond into Asia Minor, a powerful motive appears to have been desire for loot. This was achieved either by the activities of armed bands acting independently as raiders or by their recruitment as mercenaries in the endless petty wars of the decaying civilization of Hellenistic Greece. Even in this area, however, there is evidence that some Celts at least were seeking land for settlement, as is shown by the Galatae, who were allowed to settle in the vicinity of modern Ankara and who, as the Galatians of the New Testament and as late as the fourth century A.D. appear to have survived as a recognizable cultural group, even to the extent of retaining as their second language one which appears to have been recognizably Celtic. In Italy, too, as far south as Apulia and Sicily, there is evidence of Celtic raiding parties. Further north in Italy, however, the Celts appear to have been more concerned with fighting for land to settle, and in so doing contributed to the collapse of the Etruscan civilization, archaeological evidence for which has been recovered in the destruction levels of some Etruscan cities. The modern place-names of Bohemia and Bologna preserve linguistically some evidence of the Celtic tribe of the Boii, part of which migrated from Central Europe across the Alps to settle in northern Italy. When the Romans finally conquered northern Italy, eventually to incorporate it within their growing empire as the province of *Gallia Cisalpina*, Cisalpine Gaul, the name itself acknowledged the strength and durability of earlier Celtic penetration and settlement. It is interesting to note that at this time the Romans commented particularly on the intensive arable cultivation of their newly occupied territories, indicative perhaps of the successful exploitation by the Celts of land which had been so necessary for settlement.

Before the La Tène culture of the Celts was finally destroyed by Roman conquest and culture, some of its elements had penetrated beyond the continent of Europe into Britain and Ireland. Ireland remained untouched by Roman arms and largely unaffected by Roman civilization. Upland areas of Britain in the west and the north also preserved a little of Celtic culture, sufficient at least for them to experience something of a minor renaissance of what remained of that culture after the collapse of Roman military and civil control at the end of the fourth and the beginning of the fifth centuries A.D. In chapter 3 there is some discussion of the archaeological evidence for the penetration of these islands by the Celts. Ambiguous though some of it may be at present, it must be emphasized that only in the context of Britain and Ireland may any attempt be made to correlate all the evidence for Celtic culture – archaeology, native tradition and literature, some few classical references, and the not unimportant survival of a Celtic way of life into recent centuries.

In this chapter an attempt has been made both to indicate an origin for the Celts in Central Europe and to emphasize that the gestation of their culture occupied a considerable period of time. It cannot be denied that the Celts emerged in history as one of the dominant cultural groups in Europe, perhaps the most important in central and western Europe. This would imply that, as far as temperate Europe is concerned, the ancestors of the Celts and perhaps of some of the Germanic peoples too were those, who, by accident as much as by design, made a powerful contribution to the evolution of a truly European culture. It may be that Mediterranean civilization, already in decline and represented by the Christianized remnant of what survived of the culture of Imperial Rome, was to be rejuvenated by the vigour of barbarians beyond the Alps, few of whom had been subdued by the enervation of city life. It has been said that the marriage of the vigorous culture of temperate Europe and the civilization of the Mediterranean was solemnized during the early Middle Ages. The contribution made by the classical world has not been doubted since the Renaissance, and has sometimes been exaggerated. It is time that the contribution of prehistoric Europe, and more particularly that of the Celts and their forebears, was recognized adequately.

CHAPTER 2

The Celts in Europe

CELTIC culture is the fine flower of the Iron Age, the last phase of European material and intellectual development before the Mediterranean world spread northwards over the Continent and linked it to the world of today. The Celtic peoples were the first of the prehistoric peoples to the north of the Alps whose names were known to the Greek and Roman world, for they shared certain common features, including some linguistic affinity. Common political institutions gave them a unity bordering on nationality, a concept which the Mediterranean peoples could understand. They realized that the Celts were a powerful people with a certain ethnic unity, occupying wide and clearly defined territories, in process of expansion, and that they were possessed of internal political organization and formidable military strength. As enemies the Greeks and Romans respected and feared them; as neighbours they were curious about them, but of their intellectual life they had little conception.

In material culture the Celtic peoples heralded modern civilization. Their widespread use of iron enabled them to conquer vast tracts of land and to increase the amenities of life by felling forests and opening up new areas for agriculture. It revolutionized their method of warfare by making available in quantity the strong iron slashing sword and their economy by opening up hitherto unworked land, later to be controlled by their great hill-top towns or *oppida*. With the development of their *oppida* their institutions developed. Their control of important raw materials gave them a profitable trade and a developed system of barter and eventually of coinage. These things they shared with other peoples of the ancient world. Yet they were separated by a great gulf from the greatest civilizations of that world. They did not use the art of writing to any great extent and then not until near the end of their independence. They chose to record their past orally and communicated with other nations by word of mouth. Inevitably we view the ancient Celtic peoples of continental Europe through Greek and Roman eyes, for they have left no written records of themselves. Our earliest word-picture of them is in Greek and Roman writings.

The gulf between them and the civilizations of the Mediterranean was in reality an impassable one. On a nation-wide basis there was no medium of communication. The linguistic barrier was insignificant; but because of the lack of written communication the accumulated knowledge of the ancient world was a closed book to the Celtic peoples, and the history, the intellectual life, the mythology and religious experience, the eloquence and art of the formal speech of the Celts were little known to the Greeks and Romans. Among the ancient southern civilizations with their written documents, all individual experience, whether practical or intellectual, could quickly be pooled so as to become the common property of the community, whereas among the illiterate Celtic peoples experience was exchanged orally, and in certain aspects may have been fragmented. Writing has become so integral a part of modern civilization that it is difficult to remember that it is a comparatively recent acquisition, and originally very restricted in area. The Celtic peoples did not acquire it till the fifth century A.D., and to transmit their traditions and to give permanence to their thoughts they depended on the spoken word.

The languages of the Celts belong to the great Indo-European family of languages, which includes Teutonic, Balto-Slavonic and the classical languages of Greek and Latin, and even stretched as far east as India and Tocharian Asia. These languages are distinguished by the use of declensions, of conjugations, and the other elements which constitute a synthetic group of languages, as distinct from the agglutinative forms, such as Turkish and the majority of Asiatic languages. The Celtic group of this family is marked by certain well-known characteristics, of which the principal are the loss of initial and inter-vocalic *p*, as in Irish *athair*, 'father' (cf. Latin *pater*); Irish *lan*, 'full' (cf. Latin *plenus*); and the change of Indo-European *e* to *i* as in Irish *fir*, 'true' (Latin *verus*). Also the Indo-European labialized velar *gv* is represented by *b*, as in Irish *ben* 'woman' (Greek γυνη); there are other correspondences which might be noted. The Celtic languages, in fact, correspond somewhat closely with the Italic dialects.

The principal Celtic dialects may be subdivided as follows: Gaulish, obsolete except from inscriptions; Goidelic, which includes Irish, Scottish Gaelic and Manx, the latter virtually obsolete; and Brythonic, which includes Welsh, Breton and Cornish – the latter now obsolete. Pictish seems to have included a large element of Gaulish or Welsh, but of an early type no longer identical with the Welsh of today. The principal differences between the Goidelic and the Brythonic group are that the latter have very much simplified themselves in their case-endings and in the loss of the neuter gender and the dual number. The two groups also differ in the matter of initial mutation and aspiration. At what period these changes took place is still a matter of dispute, whether it was after the initial migration of the Celtic people to these islands or whether it was already completed before they left the Continent. The former view is the one most in favour, but the late Professor O'Rahilly put forward the view in his book *Early Irish History and Mythology*, published in 1946, that the changes were brought over from the Continent or even completed before. His view has not met with general acceptance, and Professor Dillon* is inclined to the more conservative view that the Goidelic invasion of Ireland took place at a much earlier date; but he holds that the changes between Goidelic and Brythonic

* In the book *The Celtic Realms* (1967), written jointly with the present author.

took place after the Brythonic peoples came to this country.

In their illiteracy the Celtic peoples were in no way remarkable. On the contrary, it is the literate peoples of the world who, at least until recent times, have been relatively few in number. Like many communities all the world over the Celtic peoples paid great attention to the development of an advanced oral technique as a vehicle for the transmission of their thoughts. Among illiterate peoples the training of the memory is cultivated to a degree undreamed of among readers of books, and the proficiency of the Gauls in this respect is commented on by Caesar. To form an efficient vehicle for the widespread transmission of thought the subject matter must be clothed in artificial form, such as poetry, otherwise it would quickly deteriorate and die out. Hence artistic speech is highly cultivated, and a high standard of eloquence is the aim of the intelligentsia among illiterate peoples everywhere. The eloquence of the Gauls impressed the Romans deeply throughout their history.

Already in the middle of the second century B.C. Cato attributed to the Cisalpine Gauls a high degree of excellence in the art of eloquence, no less than in the art of war, although this may have been influenced by contact with classical education. Diodorus Siculus, writing in the next century, comments on the succinct and figurative nature of their speech, and their use of allusion, hyperbole and grandiloquent language – all characteristic of the highly artificial Irish *retoric* and of the earliest poetry of the British heroic age, as well as the skaldic poetry of early Norse. We have a picturesque glimpse of a Gaulish orator in action, a prince of the tribe of the Aedui, in a Latin panegyric of uncertain authorship addressed to Constantine the Great, where the Gaulish prince, pleading for help for his countrymen against the invader Ariovistus, is pictured to us in retrospect as 'the Aeduan prince, haranguing the Senate, leaning on his long shield (*scutum*)'.

Even after the Roman conquest of Gaul the native Gaulish

eloquence suffered no diminution. A number of Gaulish orators are known to us by name, and the Romans were anxious to employ them as tutors to their sons. As late as the fourth century Symmachus, the greatest orator of his day, had been trained by a Gaulish *rhetor*, and almost all great masters of panegyric in the last age of the Western Empire had been trained in the tradition of the Gallo-Roman schools. At this period we are privileged to have an entrée into the great tradition of rhetorical training in the school of Bordeaux in the series of poems by Ausonius which celebrate the professors of rhetoric for several generations, and trace their ancestry to the druids of Armorica.

References to the eloquence of the Gauls and to their pre-eminence in oratory and polished speech could be multiplied indefinitely. Perhaps the *locus classicus* is the passage in which the Greek writer Lucian, who was born at Samosata on the Euphrates in the second century A.D., relates that as he was travelling in Gaul he came upon a picture of an old man, clad in a lion's skin, leading a group of followers whose ears were attached to his own tongue by little gold and amber chains of great beauty and delicacy. The men were not forced along, but followed him eagerly and heaped praises on him, and it was clear they would regret their liberty. A Greek-speaking Gaul who was standing near explained to him that the old man represented eloquence and was pictured as Heracles, clad in his lion's skin, because, said the Gaul, the Celts believed that eloquence was of greater power than physical strength, and also that eloquence attained its climax in old age. Lucian tells us further that the Celts called Heracles *Ogmios* in their native tongue, and we shall see that in Celtic mythology Ogmios is the god of eloquence in the divine community. Moreover, a temple to Heracles and the Muses is said to have been erected at Autun by M. Fulvius Nobilior after his capture of Ambracia in 189 B.C. because he had learned in Greece that Heracles was a *musagetes* ('a leader of the muses'). Traces of this traditional view of the paramount power of eloquence still linger in Irish mythology and saga (cf. p. 145 below).

The practical importance of eloquence, the paramount need of an illiterate people to make a desired impression by the spoken word, is largely responsible for many of their characteristics which appeared as childish weaknesses to their more advanced contemporaries and do so to us today. In a heroic society such as that of the Gauls, the prestige of a leader depends on his power to impress his own personality on the others, and a continuous and active propaganda must be kept up by his own boasting of deeds past and to come, by panegyrics from his bards and by elegies on his ancestors. All these are designed to impress, and must therefore make an instant impact by their force, and, if need be, by hyperbole. The same need to impress lies at the root of the love of the Celtic chief everywhere for fine clothes, fine weapons, a splendid appearance. His illiterate followers are kept loyal to him by the evidence of their eyes and ears, as well as by the praises sung by his bards, and, of course, by his protection.

The whole intellectual life of the Gauls in pre-Roman times was carried on by means of oral teaching, and closely associated with their trained eloquence was their power of memorizing. The education of the young and the intellectual life of all classes was carried on by two classes of men known as druids and seers, who taught entirely by means of poetry orally transmitted. Their subject matter was saved by the use of metrical form from the inevitable disintegration which it would otherwise have suffered, since their courses are said to have continued sometimes for as long as twenty years. Despite the absence of books their teaching was on a lofty plane and included such subjects as the stars and their motions, the nature and greatness of our earth, the power and majesty of the immortal gods, and other matters which comprised natural and moral philosophy. Among the most important of their tenets was that of the immortality of the soul. In societies ignorant of books and the written word all knowledge is regarded as a spiritual possession and acquired by spiritual means or 'inspiration', and we shall see later that the same attitude to knowledge also prevailed among the insular Celts of Britain, and especially of Ireland.

I have found it necessary to dwell on the eloquence of the Gauls because it is only by a full realization of their cultivated, polished speech that we can come to some estimate of their activity and refinement of mind. For the rest, since they have left us no written account of themselves, we are dependent on the reports of their enemies, enemies who sometimes despised them as a people of low culture, who feared them as a conquering race, and yet at times admired their bravery. It is only rarely that a classical writer gives us a glimpse of the refinement which must have inspired the grace of the art displayed in the material culture of the late Iron Age. According to Ammianus Marcellinus, who wrote in Byzantium in the sixth century, but who derived his material from Timagenes, a writer in the reign of Augustus, 'The Gauls are all exceedingly careful of cleanliness and neatness, nor in all the country, and most especially in Aquitania, could any man or woman, however poor, be seen either dirty or ragged.'

Pliny has left some notes on the niceties of their toilettes – a special soap which they are said to have invented, a special preparation for the complexion used by women; and a special perfume and other toilette devices are specified by other writers. Occasionally we are given details of dress and personal ornament and especially of armour: Diodorus refers to the famous horned helmets and the 'long shields as high as a man', which recalls the reference of the Panegyrist (cf. p. 45 above) to Divitiacus leaning on his long shield as he addressed the Roman senate.

In general, however, details of the finer aspects of Gaulish life are spare. The Romans thought of them as they knew them best, in camp life and in the field. The picture presented of the Gaulish feasts is that of a bivouac round the camp fire, with its central cauldron full of huge joints allotted according to the prestige of each of the champions present, the tradition echoed later in the Irish *Story of Mac Da Thó's Pig* (cf. p. 271 below). We have to remind ourselves continually that this is not the formal life of the Gaulish aristocracy which set value on such things as the beautifully enamelled bronze flagons almost certainly found in a grave at Basse-Yutz on the Moselle (cf. p. 225 below). The Romans meanwhile have left us both in art and in literature an ample portrait gallery of the Gaulish warriors as they knew them in the field and as they had derived descriptions from earlier writers such as Posidonius, who had travelled in Gaul in the late second century B.C. and who knew them at first hand.

The Gauls were head-hunters, and Posidonius, who had encountered the habit, is reported by Strabo as giving the following account:

> There is also that custom, barbarous and exotic, which attends most of the northern tribes . . . when they depart from the battle they hang the heads of their enemies from the necks of their horses, and when they have brought them home, nail the spectacle to the entrance of their houses. At any rate Posidonius says that he himself saw this spectacle in many places, and that, although at first he loathed it, afterwards through his familiarity with it, he could bear it calmly.*

This habit is often cited by modern scholars to the discredit of the Gauls, and apologists suggest that the Gauls may have learnt the habit from the Ligurians, a neighbouring people to the south of them, among whom the cult of the human head figured prominently in both art and religion (cf. p. 157 below). But it should be remembered that head-hunting was universal, not only in Gaul, but among the insular Celts also. Irish sagas and early Welsh poetry contain many references to it, and traces are to be found also in the medieval Welsh story of Math fab Mathonwy. Even in Norse we meet it in the story of the

*Strabo, IV, 4, 5.

Earl of Orkney, who is said to have died of blood poisoning caused by a tooth from the head of his slain enemy which he was carrying hanging from his saddle-bow. We may compare also the cult of human decapitated heads in Norse in the *Fóstbroedna Saga*, *Grettissaga*, *Bjarnar Saga Hitdoelakappa*, *Laxdaela Saga*, and *Njalssaga*.

As an example of the Romans' picture of the Gauls I will quote again a brief passage from Ammianus Marcellinus.

Nearly all the Gauls are of a lofty stature, fair and of ruddy complexion: terrible from the sternness of their eyes, very quarrelsome, and of great pride and insolence. A whole troup of foreigners would not be able to withstand a single Gaul if he called his wife to his assistance who is usually very strong and with blue eyes; especially when, swelling her neck, gnashing her teeth, and brandishing her sallow arms of enormous size, she begins to strike blows mingled with kicks, as if they were so many missiles sent from the string of a catapult.

Diodorus Siculus also stresses the 'terrifying aspect' of the Gauls and their deep and harsh voices. One might be inclined to suspect a rare element of humour in Ammianus's description of the Gaulish women warriors if we had not Dio Cassius's portrait of Boudicca, the queen of the Iceni, the Celtic tribe in eastern Britain in the first century A.D., with which to compare it: 'She was huge of frame, terrifying of aspect, and with a harsh voice. A great mass of bright red hair fell to her knees: she wore a great twisted golden torc, and a tunic of many colours, over which was a thick mantle, fastened by a brooch. Now she grasped a spear, to strike fear into all who watched her.'

Such, then, are the Celtic peoples who developed in central and east central Europe towards the middle of the seventh century B.C., in what corresponds archaeologically to the early Iron Age, or the period of Hallstatt culture, and who conquered and settled most of central and much of southern Europe from *c.* 500 B.C. until the Roman conquest of Gaul by Julius Caesar.

They are the chief people of prehistoric Europe in its closing phase, which corresponds archaeologically to the period known as La Tène. Their essential homogeneity can be seen from the name Keltoi (κελτοι) by which they were known to the Greeks from the fifth century. The Romans called them Galli, and at a later time the term Galatae is commonly used by both Greek and Roman writers.

Information to be derived from archaeology is consistent with that of references to the Celts in classical authors. Our earliest reference, which dates from the fifth century, is that of Hecateus of Miletus, who knew them as occupying the land of the Ligurians. Herodotus twice states that the River Danube has its source in the land of the Celts, and he also states that they were the most westerly people of Europe except for the Cynetes, who seem to have been in Portugal.

The permanent impression made by the Celtic peoples on European history and culture, then, is to be seen in the writings of Greek and Roman authors, in the distribution and permanence of the Celtic languages, and in their material remains. Their languages are still with us in the countries and islands which fringe the European continent – 'on the edge of the habitable world' as the Romans expressed it. As a result of recent developments in linguistics, and especially in place-name studies, we are able to trace something of their movements and expansion southwards into the more advanced countries of the ancient world. Moreover they themselves have bequeathed to us so many richly furnished sites that we are able to enter into close contact with their material and spiritual civilization. We can study their political and military organization in their great *oppida* or 'hill-top towns'; their mythology and religious ideas in their sanctuaries; their personal appearance in their own art and sculpture and in that of their neighbours; their sense of refinement and grace in their art. The La Tène art of the late Iron Age has been described as 'the first contribution of the barbarians to an all-European culture'.

It has been shown in chapter 1 that in the early phases of the Hallstatt culture Celtic tribes were settled chiefly in southern Germany and a part of Bohemia, which has preserved in its name that of the original Celtic inhabitants, the *Boii*. In later centuries Celts are seen to have occupied almost the whole of Central Europe, including Czechoslovakia and, *c.* 600 B.C., parts of Gaul. The principal Celtic expansion seems to have begun about the middle of the fifth century and is believed to have reached Spain before 450, undoubtedly by way of Gaul (cf. p. 34 above). About 400 B.C. armed bands of Celts streamed over the Alps into Italy and occupied the valley of the Po, some of them plundering as far south as Rome and Apulia and even Sicily. It was not until the middle of the second century that the Romans were able to force them back, and finally in 82 B.C. to establish the remnant at the foothills of the Alps as a Roman province, Gallia Cisalpina.

Meanwhile Celtic tribes raided in Illyria and Pannonia and the Carpathians. In 279 B.C. they laid waste Macedonia and even, under their leaders Brennus and Acichorius, invaded Greece by way of Thrace and Thessaly, and with their allies the Celtic tribe of the Volcae Tectosages plundered the temple of Delphi. Tradition vouched for by Strabo claims that the treasure from Delphi formed the vast treasure sunk in the sacred lake of the temple of Toulouse (cf. p. 148 below), and that the impiety of Brennus was duly punished by his defeat and suicide. Celtic mercenaries were frequently found in Hellenistic armies in the third century. It was originally by the invitation of the king of Bythinia that some 20,000 Galatae (Celts) were invited into Asia Minor, about half of them as warriors, and in 270 were permanently settled in something of a native 'state' in the area still known as Galatia.

The southward extension of the Celtic peoples was stimulated and in some measure coerced by fresh pressure from new arrivals from the north and east. In the latter part of the second century B.C. a people known as the Cimbri made a series of incursions from their home – perhaps in northern Jutland – seeking new lands for settlement. Such names of their leaders as have been recorded are purely Celtic, and references in Diodorus, Strabo and Pliny suggest that perhaps they spoke a Celtic language. Whatever the original nucleus of the Cimbri, however, they were joined by people known as Teutones. The latter word, moreover, is itself cognate with a Celtic common noun *tuath* (cf. Welsh *tud*, 'people') and our evidence on the whole suggests that the Teutons or Germans were a division of the Celtic peoples.

The Cimbri seem to have first turned eastwards, attacking the Celtic tribe of the Boii long settled in what was formerly Bohemia, and to have passed from there to the middle Danube and the eastern Alps, where they were defeated by the Romans at Noreia in 113. But their pressure had forced the Helvetii to leave the area where they were established between the Rhine and the Danube and to form an uneasy home in Switzerland, only to cause serious trouble later by a partial expansion southwards into Gaul. Meanwhile the Cimbri and the Teutones moved westwards and southwards through Gaul as far as Aquitania and by way of the Brenner pass into Italy. They were finally defeated in 102 at Aix-en-Provence and in 101 at Vercellae in northern Italy.

The classic area on the Continent established by the Celts was, of course, Gaul. But Gaul was not Celticized all at once or with any degree of uniformity. The north and centre were the earliest and most completely conquered, and the Celtic element diminished from north to south, where earlier cultures influenced the invaders. The original extent of Celtic settlement in southern Gaul was much smaller than in the historical period. Even at the time of Caesar's conquest in the first century B.C. Gaul was not entirely settled by Celtic peoples. Caesar himself recognized three peoples there, whom he distinguished as Galli, identical with the people calling themselves Celtae, occupying the country from the Garonne to the Seine and the

Marne; Aquitani, between the Pyrenees and the Garonne; and Belgae, from the Marne and the Seine to the Rhine. He omits to mention the region of Narbonne because it had been reduced half a century earlier to a Roman province. He tells us that the three provinces differ from one another in their language, their customs, and their laws; but he does not enlarge on these differences, and in his account of the customs of the Gauls in his *Commentaries*, especially in Book VI, he speaks always of Gauls in general.

By Caesar's time, and indeed long before, the Gauls clearly dominated a large part of Gaul, but earlier populations lingered on. At the time of Caesar's conquest the Armorican peninsula was at least partially under Celtic domination, but in more ancient times it was probably the least Celticized area of Gaul. Of the names of the five Gaulish tribes in Armorica, enumerated by Caesar, only that of the Redones (modern Rennes) in the valley of the Vilaine is certainly Celtic, those of the Namnetes (modern Nantes) and the Venetes (modern Vannes) being only doubtfully Celtic, while those of the coastal tribes of the Coriosolites in the north and the Osismii in the west are almost certainly pre-Celtic. The Ligurians and Iberians occupied relatively small areas in the south-east and south-west respectively. Already in the sixth century B.C. the Phocaeans had established an important colony and trading state in Massalia (Latin Massilia, modern Marseilles) which remained permanently in good relations with Rome, from which it was separated till the third century B.C. by the Ligurians.

To the west of the Ligurians were the Iberians, the original inhabitants of Aquitania. In general, Aquitania is limited to the course of the Garonne, and Grenier* believes that Caesar exaggerates in claiming that 'in the extent of its lands and the number of its men it constituted a third of Gaul'. In its general character it differed very considerably from Gaul proper and Strabo tells us that the peoples were much nearer to the Iberians

***Les Gaulois*, p. 152.

than to the Gauls in both their speech and physical traits. Celtic elements had already settled among the Iberians, but Aquitaine regarded herself, and was regarded by the rest of Gaul, as a distinct people, even to the end. The Gallo-Roman poet Ausonius, himself a native of Bordeaux, tells us that his maternal grandmother from the neighbourhood of Dax near the Spanish border was nick-named Maura ('a Moor') because of her dark colour. Still more significant is the passage in the *Dialogues* of Sulpicius Severus in which Sulpicius, a cultured Aquitanian, teases Gallus, an educated Gaul from St Martin's community at Tours, on the ground of his Gaulish appetite and love of large meals and good cooking. The entire passage suggests that the Gaul is regarded, and regards himself, as a rustic provincial, but though he blushes and hesitates and is diffident, he has his own pride and self-respect. He points out that the climate of Gaul does not permit asceticism, and adds, 'As I have often told you, Sulpicius, we are, in a word, Gauls.' He is proud of his nation. We note the same hauteur in the reply of the Caledonian woman, attributed by Dio Cassius to the wife of Argentocoxus, when Julia Augusta, the wife of Severus, jested with her about the free intercourse of her sex with men in Britain. She replied, 'We fulfil the demands of nature in a much better way than do you Roman women; for we consort openly with the best men, whereas you let yourselves be debauched in secret by the vilest.' The Celts were always and everywhere a proud people.

The Gaulish peoples did not enter Gaul as a single nation. Originally they appear to have been organized as military units, and they remained units both politically and economically, each occupying a more or less defined river valley with its surrounding mountains for the sake of agriculture, pasturage and woods. Thus the Allobroges spread from the Rhône to the Alps; the Sequani occupied the plateaux of the Jura and the lowlands of the Doubs and the Saône; the Aedui held from the Saône to the plateau of Autun and down again towards the

Loire. These great territories seem to have been to some extent artificial creations. Gradually in the course of conquest and settlement the separate Celtic elements formed political and military unions, both among themselves and with the native inhabitants of the country. When by about 400 they had penetrated as far south as the ancient territory of the Ligurians they at once formed a confederation with them – known to modern historians as the Celto-Ligurian League – under a single chief who led them against the wealthy Greek trading colony of Massalia. Twice the Romans relieved the colony – in 154 and 125 B.C. – and founded Provence, the first Roman possession in Gaul proper. In the last days of Gaulish independence the Gauls had lost any unity which they may originally have had, thus leaving the way open to Roman conquest.

The most recent arrivals in Gaul were the Belgae, who are believed to have crossed the Rhine into north-eastern Gaul in the fourth and third centuries B.C., pushed forward by pressure from the Germans. According to Caesar they claimed to be of pure Teutonic origin, but they spoke a Celtic language and their leaders bore Celtic names, so they were perhaps of an original backward Celtic stock with a later Teutonic intermixture. Caesar found the related tribe of the Bellovaci among his most formidable opponents, and their way of life and individual type of fortification help to account for the rapid progress of their movements westwards. Their fortresses, unlike the typical Gaulish hill-top *oppida*, tended to be of oval shape, and to be sited in river valleys, depending on rivers and swamps for defence. They showed, however, a preference for commanding promontories, cut off by a huge rampart and a broad, flat ditch with steep external sides; and also formidable entrances, often flanked by bold inturns of the main rampart. The Belgae had few towns, and their mode of life was comparatively austere.

Caesar records settlement of the Belgae as having been established in southern Britain before his arrival, and from the names of their tribes in Gaul, some fifteen in number, we can recognize in Britain settlements of the Belgae to the north of the Downs even as far west as the Bristol Channel, the Atrebates to the south of the Thames and the Catuvellauni to the south of the Wash. The Belgae probably reached the Armorican peninsula in the west of Gaul in the third century B.C.

In the days of Gaulish independence before the Roman Conquest, Gaul was divided into some sixteen separate large groups, variously known to classical writers as *civitates, populi, nationes, gentes*, ἔθνη. These political units seem to have been composed of the smaller subdivisions known as *pagi*, of which the Gaulish provinces are, in fact, collections. Caesar tells us that the Helvetii were divided into four groups or *pagi*. Among the Aedui at least six are known, including Bibracte, their *oppidum*. The *pagus* was not originally a territorial unit, but a group of men who had united as fellows-in-arms, and constituted a division of the Gaulish army. After the victory the men of the *pagus* and their families were settled on the land as their reward. The chief of a *pagus* was originally a vassal of a more powerful chief, and became in consequence his subordinate. The *pagus* represents the union of a group of men and of a land and does not differ essentially from a 'people', because before the Roman conquest the smaller peoples sought to group themselves to form a greater, or to place themselves under the protection of a greater. The *pagus* has been described as the primordial cell of Gaulish life.

A *civitas* was not only the principal nucleus of a population, not merely a city, but all the territory of a people with its inhabitants, a federal state; and each *civitas* was a self-dependent unit. All these larger divisions of a people, the *civitates*, had their own name, and frequently also their own fortified centres, their *oppidum*, their tribal centre and their 'capital'. Their name is often perpetuated in the modern province and its inhabitants: Paris, the 'capital' of the Parisi; Trier, the 'capital' of the Treveri; Chartres, the 'capital' of the Carnuti.

The *civitates* were originally governed by their own kings.

The most ancient legendary Celtic chief, Ambigat, was king of the Bituriges, and almost all the rulers of the great Gaulish nations originally had this title, but in Caesar's time the influence of the kings was giving way to that of the *vergobret*, the appointed chief magistrate. We can watch the process at work among the Aedui in Caesar's account of the struggle between the former king of the Aedui, Divitiacus, and his successor and younger brother, Dumnorix. By intrigue and carefully manipulated relations with neighbouring states, in particular the Helvetii and the Sequani, and by his popularity with the 'common people', Dumnorix had succeeded to all the hereditary privileges of kingship – the cementing of wider Gaulish military and political alliances, the military command of the Aedui as Caesar's nominal ally, even the responsibility for the religious duties of his tribe. His elder brother, Divitiacus, whom he had displaced, and who had become a *vergobret* – though the term is not used of him – appealed to the Roman senate for aid against the Germans and their allies under Ariovistus, invading from the north. He acted as Caesar's loyal collaborator throughout the invasion. Dumnorix, who would today be called a devoted nationalist, was killed in resisting. The history of the two brothers is an epitome of the death-struggle of family and peoples under the ordeal of foreign invasion.

In the pages of Caesar's diary of the Roman conquest we have, as it were, a brilliant documentary film of the political distribution of the various Gaulish peoples in the later period of their independence. From his narrative we see clearly how the number and disunity of the Gaulish states in the second and first centuries B.C. explain the conquest of this brave and noble people by Caesar and the Roman arms. Gaulish tradition claims that by about 400 B.C. the Bituriges had dominated the Celtic peoples, and seem to have counted among their subjects the important states of the Aedui, the Carnutes and others. By the second century the Celtic hegemony had passed to the Arverni, who among their other subordinate states included even the once powerful Allobroges of the Rhône valley. On Caesar's arrival he found the Aedui, the Sequani and the Arverni struggling for dominance, and so far from presenting a united front against the invader, throwing all their resources into a struggle for provincial power.

Gaul was doomed. She was in a pincer movement. The conquering Teutonic tribes were penetrating from the north, the Roman legions from the south. About 71 B.C. Ariovistus, the king of the Teutonic tribe of the Suevi, induced by the Gaulish tribe of the Sequani, invaded and defeated their rival, the Aedui. In vain Divitiacus, the *vergobret* of the Aedui, went to Rome about 60 B.C. to seek help for his tribe against the invading Teutons. Inexplicably, as it now seems to us, the senate in 59 B.C. recognized Ariovistus as 'King' and 'Friend and ally of the Roman people' (*rex atque amicus*), though Caesar himself refers to him as *rex Germanorum*. Future foreign domination, whether Teutonic or Roman, was inevitable for Gaul.

Caesar was depending in his northward march on his professed allies, the Aedui, to prevent the Helvetii under their leader Orgetorix from joining the Sequani to the west of the Rhône in their efforts to leave the Swiss homelands and to penetrate into southern Gaul; but he was hampered throughout by Dumnorix, who had married the daughter of Orgetorix and was secretly aiding the Helvetii, in the belief that if the Aedui could no longer hold the supremacy it would be better to be ruled by Gauls than by Romans. 'He hated Caesar and the Romans', and both he and Orgetorix were hoping to make themselves independent kings. To this end Dumnorix had entered into diplomatic relations with neighbouring tribes, and expended large sums in winning over the loyalty of the Aedui. But the project failed and although Caesar pardoned him, convinced by Divitiacus that this was expedient, 'he had him watched'.

After the defeat of the Aedui Divitiacus lent valuable help to

Caesar, first in his campaign against Ariovistus and his Belgic allies, and later, after the defeat of Ariovistus and in the final struggle of 57 B.C., against the Belgae and the tribe of the Bellovaci, near neighbours of the Aedui. Divitiacus so manoeuvred the Aeduan forces as to separate the Bellovaci from the Belgae, and the enemy's resistance finally crumbled. Caesar agreed to receive the Bellovaci into his protection for the sake of the respect he had towards Divitiacus and the Aedui, but he would not trust Dumnorix, and when in 55–54 B.C. he made two expeditions into Britain he insisted on forcing Dumnorix to accompany him, in the firm belief that he was still busily stirring up the chieftains of Gaul to resist embarkation, and to stand united in the interests of Gaul. Finally, Dumnorix perished at the hands of Caesar's cavalry as he made a vain dash for home and freedom at the moment of embarkation.

When Caesar was campaigning in eastern and northern Gaul he delegated to his lieutenant, Publius Crassus, the campaign to reduce the western territories between the Seine and the Loire. The rapidity of his approach and the report of Caesar's conquests shocked these western states into a temporary surrender. By the following year, however, the greatest of the four Armorican peoples, the maritime Veneti on Morbihan Bay, had induced the other Armorican states to join with them in resisting the Romans and sending a message of defiance to Crassus. Our picture of the final conquest is fuller for this little corner of Gaul than for Caesar's campaigns farther east, for in Armorica we watch the course of events, not only from the invaluable evidence of contemporary hoards of coins, but from the detailed accounts of Caesar and also of Dio Cassius, as well as other later well-informed sources, some of which would seem to be derived from eye-witnesses.

Caesar gives us our first close view of the Veneti, the leaders of the Armorican resistance. He tells us that their state was by far the most powerful of any of that sea-coast because of both their expert seamanship and their fleet, in which they were accustomed to sail to Britain. He tells us, moreover, that they controlled the ports and almost the entire trade of that open and stormy coast, and that they had as tributaries (*victigales*) almost all those who were accustomed to sail the sea. They were evidently the dominant people even beyond Armorica, for in their preparations to oppose the Romans they sent for auxiliaries to Britain, and Caesar further tells us elsewhere that in all the struggles between the Romans and the Gauls help had been sent to the Gauls from Britain. The Veneti were not wholly dependent on their fleet, however, for great stress is laid by both Caesar and Dio Cassius on the strength and number of their promontory forts or cliff castles, whose strategical importance in coastal warfare was considerable, making the approach to the Veneti fleet inaccessible from both the landward side and the sea. Caesar found that the initial approach from the landward side was hopeless and a new fleet had to be built on the Loire, adapted to local conditions.

The Romans had no experience of naval warfare in Atlantic waters, in which the Veneti were expert. In the great battle fought in Morbihan Bay between the Romans and the Veneti and their allies in 56 B.C. the fleet of the Veneti is estimated by Caesar at two hundred and twenty ships, built to negotiate the tricky conditions of that rocky coast. He describes their sails as of thin dressed leather designed to resist the Atlantic gales, and the ships themselves as built of oak and as high and massive as citadels, the benches, made of planks a foot wide, 'fastened by iron nails as thick as a man's thumb'. The Roman ships, on the other hand, were lighter and lower, and thus able to make use of oars for manoeuvring. The Romans were able to watch the battle from the cliffs above. At the first attack the great Veneti fleet had the advantage of a following wind; but eventually their great ships, immobilized by a change of wind, fell victims to the lighter Roman ships in hand-to-hand fighting, and after eight hours the battle ended in a complete Roman victory – as

Dio reminds us, 'the only Roman naval victory on the Ocean'. In Caesar's words, 'by this battle the war with the Veneti and the whole of the sea-coast was finished'.

The horrors that ensued are vividly described by both Caesar and Dio. Dio tells us that when the men were defeated and killed, the boats ripped open or set on fire and burned or towed away, the remaining crews killed themselves to avoid capture, throwing themselves into the sea rather than perish at the hands of the Romans, 'for in zeal and daring they were not at all behind their opponents'. The flight of the defeated Armorican confederates has been traced by the finds of contemporary coin hoards hastily buried along the route northwards through the countries of the Redones and the Coriosolites and even into Jersey, where thousands of Armorican coins, chiefly in hoards, have been found, and are attributed to refugees from Caesar's conquest, some, apparently, *en route* for southern England. Some of the cliff castles of the Devon–Cornish peninsula have been traced to the same period and cause, notably the Rumps, at St Minver in North Cornwall, where the defensive earthworks are typical of the cliff castles of western Brittany, and the general circumstances of the site suggest that here we have a colony of Armorican refugees from Caesar. The Armoricans had staked and lost everything and were now a conquered country, a western extremity of Roman Gaul, and their tribal centres became *civitates*, city states. The words of the great French historian Camille Jullien, in *Histoire de la Gaule*, III, V, are no empty rhetoric: 'This strong and vigorous nation of the Veneti, whose origins and power go back to the builders of the dolmens, the most ancient and original of all Gaul, ended in slavery and death.'

The conquest of Gaul by the Romans was the end of a great nation, but not of a great people. The heroic age was at an end, and with it the individuality, the pride and power of the great independent past. In exchange for these the Gauls acquired the amenities of a higher civilization, material, economic and intellectual; and the substitution of the *Pax Romana* for the wastage and uncertainties of centuries of restless warfare and military competition – the outward expression of a struggle for existence. These cultural gifts of Rome to Gaul must have been largely responsible for the development of the intellectual and spiritual pre-eminence of Gaul in the first five centuries of the Christian era, and indirectly for the rich gifts of poetry and saga – even now not fully appreciated – which Gaul transmitted to the insular Celts. It is impossible to over-rate the value of the gifts of education and literacy which Rome gave to Gaul in exchange for her liberty and which made her a partaker in the highest culture of the age.

CHAPTER 3

The Origins of the Celtic Kingdoms in Britain and Ireland

THE ROMANS IN BRITAIN

THE destruction of the Venetic fleet contributed to the final collapse of Celtic power in Gaul. But there remained a centre of Celtic power in Britain, and this constituted a possible threat to the newly-won Roman control of Gaul. Caesar made two armed reconnaissances of south-eastern Britain in 55 and 54 B.C. to assess the position, but whatever may have been his ultimate intention with regard to Britain, he made no attempt at permanent conquest. Political events in the Roman world after his assassination prevented any further plans for conquest until the following century, and it was not until A.D. 43, in the reign of Claudius, that Britain was invaded again. This time the intention was conquest, but the motives differed from those of the time of Caesar. There were additional reasons, including the important factor of the economic wealth of Britain. It is possible that the insular Celts continued to annoy the Romans in contributing to political unrest in northern Gaul, but the Britons could hardly have been regarded as a serious military threat to the security of Gaul.

On the eve of the conquest the people were still in a heroic age of society. The country was divided into a number of separate kingdoms, and there was no sort of political unity. This must have greatly facilitated the Roman conquest, for each kingdom could be attacked separately. Some had an *oppidum*, often a great hill-top citadel where many could take refuge, but apparently there was no overall 'policy', no agreement among the tribal kingdoms on methods of warfare. We have no evidence of important cities, no markets important enough to have left their traces. There was trade, both internal and with the Continent, and during the last century and a half of independence native coinage, originally introduced by the Belgae, was minted in southern Britain.

The position of the Celtic tribes in Britain at this time was roughly speaking as follows. In the south the Belgic tribes had been settling from Gaul for some time and now occupied a large part of south-eastern Britain, having penetrated as far as the Cotswolds in the west. The tribes of the Cantii of Kent, the Trinovantes of Essex, and the Iceni of East Anglia were already partly Romanized, and were prepared to enter into treaty relationship with the Romans as client states. Further afield, however, the ancient Celtic kingdoms were by no means ready to give up their independence. The Parisi of East Yorkshire, and the largest of all the old native kingdoms, the Brigantes of northern England, aimed at retaining their independence of Rome. In Wales, the native tribes saw their opportunity of maintaining their independence, and after his defeat in the south-east Caratacus, the fugitive son of Cunobelinus, who was now perhaps in control of the fighting forces of the Silures, evidently sought to make an alliance with the tribes of north-east Wales, and perhaps also with the Brigantes under their leader, Venutius. Venutius's wife Cartimandua, however, was in fact the actual reigning queen of the Brigantes, and she held firmly to her clientship with the Romans, with whom her territory marched and to whom she was under previous obligations. Accordingly, when Caratacus approached Cartimandua she handed him over in chains to the Romans. The Brigantes, abandoned by Cartimandua, were later defeated.

Meanwhile the Welsh tribes continued to give trouble, especially in the north. The tribes of Anglesey, rich in deposits of copper, doubtless felt themselves in a position to oppose the Romans and they manfully defended their shores. The distinguished general Suetonius Paulinus had just destroyed the centre of Druidic power in Anglesey in A.D. 61 when he heard of the rebellion of the Iceni under Boudicca and was forced to return south. With difficulty he defeated the rebels, including the Trinovantes who had made common cause with Boudicca. The vengeance taken on the conquered people of East Anglia left the Romans no cause to be proud, but it left them free to give their whole attention to the conquest of the north, and in A.D. 71 began the northern campaign which eventually was to extend the Roman Province into southern Scotland.

Agricola conquered the Brigantes in the north, penetrated as far into the Highlands as Inchtuthill on the Tay and there built a vast legionary fortress of fifty acres which served as winter quarters. This was as far as the Romans penetrated into Scotland in the Perthshire highlands, but they made their way eastwards via Strathmore and Kincardineshire and up the east coast as far northwards as Kintore on the River Don, and perhaps further. In the course of their eastward march they were met by a vast array of Caledonians, presumably the immediate ancestors of the historic Picts, with whom they fought a great pitched battle at an unidentified place called Mons Graupius; but they penetrated no further into the Highlands. About A.D. 100 or even earlier Roman control in Scotland was at least partly abandoned for a time.

We have reason to believe, however, that before the advanced garrisons withdrew southwards they may, to some extent at least, have trained in Roman methods of warfare the British (Celtic) to the north of the temporary boundary of the Roman province. These Celtic peoples on the frontier would presumably have been as unwilling as the Romans to be overrun by the Picts to the north of them, and would willingly be trained by the Romans in superior military tactics. A rebellion in northern Britain around A.D. 117 subsequently brought the Emperor Hadrian to Britain, and it was decided to abandon northern Britain entirely. The Roman Wall from Wallsend on the Tyne to Bowness on the Solway secured its southern limit, but twenty years later it was advanced by the building of the turf wall from the Forth to the Clyde under Antoninus Pius. Later rebellions and risings in the Scottish lowlands and the north of England destroyed the Roman defences, and although Septimus Severus early in the third century subdued the Lowlands and the Caledonians of the Perthshire Highlands, the Antonine Wall was no longer held as the British frontier, and the Romans are believed subsequently to have delegated the defence of the territory between it and Hadrian's Wall to native British tribes. It is possible to trace through later British pedigrees and other sources something of the change-over from Roman to British control of this region.

From now it was only a matter of time. A respite was gained by Theodosius in the reign of Constantius I in the second part of the fourth century, and Hadrian's Wall was repaired but advance forts beyond the Wall were abandoned. Signal stations were built along the Yorkshire coast. The Roman position was weakened by Magnus Maximus, a Roman official of Spanish origin stationed in Britain as governor or legionary officer, who in 383 was acclaimed Emperor by his troops and passed into Gaul, to reign there for three years at Trier before he was killed at Aquileia in 388. Further forts were built and re-manned southwards and westwards from the Wash to prevent hostile barbarian landings on the coast. It was formerly thought that there was a uniform system of forts against landings, but it has recently been shown that forts of different kinds were scattered round the west coast with the same end in view. A fort at Cardiff was rebuilt against Irish settlers (the Déisi) in south-west Wales, and forts at Caer Gybi, Holyhead and Lancaster were built about the same time to counter attacks of the Irish across Morecambe Bay, while Elslack and Piercebridge are believed to have been built to counter deep thrusts from the west against the Plain of York. Even the arrival of the great general Stilicho in 395 and his reorganization of the defence system could not save the province. The line of defence was now based on York, and the defences of the north were henceforth presumably based on

York also. The end came in 407. Constantine III was proclaimed emperor by the army in Britain and, employing such means for the defence of Britain as he was able, he crossed to Gaul with yet more British troops to aid the continental army, and was slain in battle. Procopius, a contemporary informant, assures us that 'notwithstanding this the Romans were never able to recover Britain which henceforth continued to be ruled by usurpers'. It was at this point, as Zosimus, a particularly well-informed chronicler, tells us, that the Britons and some of the Gauls (doubtless the Armoricans) seceded from Rome, took up arms, and struggling bravely on their own behalf freed themselves from the onslaughts of the barbarians. In 410 the famous rescript of Honorius came to Britain, formally rescinding the Roman law prohibiting the barbarians from bearing arms. According to Gildas (chapter 20), the Britons sent a letter to the consul Aetius in about 446 expressing 'the groans of the Britons' and their suffering under the depredations of the Picts and Scots; but without effect. Britain henceforth must look after herself as a free country.

The Roman occupation had not penetrated very deeply into the Celtic institutions of Britain. The Romans had, moreover, not set foot in Ireland. In southern Britain, south and east of a line from York to the Cotswolds, the most fertile part of the country, they had succeeded in implanting themselves in some depth. This was the area of Britain where something of continental conditions prevailed, and where the Roman villas are found for the most part; but in Wales and the north little more than a military occupation could be claimed, and the further west we go the fewer the traces of Roman amenities or customs.

In the greater part of the country Roman civilization had made little impression. Despite the lofty superstructure built by the late Professor Haverfield* there is no sufficient reason to believe that the Latin language was widely known or used, and

* *The Romanization of Roman Britain*, p. 29f.

the 'satis' scrawled on a tile from Silchester may be no more than an 'exeat' from a satisfied overseer to a workman who has fulfilled his quota of work. Place-names carry few Roman traces other than the Caster–Chester groups. The smaller type of Celtic fields still prevailed everywhere throughout the country. It was an essentially agricultural country, but the big plough had not yet penetrated. The Romans had been satisfied with such grain as the Celtic people could garner for them.

Nevertheless, during the occupation Roman and Briton had learned to live together, particularly in the civil zone. The Romans had been anxious to involve the native British population in local administration, and had encouraged the adoption of a Roman way of life, at least for the upper classes. But on the other hand, for example, they allowed ample provision for the native religions to flourish side by side with their own. As late as the fourth century the great sanctuary of Nodons or Nodens on the River Severn had been established, to a native god whose name is identical with that of the Irish god Nuadu Argetlám, and connected with the Welsh Lludd Llaw Ereint. It survived till the fifth century, but whereas we can trace that it was built as a Roman temple with the proceeds of the nearby shipbuilding or repairing yard on the Bristol Channel, the later repairs show signs of deterioration, while the surrounding defensive walls, first erected in the fifth century, are a sign of the unsettled times. The normal Romano-Celtic temple was the simple high, four-square Celtic pattern, perhaps copying models from the Rhineland.

Evidence for some degree of continuity of intellectual life in the post-Roman period is afforded by a number of anonymous letters, apparently dating from the fifth century, addressed by a son travelling on the Continent to his father at home. The father is evidently a bishop and it is clear that the ecclesiastical orders of the early Roman Church are still preserved in the British Church, for which there is evidence of diocesan organization in the early fourth century; but the letters seem to show the writer as having received a classical education. They are somewhat heretical (Pelagian) in tone, and carry us into a totally different atmosphere from the writings of the sixth-century churchman Gildas, or the ninth-century historian Nennius, showing Britain at this period between the end of Roman rule and the Saxon conquest as backward classical, rather than as early medieval. Reference is made in them to the education of boys in what looks like the Roman system, and we know from Tacitus that the Romans sought by their high-school system of education to place the native peoples on the same footing as themselves. Moreover, funerary inscriptions in stone show that Latin was at least understood. Communications between Britain and the Continent, and even the eastern Mediterranean, were maintained, especially by sea and from the west coast. All this suggests that Romanization among the educated classes was not simply a veneer.

POST-ROMAN BRITAIN

On the departure of the Romans the Celtic people of Britain entered upon a kind of Celtic revival. They had now not only to govern themselves, but also to foil the ever-increasing attempts of the Saxons on the east, the Picts to the north, and the Irish on the west to penetrate their defences and to overwhelm them. Obviously only a strong central government could hope for any success. The Britons had to fight on three fronts, but with the same aim – that of preserving their own Celtic integrity.

The Celts of Britain had learned much from their Roman overlords. They had learned something of the importance of unity, and of the essential value of civil government. The chief difference in the front they presented to the Saxon invaders, compared with that which they had presented to the Romans, was their realization of these two fundamentals of government. The Celtic peoples of Britain showed to the invading Romans a number of independent petty kingdoms, brave, with the courage of the heroic age, but incapable of acting together. They now sought, though not always successfully, to oppose the barbarian conquests with a united front and a central power. This they had learned from the Romans, as it would seem to us from the scattered and imperfect records which have come to us from that time. The Romans had left their own system of local government in the civil zone, and the native Celtic peoples seem to have attempted to maintain it, and to extend it to areas hitherto under Roman military control, such as Wales and northern Britain.

After the last Roman ruler had left our shores a native Celtic prince, Vortigern, seems to have taken over the command in eastern Britain and, with the help of the *ordo*, or the native Roman system of local councils, to have called in some Saxon mercenaries for help against the Picts who were menacing them from the north. We do not know who Vortigern was or the nature of his authority, but from various scattered notices he seems to have been a Romanized British chieftain from the west, probably from the Welsh border; this is the more probable since the Roman document, the *Notitia Dignitatum*, shows no defence measures around A.D. 400 along the western border of Britain. Probably the Romans here, as in the north, had left the defences in the charge of friendly chiefs. Vortigern's measure of calling in the Saxon auxiliaries was taken with the full recognition of the *ordo* and was fully in the Roman tradition. Gradually, however, the Saxons gained in strength, and as they did so Vortigern became hated for calling them in. He became, in fact, the most hated man in early British history. He is never spoken of as fighting, and indeed if we are to place any belief in traditions he must have been rather too old to bear arms, and it is his son who is spoken of as fighting in south-eastern Britain. Probably Vortigern himself in reality carried on the old régime of Roman days. We can safely dismiss all the evil tales reported about him three centuries later.

But Britain was not the only part of Europe facing barbarian incursions at this time. She received only the outer ripple of a great flood which was threatening Europe. In 406 the barbarians crossed the Rhine and inundated Gaul. In 409 and 410 Rome, 'the mistress of the world', fell to the Goths and was sacked. The contemporary anonymous Gaulish Chronicle records a specially heavy raid on Britain this same year.

It is not to be supposed that the continental countries, and Gaul in particular, were swept over simultaneously in a great conquering wave. The Franks had long been employed by the Romans as *foederati*, barbarian soldiers in Roman pay and employment, guarding the northern frontiers of Gaul. What happened in 406 or thereabouts is that the northern barbarians – the Franks and their allies – realized that they were no longer inferior in arms to Rome, and partly by force of arms, partly by purchase, made themselves masters of Gaul.

Britain could not hope to stand alone. It is not known how or when the Saxons first began to encroach on eastern Britain, but we know they came as mercenary soldiers and allies of the Romans in Britain. When and how they spread over the lowlands we do not really know in detail, apart from archaeological evidence derived from pagan Anglo-Saxon graves, and despite the impassioned pages of Gildas. No other contemporary accounts have come down to us. It is only natural that the Celtic inhabitants of Britain in the west should have transmitted legends to us – legends of which we cannot now test the validity. Gildas tells us that a last stand was made by one Aurelius Ambrosianus, 'the last of the Romans', somewhere in the west, perhaps on the Welsh border; but it came to nothing. Still later tradition, purely Celtic and oral for many centuries, would identify this Ambrosianus with King Arthur. We have no early written records for Arthur, but we have an ever-growing corpus of tradition, including one which would credit him with a victory at Mons Badonicus around 500, which held up the Saxon advance for about fifty years. Nevertheless the fact is beyond doubt that lowland England, like Gaul across the Channel, gradually became a predominantly Teutonic country.

This was not so in the west and north. The west and north – Wales and the Highlands of Scotland – remained Celtic and unconquered by any Teutonic peoples. They formed, together with Ireland, the last bulwark of the great Celtic culture which before Caesar dominated Europe. And it is a curious reflection that it was largely – so we believe – by this same Roman power that the Celtic people of Britain were enabled to retain their independence. The Celts of Britain were threatened simultaneously on three fronts. On the east the Teutonic peoples were gathering ever nearer and threatening to drive them into the western sea. On the north the powerful Picts were threatening by sea and land. On the west the Irish, the 'Scots' of early records, were rapidly winning for themselves the whole of the British Channel and South Wales and were penetrating the shores of Morecambe Bay and the Solway area and as far north as Argyll. We have every reason to believe, as we shall see, that what held the Picts in the Highlands may have been the Roman training given to the British Celts on the Border, and it would seem that on the Welsh border a similar force held. First the Roman treatment of the Cornovii of the Devon–Cornwall peninsula, and later the history of Vortigern, point in this same direction. The Romans seem to have bequeathed to the Celtic people of the frontiers some appreciation of military strategy and a superiority in arms above that of their neighbours. And in this way they may have contributed something to the salvation of the last remnants of the Celts beyond the mountains of the west, although it must be remembered that highland areas were neither attractive to the Anglo-Saxons, nor suitable for their methods of arable farming.

Our evidence for this is clearest in the north. Here we can judge from the pedigrees in a manuscript in the British Museum (Harl. 3859) that two dynasties of Romanized British chieftains seem to have policed each end of the Antonine Wall. Of these we hear most of the descendants of a certain Coel Hen whose son and grandson reappear among the ancestors of the ruling lines of chiefs of the Scottish border. At the other end of the wall Dyfnwal Hen seems to have been the ancestor of the chiefs of Galloway and Strathclyde till the time of Rhydderch Hen in the sixth century. Rhydderch Hen is a well-known historical character in his own right, and is traditionally said to have met St Columba in person. These two great lines of chieftains seem to have divided the border lands between them, and to have met to clash in Wales only at a much later date. Who they were in origin we have no clue, but as the *dux* disappeared from the *Notitia Dignitatum* in about 400 it is not unnatural to suppose that Coel Hen may have taken his place, and that his supply base may have been at York. His descendants appear in eastern Wales at a much later date. We hear little of Dyfnwal Hen in early days, but his descendants appear again much later among the ancestors of Merfyn Vrych in North Wales, as we shall see.

SCOTLAND

Scotland was a very divided country in early times. In addition to the British (akin to Welsh) population of the south between the walls, it had later, as the Teutonic element in south-eastern Britain increased, an ever-growing Anglian population in the south between the Forth and the Tyne. This is in reality an Anglian overlordship superimposed on an original British (perhaps partially Romanized) population; but the 'official' language was Anglian, and it gradually extended its sway northwards. In 685 the Anglian king Ecgfrith of Northumbria met his death at Dunnichen Mere in a northward thrust into Forfar, in which he was evidently aiming at what was at that time the capital of the southern Picts; but as the panegyric poet put it 'God favoured Brude mac Bile' – the reigning Pictish king – and the effort was never repeated. The Angles instead spread gradually westwards over the southern Scottish border till the English language came largely to supersede British (Welsh) south of the Highland Line.

Meanwhile, north of the territory dominated by the descendants of Coel Hen and Dyfnwal Hen, north, that is to say, of British Scotland between the two walls, the powerful Pictish realms had always predominated. The Picts, when they first came fully into the pages of history in the work of Bede, were divided into two realms, the northern and the southern Picts. The chief ruler of the northern Picts was at the mid sixth century a certain Brude mac Maelchon, and we gather that he held a commanding position, for he is called by Bede *rex potentissimus*; and he evidently commanded a fleet, for he had at his court a *subregulus* from the Orkneys. Adamnán represents St Columba as visiting him in his stronghold, which was probably Inverness. Otherwise we hear little of him, and his relationship to the southern Picts is not clear. The language of the Picts as shown in their inscriptions is not purely Celtic, but is thought to have been a superimposition of northern Celtic from the Continent on an indigenous language, perhaps dating from the late Bronze Age.

The southern Picts were destined to play an important part in Scottish history. They dwelt, as Bede says, *intra montes*, which seems to mean to the east of the dorsal spine of Scotland and to the south of the Mounth. They may originally have extended their influence much further west. In the historical period they occupied the whole valley of the Tay, and at the period when they first come into the pages of history they were divided into four more or less warring kingdoms, namely (1) the Athfótla (Atholl), the former kingdom of the Caledonii in the upper Tay, with its capital originally at Dunkeld (Dun Caledonii) and subsequently at Scone; (2) Circinn, comprising the north bank of the lower Tay, Strathmore, the most fertile district of Scotland, consisting later of Forfar or Angus and Kincardine and the Mearns, with its capital at Forfar; (3) Fife including Perthshire as far as the Ochils with its capital at Kilrymount (St Andrew's);

(4) Fortrenn, with a shifting capital and comprising the upper Earn and Forth.

But in the fifth century a new element entered Scotland from the west which was destined to disintegrate still further this neat framework of the southern Picts and completely change the history of Scotland, and the language of Scotland north of the Highland Line. This was nothing less than an 'invasion' from Ireland which, beginning in a small way, grew in importance till it imposed the Irish language on the whole of the Highlands in what is known today as Gaelic, and gradually extended its political sway over the Picts. What we think of today as the Gaelic culture of the Highlands began as the last and most successful effort of the Celtic peoples of northern Ireland to superimpose their sway on the peoples of Scotland after the Romans had lost their power and the northern Roman defences had come to an end. In the fifth century we have four peoples and four languages in Scotland: Pictish, the oldest, in the north; British south of the Antonine Wall; Irish in Argyll; and Anglian, the newest, just encroaching on the British as Irish was on the Pictish. In the following chapter we shall examine the growth of the Irish and the Anglian influences till they gradually occupy the whole field, and give us the northern kingdom of Scotland with its two languages, the Highland Celtic and the Lowland English.

WALES

The British of southern Scotland were obviously closely connected with the British of Wales throughout their history, but because of lack of written sources we hear little of this before the ninth century. At that time communication may have been effected across Morecambe Bay, and the shores of this Celtic pond and the neighbouring coasts may have been a centre of Celtic literary influence, as it was land-locked and offered quick and easy transport, whereas the route from southern Scotland to Wales by way of the old Roman road through Lancashire may have been more difficult. Owing to the isolation afforded to Wales by her central mountain massif she offers, in fact, a striking contrast to Scotland. Her royal houses were more stabilized; some of them had a life of eight hundred years. Moreover, they had come to regard the Romans as representing order, at least if we may judge by medieval traditions. These represent Wales as looking back to the Roman régime as a kind of Golden Age, and do not attempt seriously to trace their origin further back.

The first time that a foreign note enters the records of Wales in the historical period it comes from Scotland, however, and it is a very curious one. In the ninth-century *Historia Brittonum* of Nennius, which is our earliest source for Welsh history, we are told that a certain Cunedag (modern Cunedda), together with eight of his sons and one grandson, came from Manau Guotodin (near the Firth of Forth) a hundred and forty-six years before the reign of Maelgwn prince of Gwynedd, in the time of his great-grandfather, and that they had 'expelled the Irish for ever from those lands'. The form of the proper names and the context indicate a seventh-century date for the story. There is no hint of a migration, and Cunedag is never referred to as *rex*, or by any title. This circumstance has led most historians to conclude that Cunedag was transferred to Wales from Scotland by a customary Roman procedure; but there are difficulties in the way of this interpretation, even supposing Cunedag came by sea from Dumbarton and across Morecambe Bay. Yet the details suggest that there is some historical tradition behind it, linking the men of Scotland with an early Welsh dynastic group. In one text of the royal genealogies (Harl. 3859) appended to the *Historia Brittonum*, a list of Cunedag's sons is given in a tenth-century orthography, and at the conclusion the eldest son Typiaun is said to have died in Manau Guotodin, and his son Meridaun to have divided his share of the Welsh heritage with Typiaun's brothers. 'This is their boundary, from the Dee to the Teifi, and they held very many districts in the western parts of Britain.'

This list of Cunedag's sons is late, and we have no hint of an earlier one. It might be a composition of later times, like one which we possess of Arthur's battles, and intended to account retrospectively for the distribution of the Welsh kingdoms. All the pedigrees of the Welsh kings start at some date about the end of the Roman period, and there seems to have been in the ninth century an attempt to clarify the native dynasties of this period. We find it in the account of the sons of Erc among the Dálriada of Scotland, and even in Ireland. It was in some way a part of the Celtic revival. Moreover, the sons of Cunedag are not all found in the part of Wales most likely to have been occupied so early by the Irish, and the Irish were certainly not banished from Wales so early. But if we exclude the sons, what remains? The notice about Cunedag's eldest son Typiaun looks as if some genuine tradition lay behind the story. And the story itself is a fairly close parallel to what happened later in the reign of Mervyn Vrych – a migration of British leaders from British Scotland to north-west Wales. Did some earlier tradition of a similar movement exist?

However we dispose of Cunedag and his sons, the map of Wales, as it may be reconstructed at the beginning of the post-Roman period, is a mosaic of small states, each ruled by its own dynasty, for most of which an origin has been provided by the list of Cunedag's sons. Each has its own genealogy carefully prepared as from this time, each one inheriting from father to son.

By no means all the Welsh dynasties claimed their origin from the sons of Cunedag, who were mostly confined to the north and west. Dyfed in the south-west retained something of the name of Roman times, Demetia, and claimed origin from an Irish dynasty which had entered peacefully enough, so it seems, at some time in the late Roman period and kept its distinctively Irish character till the tenth century. This little non-

Welsh kingdom contained the site in the Valley of Hodnant (or Hoddnant, the *Vallis Rosina*) which grew into the Church of Mynyw, the monastic foundation which later became the Cathedral dedicated to St David (Dewi Sant), the patron saint of Wales. The little mountain kingdom of Brycheiniog was never conquered, and its dynasty, traditionally partly Irish in origin, was one of the most stable in Wales, lasting till the tenth century. The royal line of British kings on the Upper Wye derived an undisputed descent from Vortigern, and according to the *Historia Brittonum* (chapter 48) Gwerthrynion also traced the ancestors of its early chieftains to Vortigern from whom its name derives. The kingdom of south-eastern Wales claimed to be derived from the Silures, and to have a dynasty descended from Caratacus. The origin of the kingdom of Powys – 'the garden of Wales' – is obscure, but it was specially privileged by the Romans, and the death of Cyngen, the last king of the old native line, is entered in the *Annales Cambriae* in 852.

As we trace the history of the Welsh dynasties during this period, we cannot fail to be struck by their great stability. In this they offer a great contrast to Scotland, as we have seen. This is no doubt partly owing to the nature of our sources, which historically are much better for Wales at this time than for Scotland. Some credit must also be given to the Welsh mountains which naturally cut up the interior, and render small-scale invasion less easy and attractive. But there can be no doubt that the influence of the Roman régime had a quietening effect on Wales. The great Roman forts which ringed it round not only precluded the Celtic people of Wales from rising against their conquerors, but also protected their native chiefs from one another.

In the sixth century, the 'age of the saints', one dynasty was destined to play an important part. This was the family of Maelgwn Gwynedd, descendants in the fourth generation from Cunedag. Maelgwn is to be identified with Maglocunus, the 'island dragon' addressed by Gildas as the fifth of the wicked princes on the coast of Britain singled out by him for special opprobrium. Maelgwn had, like many other princes of these troubled times, spent some of his youth in a monastery, but had issued forth to live the life of a heroic age prince, exchanging the religious chants for the panegyrics of his court minstrels. All that Gildas tells us of the splendid and impressive figure of Maelgwn and of his court is typical of a prince of the heroic age, and he was just such a character as would be likely to attach to himself and his son the many traditions of which they were the subjects in later times.

As the sixth century draws on we find in North Wales a different world, with King Cadfan and his famous inscription on the inscribed cross in the Church of Llangadwaladr near Aberffraw. The inscription runs

> *Catamanus rex, sapientisimus, opinatisimus omnium regum*
> King Cadfan, the most cultured and renowned of all kings

The up-to-date lettering and the nature of the inscription suggest that the little court of Aberffraw on the west coast of Anglesey was in direct touch with continental culture (perhaps through the presence of literate clergy). This little monument was doubtless set up by Cadfan's son Cadwallon or his grandson Cadwaladr, for the Church of Llangadwaladr is within sight of Aberffraw and is obviously the family burial place. Here we are at the heart of the dynasty which was to move Welsh backward provincialism into the wider world, and to do battle with the Saxons from Celtic Britain.

Cadwallon, son of Cadfan, was the ally of Penda of Mercia and England's most powerful enemy in the north. He was killed in battle near Hexham, far to the north outside Wales, in 633, after his defeat by Oswald, king of the Northumbrians. The death of Cadwallon of Wales and of Urien of Rheged from the neighbourhood of Carlisle within a few years of one another may well have prevented England from becoming once more a Celtic country.

BRITTANY

Meanwhile a new Celtic state was founded to the south. Armorica had formed a part of Gaul, but the Roman régime had swept over it, and during the fifth to the seventh centuries a new Celtic population had entered from the British Isles. Gildas, in his hatred of the Saxons, calls attention to the British fleeing before them, and singing sad songs instead of sailors' shanties as they sped over the sea 'beneath the swelling sail'. Their destination, although Gildas does not actually name it, was obviously Brittany. Here colonization was, however, a carefully planned operation. The country was traditionally colonized by a prince of royal stock from Gwent in South Wales, but the majority of the settlers undoubtedly came from British Cornwall, if we may judge by the language which the newcomers imposed on the old Gaulish land. The leaders appear to have been the chieftains of eastern Wales, and the actual act of settlement is believed to have been made by the so-called saints, that is to say, the educated members of the community, qualified to make the fitting arrangements – probably partly legal – for the accommodating of the settlers. These 'saints' were often the younger sons of the chiefs. We do not hear of any clashes between the various colonists or between the colonists and the native inhabitants, and all seems to have been conducted in an orderly manner. There are indications that the chiefs at times retained their old homes in Wales along with their new Armorican settlements. In fact, the sea here, as between the west of Britain and Ireland, was a link rather than a dividing line.

The new name of Brittany, which superseded the older classical name of Armorica, is an indication of the change of front of the colony, which now looked westwards. It was divided into three principal kingdoms known as Domnonia, Cornouaille and Bro Erech. Cornouaille in the south-west has only a purely legendary history, and the reason for its name is unknown, since there is no sufficient reason to associate it with British Cornwall. Domnonia in the north appears to be more authentic historically, for although it is ignored by the contemporary historian, Gregory of Tours, we have much information about it from the life of St Samson, generally ascribed to the seventh century, and other saints' lives from the ninth century. The Life of St Samson appears to be trustworthy. It incorporates especially the whole range of Cunomorus and his relations with both the North Breton royal family and Childeberht, the Frankish king. Indeed Breton history seems to begin with Cunomorus.

The third kingdom is named Bro Erech from the king Waroch who first conquered the land from the Franks. The Armoricans of this part of the country are believed to have had relations with Britain from the early times of the Armorican navy, and to have been accustomed to draw on them for naval supplies. They are said to have been jealous of Caesar as they had the monopoly of trade with Britain. We learn much of this part of the country from Gregory of Tours, who, writing from the point of view of the Franks, has much to tell us about the long-drawn battles waged between the local Bretons and the French of the south-east. The Franks regarded themselves as the natural heirs of the Romans, and sought to retain their hold on this, the richest part of the country – the ancient domain of the Veneti. The Bretons, on the other hand, in their eastward progress, sought to enlarge their domain at the expense of the Franks, and Gregory describes for us the frequent raids over the border into Frankish territory. This border warfare between Bro Erech and the Franks, in fact, lasted for years.

We have no contemporary records of the British settlement, and the earliest Frankish records cannot be trusted as they are probably contaminated by Gildas, who is known to have been read at Landévennec by the ninth century at latest, but we may be sure that the country of Domnonia would not have allowed the immigrants to settle had it not had a use for them. The whole of at least the north-east of Brittany must have been thickly populated, but the interior of the land was densely covered with forests, and our traditions are full of the forest and the clearing operations effected by the colonists. This I take it was the chief cause of their welcome. Some kind of a *modus vivendi* evidently evolved, especially in the north. In the south the forest clearing seems to have been less drastic, and the colonization on the whole less thorough. The great forest of Brocéliande in the south-east was never cleared.

IRELAND

West of the Britons were the Irish. We have seen that they were already encroaching on the western shores of Britain in the Roman period, and that the Severn Sea and South Wales were already largely in their hands. The kingdom of Dyfed was bilingual and largely Irish in its ruling dynasty. For West Wales our evidence is largely in the form of sagas; but for Holyhead, the fort of Caer Gybi, the excavations of Segontium (near Caernarvon) and the Roman landing place on the sea-shore place us again on relatively firm ground, as do the Roman fort at Lancaster and those at Elslack and Piercebridge which seem to have been built against Irish encroachments across the Pennines. It is coming to be realized also that in the south-west of Scotland the Irish menace was a real one; but it was only in Argyll, beyond the last Roman defences, that the Irish got a foothold which spread over the mainland of Scotland.

Ireland herself was never conquered by the Romans. Tacitus tells us how Agricola, standing on the western edge of Scotland, looked across with the eyes of a general and calculated that it would require only a single legion and a modest force of auxiliaries to conquer Ireland; but he was not destined to make the attempt. That he seriously thought of it is shown by the fact that he retained at his side an Irish chieftain who had fled from Ireland and taken refuge with him, and whom he hoped to use should he ever cross; but Rome had no serious business westward, and Ireland has remained the last great stronghold of the early Celtic people.

It must also be emphasized that, however it came about, the Irish language is the most conservative form of Celtic (see p. 44). Whether or not this was always so (and the question is still under debate), there is no doubt that Ireland as a whole is an extremely conservative country, and the nearest we can ever hope to attain to the original Celtic people. Despite later invasions, it has, to a great extent, been left behind by time, and we can there study something of the ancient Celtic world.

As in the case of the Celts of Britain, the historical period in Ireland began in the fifth century, when writing was first introduced there with the coming of St Patrick. But, as in Britain, we can gauge something of Ireland before this time owing to the high development of her oral tradition and the legends of previous days which remained as living memories till the age of written records. Of these the chief is *Táin Bó Cualnge* (*The Cattle-raid of Cooley*) which gives us a picture of an Ireland quite differently divided from that of historical times. From this and other sagas we can also visualize an Ireland with a population different from that of the dominant peoples of history. Before the fifth century, in fact, we find ourselves in a different world.

In this prehistoric period, Ireland was populated by a people called the Erainn (Ptolemy's *Iverni*) and in *Táin Bó Cualnge* they are found divided into four chief peoples. This is in fact the period known as the *Coiced* 'Fifth Part', though only four divisions are certainly known, the fifth being disputed. *Táin Bó Cualnge* is, in its final form, the story of the carrying away of the bull owned by Conchobar mac Nessa, king of Ulster, by Medb (Maeve) queen of Connachta (Connaught), and the defence of the Ulster men, disabled by a mysterious sickness, by their champion Cú Chulainn, who was of a different race, and was immune from the disease. In this phase the whole of the north of Ireland (Ulster) was subject to the Ulaid under Conchobar.

The west was known as Connaught, and subject to Maeve and her consort, Ailill, but it is made quite clear that Maeve was the real ruler. The rest of Ireland was divided between Leinster and Munster, which play only a subordinate part in *Táin Bó Cualnge*. Leinster is thought to have been occupied by relatively new invaders in the prehistoric period, but Munster is ancient and throughout history seems to have kept up a communication with the Continent, and in early times at least to have been responsible for certain cultural changes. The fourth-century King Cormac mac Airt is represented as ruling at Tara, and seeking to enforce tribute on the people of Leinster, who resented and resisted it. The struggle between Leinster and central Ireland, which sought to enforce the tribute, went on intermittently for centuries, and reached its climax in the Battle of Allen, the last great battle of Ireland in the heroic age.

In the fifth century we emerge from myth and legend into the world of history. At this period a certain Niall Noígiallach ('Niall of the Nine Hostages') is found ruling at Tara. His origin is unknown although his mother may have been British, but he and his sons conquered the centre (Meath) and part of the north of Ireland, and imposed tribute on the peoples who thus became subject to them. Niall himself is generally thought to have come to Ireland by sea, and to represent the northern Goidels, but it is quite historically possible that he belonged to one of the peoples settled round Tara who may have risen to power under circumstances unknown to us. However it came about, he and his sons ultimately divided Ireland into two portions, themselves taking the northern half, where they became known as the northern and southern Uí Néill, while the southern half of Ireland fell to Munster, which later had its capital at Cashel. The eldest son of Niall was Leary (Loegaire, modern Laogaire), who was the first king of Ireland of whose accession we know the date (A.D. 427 or 428), and he occupied Tara. Three of Niall's youngest sons occupied the north of Ireland, and were known to after ages as the northern Uí Néill, while the rulers of Tara, the senior branch, were known as the southern Uí Néill. Conall Gulban occupied what is now Donegal, and Eógan occupied the country to the east of him, gradually overcoming the whole of the ancient *coiced* of the Ulaid save for a narrow strip on the eastern edge. The third son, Enda, gradually disappears from the records, but Eógan and Conall occupied the Gríanán Ailech, the splendid prehistoric fortress a few miles west of Derry, commanding views of Lough Swilly, and Lough Foyle to the north, and to the south as far as the Nefin mountains and the heart of Ireland. The northern Uí Néill held together in amity till the eighth century.

Niall and his sons come just at the turning point between poetry and prose. That is why they herald the historical period. We know little about Niall from prose, but in scattered snatches of panegyric poetry he is said to have had hair 'yellow as the primrose', and to be the son of Cairenn (Latin Carina), who is thought to have been a British princess carried off in a raid on Britain by Niall's father, as the name is unique in Irish. Certainly the family were great raiders. Niall himself is said to have perished *i Alpi*, which is generally understood to be a reference to the Alps, but more probably means 'in Alba', and he is also associated with 'the Ictian Sea', i.e. the Isle of Wight.

In the reign of Niall's eldest son Leary at Tara, St Patrick came to Ireland, and Patrick's earliest biography by Muirchú relates his having come to the court there before moving northwards to Armagh. It is undoubtedly with St Patrick that Ireland was opened up effectively to new ideas from Europe, and in his period at least writing came to take the place of oral tradition. It was long before chronological reckoning came to take the place of saga, and before our earliest written records came to be made, probably not before the mid seventh century. Probably local records had been kept separately in various small churches; but we have no reason to suspect any writing before the fifth century. The two oldest written documents which we possess are from St Patrick's own hand – the *Confession*, and the *Letter to the Soldiers of Coroticus.* He is pictured in the earliest documents as essentially haunting the north of Ireland, and his great sanctuary is Armagh, which is only two miles to the west of Emain Macha, the dwelling of Conchobar mac Nessa in the heroic age. When Niall conquered Armagh he obtained at a blow the sanctuary of St Patrick and the heart of the old *coiced* of Ulster. Henceforth St Patrick became the prime saint of Ireland and of the Uí Néill.

About the time when the Uí Néill were spreading over the north of Ireland, Munster and Leinster were quietly consolidating themselves. They had their rivalries too, but they do not seem to have had much to do with the north, and one gets the impression that Munster faced southward, and from the earliest times was in touch with the Continent. Foreign mercenary soldiers have been traced in Munster who probably came from Gaul at the time of the barbarian invasions, and in the Christian period we shall see other continental influences in the valleys of the Suir and the Barrow, and at the later monastery of Lismore in particular. Already in the heroic age we find Corc, son of Lugaid, taking refuge in Scotland from his usurping uncle, and ultimately returning with a Scottish bride to rule in Munster. The Munster stronghold of Cashel itself is a growth from the heroic age, and has a magnificent strategic position. It is probably partly because there were fewer Munster chronicles that we hear less of her than of the north, but the one Munster Chronicle, the *Annals of Inisfallen*, though it has a common source for the period under discussion with the *Annals of Ulster*, is more selective and pays more attention to Munster affairs than to those of the north. In fact, from the beginning of the historical period Ireland may be virtually divided into two realms, known as *Leth Cuinn* ('Conn's Half'), and *Leth Moga Nuadat* ('Mug Nuadat's Half'), from an old tradition according to which Conn and Mug Nuadat had divided Ireland between them. The south of Ireland becomes prominent in the Viking Age, but for the first millennium of its history it is comparatively little heard of, and as MacNeill said, 'probably enjoyed greater tranquillity than any other realm in Western Europe'.* Of the north, we hear much more.

Before leaving the northern Uí Néill we must return for a moment to their gradual encroachment on the peoples to the east. Just beyond their orbit the little kingdom of Dálriata on its rocky promontory on the north coast cast its eyes to Scotland. Dálriata (the modern Dálriada) was a remnant of the ancient Ulaid, a different people from the encroaching Uí Néill. They were of the older Érainn stock. Whether for this reason, or possibly because of the approach of the Uí Néill, a small contingent left their old home at some time in the fifth century and sailed to Scotland. They were, in all probability, not the first who had made the expedition, but they were the first reported to impose their dynasty on the coast of Argyll. Nothing is said of fighting or any opposition being offered to them. Bede seems to indicate an earlier invasion, but the date is undetermined. By the fifth century the Irishmen from Dálriada had colonized part of Scotland north of the Antonine Wall, and while their original Irish home diminished in importance, the new colony grew apace. It was joined in the following century by St Columba, a member of the northern Uí Néill. We shall trace in the next chapter the growth of this Scottish colony from Irish Dálriata till it reached its zenith under its king Kenneth mac Alpin and finally in the Lowlands gave way before the Angles. It must be borne in mind, however, that one reason why we have fuller records of Scottish Dálriada than of the Scottish Picts is that they were literate, whereas for the powerful kingdom of the Picts we are still dependent on oral tradition, especially for the north. Their inscriptions, almost entirely in the Pictish language, have never yet been translated.

* *Phases of Irish History*, p. 126f.

CHAPTER 4

The Development of the Celtic Kingdoms of the West

SCOTLAND

In the last chapter we found Scotland divided between four nations, speaking four different languages. In the present chapter, which is concerned with the fifth to the seventh centuries, we shall find these reduced to two, as has remained the case till the present day. There are the Irish of Argyll, who have succeeded in spreading over the whole of the Highlands, utterly ousting the Pictish language; and the Anglians of the Lowlands. The Teutonic invaders have now encroached as far as the Highland Line. It is clear, indeed, that Athelfrith of Northumbria at the beginning of the seventh century aimed at conquests still farther north. Ecgfrith, a later king of Northumbria, was killed in 685 at what is now Dunnichen near Forfar, which, as we have seen, is in the heart of the country of the southern Picts, and no later Teutonic lord ventured to cross the Firth of Forth until the time of the Anglo-Normans. Until then the Teutonic element was confined to southern Scotland.

The Picts seem to have been contained behind the Forth-Clyde line, but we know little of them after the settlement of the Irish in Dálriada. This may be in part due to the accident of their leaving no written records, for we hear from time to time of clashes with the Scots of Dálriada which must have left their mark on contemporary history. On the other hand we hear from time to time of notices *in veteribus Pictorum libris* ('in old books of the Picts'), and if these refer only to notices in church registers they must betoken a people at least partly literate, though they may, of course, refer only to the southern Picts. Moreover they must, by some means or other, have kept lists of their kings, but these are unreliable before 550, being mainly lists of names, occasionally with later notes added.

On the other hand, from about 550 the names of the Pictish king-lists are evidently genuine, for they can be checked from the Irish Annals and from other historical works. We know much more of names and events at Dálriada, for, the kingdom being Irish, its events were treated as those of Ireland proper by the annalists, who had been literate from the sixth century, and though the Irish Annals in their present form are much later, they can often serve as a check to the records of Scottish Dálriada. It is also important to bear in mind that Scottish Dálriada had kept a short Chronicle, doubtless on the island of Iona, from at latest the seventh century, and though this consisted in its early years of brief notices of church festivals and a *computus* for the Easter reckoning, it ultimately developed into a Chronicle which served as a basis for certain entries in the Irish Chronicles. If we view Iona and Scottish Dálriada from the point of view of the sixth century, we see that they were in the forefront of the Celtic world, on the shores of a busy land-locked sea, and, moreover, on the eastern shore. They were in a position to give a lead to much of the Celtic world of that date.

The Scottish king-lists are therefore relatively reliable, and can be checked in a number of Irish sources. They trace the kings from a common ancestor Erc, whose three sons are said to have landed with a hundred and fifty warriors and settled in what later became Argyll and the adjacent mainland and islands. The lengths of their reigns can be traced from a number of Irish sources. Of the three brothers, Angus occupied Islay and Loarn occupied the north of present Argyll, with his seat at Dunolly near Oban; though little is said of this settlement in the *Forfes for n'Alba*, it was of importance for future relations with Ireland. The third brother was Fergus, who died in about A.D. 500. Little is known of him, but his descendant, Gabrán, had his stronghold at Dunadd, at the head of the little river Crinan; the most eastward of the settlements. It was a strong position, a natural rock citadel, entirely surrounded by Crinan Moss, and accessible nowhere from the land, and from the sea only by the river. What is known of Gabrán and Loarn forms the basis of the internal history of Argyll, as the two appear to have been rivals for supreme power.

For the future of Scottish history the most important man of this Irish settlement during the last quarter of the sixth century was Aedán mac Gabráin. He it was who seems to have either overcome or placated the Picts and established the kingdom of Dálriada as the ultimate nucleus of Scotland, and it was he who attracted the great St Columba to his court, and retained his loyalty and his friendship throughout his life. What could have been the original attraction of this great saint, a scion of the Uí Néill and possessor of the *rigdamna* (the right of eligibility to the kingship of Ireland) to this remote spot we do not know, although tradition would attribute it to self-imposed exile as a penance, following a serious dispute in Ireland. We would be glad to know also whether it was the wisdom of the saint or the heroic politics of Aedán which governed the growing prestige of the Cénel Gabráin (the descendants of Gabrán) throughout the sixth century. Adamnán would have us believe that it was the former. But we know enough of Aedán's personal problems to realize that he was an outstanding figure. He seems to have been present with Columba at the convention of Druim Ceata in 575, and according to the *Annals of Ulster* he made an expedition to the Orkneys in 590. In 578 the Irish annals record his having been present at a battle in Manau, and for the next four years he seems to have been active in the Isle of Jura in opposition to Baetán on the coast of Antrim. But his most permanent achievements were undoubtedly against the Picts, and already in 628 the *Annals of Ulster* refer to his son and successor, Eochaid Buide, as *rex Pictorum*. Dálriadic penetration into eastern Scotland had probably been going on for a long time. Indeed the name Atholl (Ath Fhotla) means 'Second Ireland', and can only have been given to it by the Scots at the beginning of the eighth century. Only in his southernmost movements against the Northumbrians was Aedán unsuccessful. In 603 he marched south against Athelfrith of Northumbria, who was seeking to invade the southern Picts, and was severely defeated at a place which Bede calls Degsastan, possibly in Liddesdale; and, adds Bede, 'from that day until the present no king of the Scots (i.e. the Irish) has dared to invade Britain to make war on the English'. It will be seen, nevertheless, that Aedán's warfare extended in every direction from his home in Argyll. He is believed to have died in about 608, leaving a reputation as the greatest king of Dálriada, and making it a force in the future history of Scotland; but there was a long and stormy time to intervene before it amalgamated with the Picts.

The years of the seventh century were chiefly occupied by struggles for supremacy among the Scots of Dálriada, and it has been conjectured that they were in some form of agreement with the Britons to the south of them. Certainly Aedán must have had British sympathies, for he called one of his sons Arthur, and other British names, such as Rigwallan and Morgan, were current in the royal family about this time, or soon after. But he himself is called Bradawc, 'treacherous', which suggests some sort of a quarrel with his southern neighbours. The alliance broke down under his successors, and we hear little more of relations between the Britons and the Scots. In 741 the Irish Annals record a *percussio Dalriatai* (a 'devastating attack') by the Pictish king Angus, but this must be an exaggeration, for we hear after this of the long and brilliant reign of Aed Finn, who is said to have ruled Dálriada from 748 to 778 and to have distinguished himself in fighting against the Picts of Fortrenn. On the other hand, there is ground for believing in the introduction at this period of Dálriadic elements into the Pictish royal family. Actually we are ignorant of the relations between the Picts and the Scots during the eighth century and until the time of Kenneth mac Alpin, who must have been Pictish on his mother's side; but the long reign of Aed Finn certainly does not suggest that the Scots of Dálriada were 'wiped out'.

The period on the eve of the union between Dálriada and the southern Picts is unfortunately obscure as the Irish Annals, which were our chief guide to the history of Dálriada, fail us about this time; but it must have been an important phase in Scottish history. We are gradually approaching the final union of the Scots with the great Pictish nation, which culminated in what is today Highland Scotland. We must suppose it to have been the conclusion of a gradual process, probably of intermarriage. The law of succession among the Picts was through the female, and there are grounds for thinking that the bridegroom was usually a visiting prince, and that the marriage arrangement was not regarded as permanent. The Irish story of Corc, son of Luigdech (cf. p. 87 above), who carried off his Pictish bride to Munster is probably typical in this respect. This would help to account for the fact that the Dálriadic kings often have Pictish names after 781, though there is no hint of a Pictish conquest to account for it. Indeed this Pictish law must have greatly facilitated the union of the two peoples by intermarriage.

However we view the Pictish marriage customs we do not really know how Angus mac Fergus, the most powerful of all the southern Pictish kings, obtained the supremacy for which the southern Pictish kings had been struggling throughout the seventh century. His kingdom seems to have been Fortrenn, but the Picts of Fife were evidently associated with him, and possibly also those of Angus (Forfar). If so, he must have already had a successful career of conquest before he appeared in the Irish Annals. But he seems to have had a chequered course at the beginning of his career against Dálriada. We have mentioned (p. 92) his attack on Dálriada in 741, but in 749 we hear of the 'ebbing' of the power of Angus. In 768, we hear of an invasion of Fortrenn by Aed of Dálriada in terms which suggest that the

Scots are now in the ascendant, and that they are predominant in Atholl, west of the Tay, and in Fife to the south. They seem, in fact, to have gained the mastery of the Picts in the lower Tay Valley.

The actual union of the Picts and Scots seems to have taken place about the middle of the ninth century under Kenneth mac Alpin, traditionally about 843, possibly as a result of his having attacked them, as Henry of Huntingdon tells us, immediately after they had suffered heavily at the hands of the Danes. Kenneth's father, Alpin, belonged to the royal line of Gabrán, but he was killed in fighting against the Picts, who are said to have 'cut off his head'. Both Alpin and Kenneth appear to have been celebrated in elegiac poetry which is reflected in our records, and it is therefore not surprising that our records describe Kenneth as ruling the Picts happily for sixteen years after he had *delevit* ('wiped them out') and brought about their *destructio*. No record of such a conquest is given in any Irish, British, or English records, and all the annals simply call him king of the Picts in recording his death. The title remained in use by the Irish and Welsh annalists till the time of his grandson; but their subjects are referred to as Scots, and the Picts soon came to be thought of as a people of the past. Kenneth himself died in his palace at Forteviot in Fortrenn, it is thought at about 860, but the kings of what we must now call Scotland kept up the old Pictish customs. Henceforth their chief seat was at Scone, the old palace of the Pictish kings of the upper Tay.

We can trace the Britons to the south of this battle-ground of Picts and Scots throughout the sixth century, but little of outstanding importance is reflected in the Annals, and we gather the political status of the British was that of a heroic age, guided by such remnants of Roman prestige as they had acquired and as had collected to the south of what remained of the Antonine Wall. As this was only thirty-seven miles long it did not require serious policing as a frontier. These northern British peoples have left no written records, but a northern scriptorium must have existed, for we have their minutes incorporated by Nennius in his *Historia Britonnum* from chapters 57 to 65. From this we gather that in the second generation after the death of Urien of Rheged (cf. p. 80 above) an expedition had been made, headed by a certain Flamddwyn, from somewhere near Edinburgh into England, which had been a signal disaster for the northern British. The tragic story is told in the long 'palm' (or collection of poems) known as *The Battle of Catraeth* (probably Catterick), where the British force was annihilated to a man. After this we hear of no further activity against the English.

From now onwards our knowledge of the northern Britons comes to us through north Welsh sources. The Welsh always recognized their kinship with the men of southern Scotland, calling them the *Gwŷr y Gogledd* ('the men of the North'), meaning 'our northern neighbours', as they called the people of south Wales the *Gwŷr y Des* ('the people of the South', cf. p. 76f. above). But Lancashire was not easy country to negotiate physically, and the natural means of communication was across Morecambe Bay, which was a quick and easy means of transport, with the Isle of Man as a convenient landfall. Indeed from the earliest times we find British (Welsh) and Irish records side by side in the Isle of Man, as soon as the stone inscriptions occur.

WALES

The Angles of the North – the Bernicians – gradually extended over the whole of southern Scotland, as far as the west coast, and we have seen that the British chiefs, descendants of Dyfnwal Hen of Dumbarton, the capital of Strathclyde, were previously spread over this area. It would seem likely that before the oncoming tide of Teutonic settlers some of them would have taken to their boats and sailed across Morecambe Bay to Wales. At the end of the eighth century the male line in Gwynedd seems to have failed and, as Sir John Edward Lloyd put it, 'a stranger possessed himself of the throne of Gwynedd' (*History of Wales*, Vol. I, p. 323). This was Merfyn Vrych. When, however, we examine his pedigree he seems not to be exactly a stranger but a direct descendant from the ancient ruling line, a son of Erthil, a direct descendant of the ancient line from Maelgwn. In fact, his ancestry could not be better. His male line presumably goes back, apparently through the Isle of Man, to the men of the North, to Llywarch Hen, a first cousin of Urbgen (Urien) of Rheged, the highest in prestige of them all, a direct descendant of Coel Hen.

Merfyn's court seems to have been cosmopolitan. It is called an *arx* ('citadel'), and we have a letter from him relating to some Irishmen who paused at his court on their way from Ireland to the Continent. At Merfyn's court they were subjected to an intelligence test and had to show their credentials, and we have reason to suspect that Merfyn's court was a regular port of call for people going from Ireland to the court of Charles the Bald at Liège. In a letter which is still extant Merfyn 'greets Concenn' – and as we know that Merfyn married the sister of Concenn, prince of Powys, who died at Rome, it looks as if, in addition to Merfyn's original north–south journey across Morecambe Bay, he was also on an east–west route. In fact, he seems to have lifted North Wales out of the isolation in which it had lain since the death of Cadwallon into the world of the Continent. And the interesting thing is that the route appears to be an inland one. His capital lay on the north coast.

We have seen that no written records are preserved from the British of southern Scotland, although they were Christians and seem to have been under Roman influence. We have seen, moreover, that the jealously guarded oral tradition has preserved their legends intact. These legends, however, came to be written down, not in the North, but in Wales. It is very likely that Merfyn would have brought a crop of these legends, his own credentials, with him when he came to Wales; in particular his own pedigree. We see that the fuller source of all these legends and genealogies in Wales can be traced to Rhodri Mawr, Merfyn's son and successor, and it appears most probable that it was at Merfyn's court, which we know to have been literate, that all the lore of the North was collected and written down in the reign of Rhodri Mawr 'Rhodri the Great'.

Yet another indication of the high cultural level of the court of Gwynedd under Merfyn and his son Rhodri is their substitution of policy for warfare. Merfyn owed his throne to a royal marriage. He further enlarged his realm by marrying the sister of Concenn, and presumably he inherited Concenn's domain, adding Powys to Gwynedd. His son, Rhodri, followed the same plan, marrying Angharad, the sister of Gwgon, the drowned king of Cardigan, and again presumably inherited. And in their turn Rhodri's sons are known to have inherited likewise. The dynasty never struck a blow, but by policy came to inherit a large part of Wales. The memory of the proper names of his sons, and their identity with those of the counties of Wales, suggests that the policy was recognized.

There is an indication that the link of Merfyn with the court of Charles the Bald on the Continent may have continued with his son Rhodri. Rhodri's court must have been a brilliant one if we are right in thinking that the writing down of the lore of the *Gwŷr y Gogledd* is ultimately due to him. The fact that the pedigrees of the Welsh kings are traced to him in the Welsh manuscripts certainly bears this out. But he was also a warrior, and is named in the *Annals of Ulster* as having slain Horm (Norse Gormr), the Danish chief, off the coast of Anglesey (see p. 103). This was the outstanding victory, which in all probability would reach the ears of Charles the Bald at his court of Liège where he was seriously threatened by the Danes encamped in strength on the River Seine. At his court was an Irishman, Sedulius Scotus, who about this time composed an ode on a victory over the Danes, which was almost certainly Rhodri's. In 876 the *Annals of Wales* record a 'Sunday Battle' in Anglesey, fought no doubt against the Danes, and this is doubtless the explanation of Annal 876 (*recte* 877) in the *Annals of Ulster* recording how Ruaidri (Rhodri) son of Muirmenn (Merfyn), 'king of the Britons', came to Ireland fleeing before the Black Foreigners (i.e. the Danes). The following year (877) Rhodri's death and also that of his son Gwriad at the hands of the Saxons is noted in the *Annals of Wales*.

Rhodri, like the *Gwŷr y Gogledd*, had been forced to fight on two fronts, and his death was a heavy blow to the Welsh. On the west the Danes were an increasing threat. In the east the English in Wessex and Mercia were an ever-increasing menace. By Rhodri's inheritance of Powys he had inherited the 'garden of Wales', but he had also inherited the feud along its borders which is witnessed by Offa's Dyke. In 822 the *Annals of Wales* record the destruction of Deganwy by the Saxons, who also took the region of Powys into their own power (*in sua potestate*). In 828 the *Anglo-Saxon Chronicle* reports the West Saxon king as conquering Mercia and reducing the Welsh to submission, thus bringing Wessex into direct conflict with the Welsh. A generation later we find the Mercians under their king Burgred reducing the country of Wales with the help of the Anglo-Saxon king Athelwulf and the West Saxons. North Wales now had to watch Wessex as well as Mercia. Asser (a monk of St David's, later bishop of Sherborne, friend and biographer of Alfred the Great) tells us that after Rhodri's death his sons worked together against the southern states, and he emphasizes the persistent effort of Anarawd, Rhodri's eldest son, to make a compact with the Northumbrians, even after Rhodri's death.

By inheriting Powys, Rhodri had reached the border of the ruling power in South Wales – that of Hywel Dda – whose policy was the reverse of his own. North Wales had always been anti-English. It had identified itself with the men of the North from the days of Cadwallon, who died with Penda fighting against Oswald the Northumbrian king, and who had in all probability nearly succeeded in driving the Anglian invaders over the North Sea. Rhodri and his sons followed the same policy. Anarawd, the last, was to join in the South Welsh policy of Hywel Dda.

With the death of Rhodri we come to the end of the old order. The brilliant Celtic heroic age had always seen Wales as the champion who would hurl the Saxons back across the North Sea, and the tradition of Cadwallon survived for centuries after his death. Rhodri had found Wales a collection of small states and left it to his sons almost a united realm, but he showed to the last no signs of uniting with England, or creating a wider whole. I have no doubt that it was as a part of his dream of a united Celtic realm that he caused to be put together the traditions of the North.

His grandson, Hywel Dda, came of a different tradition. He belonged to South Wales, which was in close touch with English thought and English tradition. He seems to have acquired a mint, and he has left behind him a tradition as a lawgiver. He signed regularly when Athelstan summoned the *subreguli* to the meetings of his *witan* or council, where they regularized grants of land, and from 928 to 949 his name always appears in the first place wherever the Welsh princes appear among the witnesses. He was apparently a great admirer of Alfred the Great, visited Rome, and called his son Edward, probably as a compliment to the son of Edward the Elder, who died in 933. In the *Anglo-Saxon Chronicle* we read that Hywel of the West Welsh, and in fact the whole of South Wales, submitted to Athelstan, and when two years later the tributary princes leagued themselves against Wessex, only the South Welsh seem to have stood aside, probably due to the influence of Hywel. Everything testifies to his English sympathies. He died in 949 or 950.

In bringing Wales out of her isolation Hywel had completed the work begun by Alfred the Great. Alfred's part in Welsh politics has never been appreciated as it deserves, the *Anglo-Saxon Chronicle* being too full of Alfred's achievement against the Danes to have much interest in what he did in Wales. But Alfred's problem was much like Rhodri's. He was obliged to look to two fronts, and he could not afford to have a disaffected Wales in his rear. He temporized with the Irish and the Welsh, and Asser tells us something of this side of his activities.

He made a substantial annual contribution to the Irish Church, perhaps through St David's, and took an active interest in Irish affairs, as we see from the arrival of the three Irish pilgrims at his court in the *Anglo-Saxon Chronicle* (MS. A.891) and the unique notice in the same entry of the death of the Irish scribe Suibhne (Sweeny) mac Maelumha of Clonmacnoise. He kept himself in touch with the Irish affairs of Dyfed, and above all with South Welsh policy, by having Asser of St David's spend half of each year with him. It is Asser who tells us that all the Welsh kings came to him and paid him homage, but last of all Anarawd of North Wales, the son of Rhodri Mawr. Alfred had joined Wales to England in a bloodless revolution, and in the end the North joined him. He had brought Wales out of her heroic isolation, and into the conditions of Anglo-Saxon England and continental Europe. At the same time Wales no longer looked westward across the Irish Sea, but now turned eastwards to the continental area. Something similar was happening to Scotland. Both these Celtic fringing countries of our island abandoned the west coast, the land-locked sea, and turned eastwards. They were no longer a maritime population, facing the Irish Sea, but formed a landward facing country. The change came about almost simultaneously in both countries, in the ninth century.

IRELAND AND THE NORSE

We have watched the reaction of the Celtic people of Gaul and part of Britain to Roman domination; and we have seen them first overwhelmed and later once more raising themselves up as independent principalities when the Frankish invaders overwhelmed their conqueror in Gaul. We have seen the Irish Sea lose its importance for Britain as Scotland and England gradually turned eastwards and became no longer principally a maritime but a landward power. Ireland, meanwhile, had been left in peace and had developed on her own lines. About this time, however, towards the end of the eighth century and early into the ninth, she suffered an invasion of a totally different kind, a belated invasion, not from a Mediterranean civilization from the South, but from a Teutonic people spreading southward from Scandinavian lands. We have referred to this invasion from time to time as it affected Scotland, Wales and France. By far the chief sufferers were the Irish, and we have left the chief consideration of the Vikings till now because parts of Ireland, hitherto immune from foreign attack, were so overwhelmed by the Vikings as to be transformed from a cattle-keeping country, with an exclusively internal economy, to one in which the coastal areas now boasted towns, trade, and the units and measures which invariably accompany them. In Ireland, hitherto free from Teutonic invasion and Teutonic influences, the old order still continued, up to the arrival of the Norse. The Uí Néill still ruled the North, the Rock of Cashel the South.

The first attacks on Ireland came from Norway, perhaps by way of the Island of Lewis, for we read of 'the sea-king of Lewis' quite incidentally. This island was more Norse than any other part of the Hebrides or of Gaelic Scotland, as place-names make clear, and may possibly have been in early medieval times an independent kingdom. At the start, it was the headlands and outer islands of Ireland which were attacked, and this quickly put an end to the island sanctuaries off the west coast. We read in the Irish Annals that Etgal of Skellig was carried off by the raiders and died soon after of hunger and thirst; and this was only in line with the attacks on Inishmurray off the Sligo coast. At this stage the tip and run policy was widespread, and the islands at the north of Wexford harbour and the coastal monastic settlements, such as the monastery of St Comgall of

Bangor (Co. Down) were attacked. But in the ninth century the attacks rapidly increased, especially in the west, which at this period was undoubtedly the natural entry into Ireland, leading by the great rivers into the interior of the north and east. The Norse fleets were stationed on the great loughs – Lough Neagh and Lough Ree – and Armagh was attacked from the west. We are told in *Cogadh Gaedhel re Gaillaibh* (*The War of the Gaedhil with the Gaill*) how Audr, the wife of Turges, stationed herself on the high altar of the church at Clonmacnoise, which reminded her of the Norse heathen magic platform (the *seithr hjallr*), and from there performed the Norse heathen rite of *seithr*. It was undoubtedly from the west that the Vikings in the first half of the ninth century penetrated to the east, and it seems that the kingdom of Lewis may have been the ultimate basis of this penetration.

Throughout the ninth and tenth centuries Norse penetration continued, but now the east as well as the west was directly affected. Large towns sprang up. Dublin, which had been called under the Irish simply Ath Cliath ('the hurdle ford'), was already in 841 fortified by the Norsemen, and Norse sea-ports developed at Wicklow, Waterford, Wexford and Cork. Each was the centre of an independent kingdom, prepared to make independent alliances with other Norsemen or with the Irish themselves. There was no central government. But when an Irish resistance movement began in the middle of the ninth century the Norse supremacy could not stand up against it. Their leader was defeated in a great battle in Carlingford Lough. This first defeat, however, was inflicted, not by the Irish, but by Danes, who had arrived from the east. From now onwards the basis of Norse operations was from the east of Ireland, and the Irish Sea became their centre. In fact Ireland seems to have become little more than a battle-ground of the Danes against the Norwegians, of the eastern Vikings against the western.

About this time the Norwegians shifted their power to the east where they remained throughout the third phase of the wars, and although the Danes had a formidable fleet, with the arrival from Norway of Amlaim (Norse Óláfr), the son of the king of Lochlann (Rogaland), perhaps Óláfr the white, they regained possession of Dublin. In 870 (*recte* 871), the *Annals of Ulster* tell how the same Óláfr and Imharr (Norse Ivarr) came again to Dublin, and from now onwards they made Dublin the chief Viking centre, using it as a base for their fleet in its raids on the countries around the Irish Sea. Everything we know about the Norwegians at this time shows their determination to expand and colonize from Norway. Their arrival in Ireland about the middle of the ninth century, and the establishment of their base, seems to have introduced a time of relative peace from further external invasion, but the *Annals* tell with horror of the desecration of the ancient sanctuaries and the plundering of the grave-mounds, for 'they left not a cave nor a hole underground that they did not explore'. Meanwhile in the closing years of the ninth century and the beginning of the tenth the Danes were establishing the Danelaw in England, and threatening the Norwegians in Dublin from eastern Britain. The danger was a very real one.

In general, the mobility of Óláfr is astonishing, as we hear of his carrying the war into the enemy's camp by pillaging Fortrenn and Dumbarton, and though his gain here is not clear, owing to our lack of annals for Scotland, it must have given him some advantage, for it is noted in both the *Annals of Ulster* and the *Annales Cambriae*. The poverty of Wales won her in general immunity from the Viking depredations, but Anglesey, 'the granary of Wales', was too valuable to escape, and in 853 it was devastated by the 'Black Foreigners' as the Danes were called, probably under their leader Horm who is believed to have beaten the Norwegian fleet in the battle mentioned earlier at Carlingford Lough. However, we have already seen how he was slain by Rhodri Mawr in 856. Henceforth we hear little of Danes in the area. The Norwegians seem to have been predominant in the latter half of the tenth century.

It was probably at about the beginning of the tenth century that the Isle of Man was first permanently settled by the Norsemen. We know very little about Manx history, and all three languages – Irish, Welsh and Norse – are attested, but without chronology, for we have no written records for them till a late date. The Isle of Man is exceptionally rich in remains of the Vikings, especially after the expulsion of a large number of Norsemen from Ireland in 901 (*recte* 902) as recorded by the *Annals of Ulster*. In 902 there was something of a national comeback for the Irish in Dublin, and many of the *gennti* (foreigners, Vikings) were expelled. But the central position of the Isle of Man must have made it a natural halt for the Norse at all periods.

It may be in this period of comparative quiet that the Norse occupation of south Lancashire and parts of western Cheshire took place. This seems to have been a peaceful settlement resulting in an agricultural way of life. We have no monastic remains for so early a period in this part of north-west England, but the place-names are unmistakable on the low-lying land between the forest hills of the Pennines and the sea – Ainsdale, Birkdale, Meols Cop, Blowick, Scaresbrick, Ormskirk, Hoscar, Skelmersdale, Formby, Crosby, Kirby, Whitby, Kirkham, Blundell – a little colony of settlements all within easy walking distance of one another. The silence of our records on these extensive Norse settlements gives us a clue as to how much we must disallow for the monastic records of Ireland. No doubt the Norse depredations were very terrible in Ireland, but we have to allow for the rise of schools of stone sculpture there at precisely the time when we should have expected the Viking terror to be at its height.

In 919 Dublin was recaptured by the Norsemen and the leaders of the resistance movement for the most part were slain.

It was in the following period that the sea-port towns were developed. Dublin was strengthened by being joined to the Danish kingdom of York, and Limerick consolidated its territory in Munster; but in West Munster towards the close of the century the Dál Cais on the Clare border was able to enlist the help of Connaught against the Limerick Vikings. Munster became very active during this century and by the middle of the tenth century the Eóganact dynasty of Cashel lost its supremacy to North Munster, or Thomond, and to Cenetig, the ruler of the Dál Cais and his son Brian Bóruma (Boru), who led the attack against the Vikings at the Battle of Clontarf in 1014. This great battle put an end to the Viking supremacy in Ireland. The importance of the battle is at times disputed, and the issue between the Irish and the Norse is not really a clear one. Sihtric, the Norse king of Dublin, took no part in it. Leinster supported the Dublin Vikings, for she was always against Meath from the earliest times, and the Limerick Vikings, always hostile to the Dublin dynasty, seem to have sided with Brian. The Irish victory was marred by the death of Brian, and although the outcome was undoubtedly an Irish victory there was no real break. The Norse and the Irish had lived together in a small country for two centuries; intermarriage was frequent; and conversion of many Norsemen to Christianity had tended to induce a mutual understanding. The leading bards of the Irish and the Norse were fraternizing. Brian had married Sihtric's mother, and Sihtric had perhaps, in his turn, married Brian's daughter. What was there left to fight about?

The true significance of Clontarf lay in its site. It was the gateway into Ireland. The presence there of Sigurd the Stout, Earl of Orkney, who died in the battle, gives us the clue. It is inconceivable that he would have left his Orkney jarldom, which he had from Harald the Fair-Haired, for the sake of a quarrel between Dublin and the rising state of West Munster. His hope had been the extension of his earldom by the acquisition of Ireland. As the Norsemen had obtained Normandy he hoped to acquire small but fertile Ireland, and perhaps from there to obtain western Britain as an extension of the southern Norse colony. Nothing less would have tempted him so far south with his famous raven banner – his own 'devil', which had been foretold to bring victory and death to its bearer. It was this ultimate political aim rather than the immediate result of the battle which gives so much significance to the death of Norwegian hopes of colonization in the south-west. To the Norse saga-tellers the battle was fought out, not only by the men on the ground, but, making use of the old convention of the *Battle of Allen*, even more by supernatural powers. Throughout the Celtic world there were dreams, portents and visions. A man in Caithness saw in a vision supernatural women weaving the battle on a loom of slaughter, where men's heads were the weights, and men's entrails the warp and woof, and he has embodied his vision in an unforgettable Norse poem the *Darrathar Ljóđ*, (the *Song of the Dart*). In Ireland the prose narrative *The War of the Gaedhil with the Gaill* is unequalled in its excited flow. There has probably never been a battle in northern or western Europe which has excited such a reaction. It can only be accounted for by the major issue involved.

The intellectual loss to Ireland caused by the Viking régime was enormous. Treasure, including illuminated manuscripts, liturgical vessels and reliquaries, were lost, and the techniques which had inspired them were scattered. The monastic houses, the homes of all such fine work, were destroyed. Many of the monks sought asylum on the Continent, and were welcomed in France and Italy; perhaps only a small proportion of the great treasures of this period were preserved in the little western isle. What they have left us in the continental libraries shows us the extent of our intellectual and artistic loss, which is incalculable and irrecoverable. But the Celtic way of life survived, and so ensured the continuation of the basic farming economy. The structure of Celtic society, under its chiefs or kings, was maintained, and wherever Celtic society was sufficiently stable the monasteries revived. Following the Viking Age there was something of an intellectual revival which we can recognize from the metal work and stone crosses. This is usually attributed to the stimulus of freedom from foreign offensives, but it amounted almost to a renaissance, and here the Viking connexion may have contributed a ready market as well as a source of pillage. This would seem to be the case if we judge by the number of Irish objects found in Scandinavia, although most finds had probably been looted from the monasteries. We have to bear constantly in mind that our literary evidence for the Vikings in Ireland comes to us almost exclusively from the monasteries which were the chief objects of Norse depredation, and therefore their bitterest accusers. They were, in fact, the only people able to give us a written report.

Taking a longer view, however, Ireland gained from the Vikings in her position in the modern world. She has been likened to a saucer, with the rim neglected in pre-Norse times and the internal economy fully developed as a pastoral country when the bog had been cleared. She had no towns and no trade. The old royal sites – Tara, Cruachan, Emain Macha – were permanent forts, occasional meeting-centres rather than cities. The Vikings, on the other hand, concentrated on the coastline, and although we find them in Armagh and Clonmacnoise, this was because they had then taken over old Celtic sanctuaries. Their own creations were such as depended on their fleets. It therefore transpired that the Vikings gave to Ireland some appreciation of the value of her coastline, with the development of trade and harbours, especially in Dublin, Wexford, Waterford, Cork, Limerick. All her terminology of shipbuilding and trade, weights and measures, was Norse, and the first coinage struck in Ireland was that of the Vikings of Dublin, which soon afterwards found its way across the Irish Sea, as in the hoard discovered at Bangor in Caernarvonshire. The Vikings introduced commerce to Ireland.

Naturally the Irish law tracts were less affected than the ad hoc arrangements made to suit this new order. The Irish law tracts were an immensely old institution, and their written expression had become sacrosanct. It is, indeed, difficult for us to see what their practical bearing could be when the lawyers came to apply them. Clearly they could have little bearing on the Ireland of the Viking Age, and the age-old tradition of Irish society underwent at this period what has been described as 'a watershed for the history of Irish society'.

Thus it came about, although slowly, that the Viking Age encouraged Ireland, in common with other surviving Celtic areas, to develop into a nation from a number of small states, and so, in theory at least, into a single independent monarchy, analogous to Scotland, Wales and Brittany. Her rulers did not, like Charlemagne and Alfred the Great, go down to posterity with the outstanding epithet of 'great'. She did not even leave an aftermath of grateful clerks to call her last independent king the 'Good' like the Welsh Hywel. Her position was too isolated and her politics too local to challenge comparison with the great monarchs of western Europe.

Looking back over the development of the Celtic countries which fringed western Europe we are aware of a distinctive if limited similarity in their development. Each had begun as a series of small settlements, seeking to exploit the land, interested in fighting only in so far as it was necessary to maintain its footing. The Dálriada of Argyll seem to have amalgamated with the Picts happily enough by intermarriage. The princely houses of the Britons of southern Scotland moved southwards into Wales when the Anglian kingdom encroached too fully into their Scottish domain. The North Welsh under Rhodri Mawr followed the heroic age policy of nationalist aggression against the Anglians of North Britain till the policy of Alfred the Great in the next generation united Wales, first through Hywel Dda, later under Athelstan; and Wales, with no conquest, became virtually a part of England. The Bretons made a gradual union with France under the Breton chief Nominoé and his successors. Ireland, the oldest and purest of the Celtic countries, had remained longest as a collection of little states, but by her own nationalist risings, and by Viking pressure, had developed, for a time at least, a strong centralized monarchy. Fighting had been a necessity from time to time, but in general was only resorted to when absolutely necessary. First the Romans from the Mediterranean, then the Teutons of the North have gradually edged the Celtic peoples farther and farther to the West, to 'the limits of the habitable world'. We have watched the progress, and the struggles of the Celtic peoples to obtain and retain a foothold on the edge of the continent of Europe. It has been a long struggle and is not over yet.

CHAPTER 5

Institutions and Way of Life

By far the earliest detailed information which we possess about the institutions of the early Celtic peoples is derived from Ireland, for the earlier comments of classical writers are inadequate on this subject. Here no trace of later legislature came to disturb the native system till the Viking Age, although perhaps the influence of Christianity should not be discounted. Moreover, here we have preserved a large number of ancient law tracts, not so much a legal system as a number of treatises devoted to special subjects. Many of these go back to early times, the seventh and eighth centuries and perhaps even earlier, for there are signs that some of them were originally composed in poetry, which suggests that they were composed to be remembered and handed down orally by the *filid*. A very curious and very early example of this kind is the tract on 'sick maintenance', which contains what purport to be 'the Judgements of Dian-cecht', the Irish god of healing. This contains passages of verse which are probably as early as the sixth century; we know that this archaic custom of sick maintenance was already obsolete by the eighth century, for the *Crich Gablach*, which cannot be later, declares that there is no such practice, and describes the old procedure as we find it in *Bretha Crolige* ('Judgements of Blood-Letting').

The Irish laws are probably the oldest surviving in Europe in their inspiration, unaffected as they are by Roman law and the laws of the Mediterranean countries. They are the laws of an essentially pastoral people superimposed on a still earlier tradition. The early Irish had no towns whatever, and their earth or stone forts were of primarily military significance. They served, however, some of the functions of towns proper, being used as meeting-places, markets, or the like, and an *oenach* or fair seems to have been attached to each true fort of whatever size; larger centres, such as Tell-town and Tara, held large annual fairs. Their fines and commercial transactions were assessed in cows, the unit being the *sét*, which was half the value of a milk-cow; there was no coinage till the Viking Age, barter prevailing instead. A coinage has little meaning to a people whose wealth consists principally of cattle. As frost and snow are almost unknown in the interior of Ireland cattle could be left to fend for themselves out of doors all the year round, and they provided much of what was needed in the normal economy.

On the other hand many of the customs may show adherence to an older and more widespread tradition. Those which governed the institution of a king and his royal marriage with the *flaitheus h'Erenn* ('the sovereignty of Ireland') for example, have been thought to have affinities with the Indo-European systems as we can trace them in ancient India. Ireland, like India, is situated on the periphery of the Indo-European world, and it might therefore be supposed that the ancient institutions of both countries would have preserved traditions somewhat more archaic than those nearer the centre. This may be seen, for example, in certain features common to the Druids and the Brahmins. The study of early Celtic society in Ireland presents additional problems of interpretation in that it is difficult to disentangle what might be regarded as a specifically Celtic contribution from institutions already in existence, which themselves were in origin of Indo-European derivation.

Early Irish society was hierarchical in that there were clearly defined distinctions between the classes. The laws also sometimes defined degrees of status within individual classes. The country was divided into a number of kingdoms, perhaps as many as a hundred, differing in size and importance. Each kingdom was occupied by a *tuath* ('tribe' or 'people'), at the head of which was the *rí* or king who, if he were king of a small tribe, might be bound by personal allegiance to a *rí ruirech*, an 'over-king'. It is difficult to estimate the real extent of a king's powers or duties, but, as in many societies, these almost certainly included ritual functions. This appears to have been true of the pre-Christian period, as is suggested by the ritual ordeals of the Dagdá (cf. below, p. 171). Some similar rituals may have been practised later in the Middle Ages, as is suggested in turn by an account given by Giraldus Cambrensis of the inauguration of a Celtic king. It is perhaps significant in this context that royal sites, such as Cashel and Tara, were important ritual centres. Succession appears to have been agnatic; that is, the king was chosen from among the male descendants of a common great-grandfather. We find few references to the *rí* and the *rí ruirech* in the sagas. Theoretically, however, and no doubt practically, the inferior king gave hostages to his overlord and perhaps received from him a stipend in token of his dependence. This probably amounted to service in time of war, and there is no certain evidence of any other form of mutual obligation. This arrangement, as long as it was left undisturbed, must have worked admirably for keeping the peace according to a rough and ready balance of power. Small-scale raiding in case of local food shortage was the only likely serious breach of the peace or occasion of warfare, although the sagas seem to provide evidence of many personal occasions of quarrel.

Below the king, society was divided into three principal classes, similar to the *druides*, *equites* and *plebs* of Caesar's Gaul. There was the warrior aristocracy, landowners and patrons of the arts – corresponding to the *equites*. Of comparable social status were what we might term the intelligentsia, the *aes dána*, who in pre-Christian times and later included not only the druids, but also bards, jurists, physicians, historians, artists and skilled craftsmen. The third class, the equivalent of the *plebs*, comprised the body of freemen, commoners, minor craftsmen and small farmers, who formed the basis of society. In addition, there were slaves, but not surprisingly little is known of their position in society.

The obligations and rights of each freeman within a *tuath* were defined clearly and enforced by customary law, although there was nothing even approaching a police force to enforce the law. The power of custom appears to have been adequate. In pre-Christian times an important factor may have been the threat wielded by the druids of the virtual outlawing of a transgressor by denying him participation in ritual observances. In general, it appears that parties to legal disputes agreed in advance to accept the ruling of professional jurists (the *brithem*). The surviving legal codes show clearly that most causes of dispute from murder downwards were provided with means of redress, not by imprisonment, but by some form of 'honour price' (*lóg n-enech*). An additional stabilizing force was the practice of suretyship, by which a guarantor, often of higher status than that of the offender, was responsible for the actions of the offender. But most important, as is discussed below, was the fact that the individual counted for little in law. It was the kinship group which was ultimately responsible for the actions of its individual members. This was the basis of the stability of ancient Irish society. Beyond the boundaries of his *tuath* an individual could not rely on legal protection, unless there was some form of reciprocal agreement between different *tuatha* as, for example, when a minor king owed allegiance to an over-king. The *aes dána* appear to have been exceptional in that the members of this class, whose status was not determined by birth, seem to have been allowed to move freely around Ireland, and in so doing contributed to cultural unity within the country.

As we should expect in a largely pastoral community the most striking feature of the native institutions of Ireland is their apparently non-individual character. This is seen at once in the inheritance system and its system of *fines* (kindred). In Irish systems privilege and responsibilities alike rested on the kindred, the *derbfhine*, of the freeman, extending for four generations. Obviously marriage was thought of as taking place early, so that potentially the act of one individual might affect the whole kindred of four generations. This tie of the 'kindred' was the strongest of all their early institutions. Any member of the four generations descended from a great-grandfather was a *rigdamna* ('the subject suitable for a king' or for any other form of inheritance) and could claim his share. Conversely he was obliged to take his share of responsibility for any fines payable by any member of the 'kindred'. There was no personal payment. The 'kindred' stood or fell together. In this way they were responsible for one another and would obviously keep a close eye on one another's doings. In this way too every 'kindred' group would see to it that the kindred did duty as both police and judges. There could have been no better way in such a society of keeping justice on an even keel, and this helps to explain the relative scarcity of legal machinery which a study of so many legal tracts implies.

As regards the wider provincial kingdoms, the *cóicedach* and the *ruired*, we have seen that there were five of the former in proto-historic times. Their names are unknown, but they correspond to modern Ulster, Leinster, Munster and Connaught, with Meath as a separate kingdom in the midst, having its capital at Tara. The *cóiced*, however, already belonged to a past order before the time of our earliest historical records. At the beginning of the historical period the north consisted of the three kingdoms of Ailech, Airgialla (Oriel) and what remained of the Ulaid. Munster, with Ossory, and later with Cashel also and South Leinster, contained the rest of the south. In the eighth century Meath, the central kingdom, lost Brega which consisted of the present Co. Meath, South Louth and North Dublin, but it survived only until the eleventh century when Brega was again a part of Meath. This is roughly the political state of Ireland as it appears in the old law-tracts. But from the ninth century the provincial kings, especially in the north, tried to establish themselves in a high-kingship which should cover all Ireland. This in fact was not achieved until the time of Brian Bóruma of West Munster at the beginning of the eleventh century.

In the absence of a central organization the small kingdoms also joined themselves together by the system of fosterage, in which, till they reached adult years, some of the sons of the *flaith* ('the nobility') were placed out to be fostered by their neighbours, often those of higher rank. In this way close bonds of loyalty were established between foster brothers which were to be useful later in life. In the sagas the fosterer often became to his fosterling in later life an adviser and something like a grand vizier. We have no exact parallel to this practice in the Teutonic laws, but traces of it remain in early Britain where the father was called a *nutricius*, or *nutritor*. An example is found in Gildas, who speaks of the two royal princes of Devon being torn from the arms of their *nutricii*; and Adamnán represents Brude mac Maelchon of the northern Picts as having a *nutritor* whose name was Broichen and who resented the intrusion of St Columba into his domain.

Otherwise we hear little of family life. Marriage seems to have been a close tie in the sagas, but in the older law tracts we notice various degrees of marriage and concubinage. Nevertheless the position of women seems to have been high. In Britain the sagas tell us of households which trained the heroes in arms as well as gnomic wisdom, and to which the Irish heroes repaired (cf. below). A particular case in Irish literature is Cú Chulainn, trained by Ailbe and Aife in Alba (Scotland); in Wales there is Peredur in the Mabinogi. We find the 'seven witches of Gloucester' who have a similar establishment, possibly reflected in the Breton *Life of St Samson*, whose clerk is pursued by a *theomacha*. These are exceptional fragments of old lore, but we find a number of instances which seem to support the memory of a time when there were women rulers in the ancient Celtic world. Maeve is an instance in Ireland, and in Britain there were Cartimandua of the Brigantes and Boudicca the queen of the Iceni. The burial from Vix may be significant in this context.

We can see that in ancient times the Welsh laws had a similar basis to the Irish ones though in Britain they were more complex, and have been overlaid with the later Teutonic system. The institution of the *cenedl* ('kindred') may be traced in its four generations here as in the Irish *fines* despite differences in details. The Welsh people, like the Irish, were divided in pre-Norman times into three chief classes: (1) the so-called free tribesmen, known indifferently as *uchelwr*, *bréyr*, and *innate bonnedig*; (2) the subject population known as *theog*, *aillt*, *alltud*; and (3) the slaves. The first claimed relationship to one another, and presumably claimed descent from the *cenedl* or ancient conquering population; the second, whatever their origin, were not included among the tribesmen and, though not slaves, were responsible for a large part of the agricultural work. They were doubtless often foreigners, as their name implies; but in essence they were men who had no claim upon any land in the district. The slaves were probably originally largely won in war, and were the absolute property of the owner and belonged to the *cenedl*. They were largely responsible for the field-work of the homestead and much of the rougher household work.

Here also the 'kindred', claiming blood relationship, was a fixed institution, constituting the very heart of the law of inheritance. Giraldus Cambrensis observes that in Wales 'the most ordinary folks among this people keep careful count of the family pedigree'. Apart from its importance for the law of inheritance, perhaps the most striking illustration of the function of the *cenedl* is in the *galanas* ('blood-feud'), in cases of murder and homicide (from *gal*, *gelyn*, 'a foe'), or, in the case of lesser crimes, the *sarhad* ('insult', 'injury'). The vendetta was an active institution in Wales. Giraldus declares that the Welsh were ready 'to avenge not only new and recent injuries but also ancient and bygone ones as though but recently received'. To avoid a perpetual state of private warfare a system of compensation gradually evolved, and, in the case of *galanas* or enmity arising out of violent death, the honour of the clan of the injured man and the safety of the offender could be paid for by a fine of an amount exactly fixed in a scale according to the rank of the injured party. However, this fine was payable not by any individual person but collectively by every member of the *cenedl*, who had to contribute a share fixed by the degree of his relationship to the *cenedl*, and every member of the *cenedl* of the injured man received a share similarly calculated. The antiquity of the custom can be seen by its survival, in the form *galnes*, *galnys*, of 'satisfaction for slaughter' among the Strathclyde Britons. Traces of these customs remained in both Scotland and Wales, and indeed the Teutonic system also shows elaborate enactments and precise fines in Anglo-Saxon laws for the *wergild*. The chief difference is that in Teutonic law individualism has developed, whereas in Celtic law the responsibility for payment rests with the *cenedl*, and the payment is mostly in cows. The laws of King David of Scotland show distinct traces of the responsibility of the *cenedl* for the payment of the *wergild*, mostly in cattle. Even as late as the twelfth century 'the law which is called weregylt' was still assessed in cattle, and the continued right of the kindred of the slain recognized. Here also the social claims continued to be referred to under certain Celtic titles. In a particularly interesting late code of north British law known as the *Leges inter Brettos et Scottos*, the compiler has used an older legal system of Cumbria, whose early terminology shows relationship with Welsh. Here the fines for certain legal offences are referred to under their Welsh terms, all assessed in cows, and probably dating from the eleventh century when an attempt was being made to regularize relations between the different peoples of Scotland.

The most important of the Celtic institutions, in Ireland and Wales alike, is the kingship, which is always non-hereditary; but we cannot be at all certain that the word denotes the same function in all cases. The institution of the Pictish king is far from clear in the early period, as is also the relationship of the various princes to one another. What, for example, was the relationship of Bede's *rex potentissimus*, the king of the northern Picts, to the Picts of the Four Kingdoms, the southern Picts? And what was the relationship of the kings of the southern Picts to one another? We read in one of the medieval surveys of *regona* and in the Irish Annals of a 'king of Fortrenn', and though Bede speaks (V. 28) of a *rex Pictorum* he refers rather vaguely to the Picts under various terms, *gens*, *provincia*, and *natio*. Clearly he did not know the niceties of their nomenclature. Adamnán refers to a *regulus* ('petty king') of the Orkneys as if he were in some relation with Brude mac Maelchon. Moreover, in the ninth century the Pictish kings do not seem always to have been resident in one place. When Kenneth mac Alpin was at Forteviot his sons appear to have been resident there with him, but his wife was in Moniki, in Forfar, and Kenneth appears also to have had a residence at St Andrews.

An interesting feature of Pictish institutions was inheritance through the female. Bede had thoroughly grasped this, for he explains it fully. The antiquarian tracts bear out Bede's statement, for in the third and most reliable Pictish king-list only two kings are recorded as having fathers who have reigned; there is no clear evidence of succession through the father's line till the ninth century. Although kings married and had families, their sons did not succeed them. The system must have entailed a way of life quite different from what we understand, and probably goes back to something very old. We can trace it working in the saga of Corc son of Lugaid (cf. p. 93 above), and it seems to have involved visiting princes and a system of purely formal marriages, highly organized and intricately provided for. The organization of the royal family seems to have been at times matrilocal as well as matrilinear, but not usually matriarchal.

Apart from Celtic institutions of a general and universal

character, such as the *cenedl* and its system of consolidation and inheritance, and the systems of *galanas* and *sarhad*, which were dependent on it, and which had their roots in the ancient pan-Celtic economic way of life, we have in Wales a totally different system of law which had obviously been superimposed on this earlier system without destroying or even fundamentally modifying it. This system was much later in origin than the one which the Welsh shared with the Irish, and has reached us in a much more comprehensible shape, in the form of a code, rather than in the form of separate treatises, and so possesses a certain unity, and some resemblance to the Teutonic codes. This unity is discernible everywhere, though many and various forms of the code appear, and it always concentrates itself in the person of the king. This is the first and greatest characteristic of the Welsh laws in which they differ fundamentally from the earlier Irish law tracts.

The Welsh laws are all prefaced by a statement in which they claim to have been enacted by the Welsh king Hywel Dda, who is said to have summoned a representative assembly, in which each cantref of Wales was represented by six men, to meet at his court which was called the White House on the River Taff (identified in modern times with the village of Whitland in Carmarthenshire). It is implied that the laws were not the creation of any legislative body, but were the organized statement of the ancient customs of the race, which had hitherto been carried on by oral tradition. They could only be altered by a national body such as the one which apparently had now been summoned by Hywel. One version, known as the *Venedotian Code*, enacts that no part of the laws of Hywel can be abrogated save by a body as large as that which met at Hywel's behest. Here we see the important part which the king has come to play in legislature, and the large and representative body held responsible for the laws which follow. This meeting seems to have taken place soon after 940.

We have no external evidence vouching for the genuineness

of the prefaces to these laws, and the earliest manuscript was not written before the end of the twelfth century. Accordingly it is not surprising that many scholars have regarded them with some suspicion, but the unanimity of their ascription throughout Welsh literature, and the absence of any suggestion of a rival constitution, are a very strong indication of their genuineness. Further, the act is consistent with what we know of Hywel from other sources – his admiration of Alfred the Great, whose laws he must have known, his unfailing attendance at Athelstan's meetings of the English *witan*, his general approval of everything politically English; all these must naturally have led him to extend his power to a synthesis of Welsh law. Many lawyers must have helped him in his task, and we hear nowhere else of such a unified body turning their efforts to so great an undertaking. What we learn of 'that most learned man Blegyrwyd' (he is described as a teacher of law to Hywel's household, and other incidental allusions are made to his fame as a lawyer) suggests that he also lent his aid and advice to the king. Incidentally it may be mentioned that there are also allusions in the text to the 'Code of Hywel', and there were certainly lawmen in Wales capable of collecting and formulating such a code. Evidently, there had been written law-books before these of Hywel, and these may well have borne some resemblance to the less unified Irish tracts.

Apart from minor variations in the texts of the laws, three principal versions of the Code have survived, which are believed to have been compiled by lawyers from the original version over the intervening years for the use of particular districts or communities. These are distinguished commonly as the *Venedotian Code*, of which the oldest manuscript, the *Black Book of Chirk*, would seem to date from about 1200; the so-called *Gwentian Code*, though there is no evidence for the ascription to Gwent or Morgannwg, and the compilation might with more appropriateness be ascribed to Morgeneu and his son Cyfnerth; and the *Dimetian Code*, probably the closest to the original text, but obviously much amplified and preserved only in a late manuscript. In addition to these, and of earlier date, are the extant Latin versions which, however, clearly show themselves to have been translated from the Welsh originals, and to have been based on texts older than any of those which have survived.

A glance at the contents of these different Codes will show how far they must differ from the original enactment of Hywel, in the additions which have been made in accordance with local requirements, the local emphases which have been thought necessary, and perhaps a certain amount of omission. But all make clear the royal nature of the document in its original form and its orientation towards the court and the king. On the whole the document perhaps tells us more about the later period of Welsh pre-Norman history than about earlier times, and it is obvious that it has been much influenced by the English legal codes. However, we get a fair idea of the court of the period, which was probably slow to alter. We gather that the court consisted of some twenty-four officers, though the number ought not to be insisted on for any given period; and the duties and payments of these officers throw abundant light on court life in its external aspects, even on the clothes of the officers.

Perhaps the most interesting and conservative features relate to the bards. The *penkerdd*, ('the chief of song') has a free holding of land and sits next to the *edling* (the king's heir) in the hall, and has the right to sit next to the king. The *bardd teulu* ('the household bard') also has a free house and land from the king, and his harp and a gold ring from the queen, but his status is lower than that of the *penkerdd*. The section on penal codes for *galanas* and *sarhad* (cf. p. 116 above) may well be older, and probably original, and the law of inheritance is included. Values and fines have a section to themselves: the valuations given for various kinds of property include one for a harp and its tuning key – both separately assessed – and for various kinds of livestock, including bees, whose origin is said to be in Paradise, a belief which is understandable enough before the days of sugar. The penalty for killing a cat which guards the king's barn looks old, and has parallels in early Norse literature: 'Its head is to be held downwards on a clean, level floor, and its tail is to be held upwards; and after that wheat is to be poured about it until the tip of its tail is hidden, and that is its value.' Here the glossator has added his note on the *teithi* ('points') of a well-bred cat: 'It should be perfect of ear, perfect of eye, perfect of tail, perfect of teeth, perfect of claw, and without marks of fire, and it should kill mice, and not devour its offspring, and it should not be caterwauling every new moon.'

Nothing in the surviving laws of any Celtic people suggests the existence in early medieval Wales and Ireland of town or communal life, and the absence of a native coinage suggests that barter was the universal rule, at home and abroad. There is still some slight hint of a tin trade, and pottery and beads suggest trade with the Mediterranean at Bantham in south Devon, at Tintagel and Gwithian in west Cornwall, and even as far north as Dunadd in Argyll, but in general the Celts at this time reckoned their wealth in cows, and these finds are limited to coastal districts. Agriculture was practised, though perhaps only on a small scale, and place-names show the seasonal transhumance of the Welsh, in particular *hafod* and *hofoty* ('the summer pasture', 'summer dairy') and its *ty* ('cot'). Their cattle raids hardly exceed what we should expect in a country devoid of shops and permanent purchasing centres. The life of Ireland is that of an aristocracy living mostly in the open air, and that of Wales is pretty much the same. In all the Celtic lands the life of the aristocracy centred largely on hunting and all that goes with it: that of the lower classes in waiting on them, and in carrying on such agriculture as prevailed. The men of the North have left us an unforgettable little picture of their life of hunting and fishing in the open air in a little cradle song which I cannot resist quoting:

When thy father went a-hunting
With spear on shoulder, and cudgel in hand,
He would call his big dogs,
'Giff, Gaff': 'Catch, catch!': 'Fetch, fetch!'
In his coracle he would spear a fish,
Striking suddenly like a lion.
When thy father went up the mountain
He would bring back a roebuck, a wild boar, a stag,
A spotted grouse from the mountain,
A fish from the falls of Derwenydd.
As many as thy father caught with his spear
None would escape except those with wings.

To a limited extent archaeological evidence supplements that of the literature of Ireland and Wales for certain aspects of the life of the insular Celts, and that of classical writers for the pre-Roman period both on the Continent and in Britain. In this section there is no reference to Celtic religion and art, as these subjects are discussed respectively in chapters 6 and 8. One fact of interest which emerges from their study, however, is that the evidence derived from burials not only emphasizes the hierarchical basis of Celtic society in pre-Christian times but also, in the case of richly furnished burials, underlines the wealth of the aristocracy and its love of personal display.

Until the Celts either came into relatively close contact with the classical world of the Mediterranean, or were conquered by the Romans, their standard of architecture remained at a level very little different from that which had existed in temperate Europe since the Neolithic period. Their buildings were generally of wood; when of stone they were normally of dry-stone construction. There is therefore little surviving evidence of elaborate architecture dating from the pre-Roman period in Celtic Europe. Even during the early Christian period in Ireland, native building techniques were adapted for ecclesiastical purposes (cf. below, p. 215). Among the field monuments of the prehistoric and early historic periods there are few substantial remains of Celtic structures, other than fortified sites, particularly hill-forts. These latter constitute a not inappropriate legacy of the Celts, but the only widespread visible remains of domestic structures, found commonly in the stone-bearing areas of Britain and Ireland, are the so-called 'hut-circles', stone foundations of circular houses, and even many of these may be proved to belong to a Celtic context only after excavation.

It will be appreciated that from stone foundations of the post-holes or sleeper trenches surviving from a wooden building only the basic framework of a structure may be reconstructed. Archaeology in temperate Europe can rarely hope to recover details of any superstructure, and still less of decoration. Reference to more recent primitive peoples, however, such as the North American Indians of British Columbia for example, provides a reminder that timber buildings could be both spacious and decorative, with carvings and paintings. Some descriptions of buildings in early Celtic literature, while obviously exaggerated and fanciful, suggest that princely residences were anything but austere, at least internally. It nevertheless remains true that archaeology can reconstruct little more than the ground plan and any associated artifacts. Mention is made in chapter 1 of the Heuneburg, a possibly fortified princely residence of the Hallstatt period on the upper Danube, and some indication of a more modest dwelling, of the same period, but one superior to that of a simple peasant farmer, is provided by the foundations of a house found below a nearby burial mound. This was an apparently plank-built rectangular house of four or five rooms set within a palisade. A large, elongated rectangular earthwork at Tara is commonly referred to as the 'Banqueting Hall', and it has been suggested that this may represent the remains of an aisled building at Tara described in medieval texts, and named *Tech Midchuarta* ('house of mead-circling'). These descriptions refer to compartments or open-fronted cubicles assigned to particular grades of guests, according to social status. As the earthwork has not been excavated, this identification cannot either be proved or disproved. It is possible that it dates, as do some other ritual monuments on the Hill of Tara, from pre-Celtic times.

The houses of the peasant farmers, and perhaps indeed those of the minor aristocracy, differed little from those of the Neolithic and Bronze Age. On the Continent in pre-Roman times the houses were normally timber-built and rectangular on plan. They were grouped together in small nucleated settlements which were sometimes encircled by a palisade or bank and ditch, or both. In contrast, many Celtic houses of the pre-Roman period in Britain were normally circular on plan and, although often accompanied by other buildings, formed the nucleus of an independent farmstead. A few villages have also been identified. Circular houses are also known to have been built in Ireland at this time, and this tradition was maintained into the early Christian period and beyond. Rectangular, square and even trapezoidal buildings are also known. In the west houses were normally built largely of stone, but elsewhere in Ireland timber buildings were common.

Most settlement sites, whether nucleated or individual, were enclosed. In many instances security was provided by a timber palisade, but others were given more substantial protection in the form of either a massive stone wall or a bank and ditch. These more substantial defences frequently appear to have been more appropriate respectively to an Irish ring-fort or to the more widespread hill-fort of Celtic Europe. It is indeed sometimes difficult to distinguish between a defended settlement and a true fort, apart from considerations of size. This is understandable when considered in the context of feuding and raiding, evidence for which is provided abundantly both from archaeological and literary sources. A feeling of insecurity appears to have affected even simple farmers who otherwise appear to have had little desire, or opportunity, for fighting. Some of the surviving stone foundations of circular huts are often more massive than would have been necessary merely to support a superstructure.

Reference may be made in this context to a type of underground structure found in Brittany, Ireland, western and northern Britain. This is the *souterrain*, sometimes referred to in Cornwall as a *fogou*, and in Scotland as an 'earth-house' or 'weem' (*uamh*, literally 'cave'). Souterrains consist of stone-lined trenches, often of considerable length, and, particularly in Ireland, sometimes providing access to one or more underground cells or chambers with corbelled roofs. There is some uncertainty as to their function, and this is aggravated by variations of size, proportions and complexity of plan within the class as a whole. Although many may have been used for the storage of perishable foodstuffs, others almost certainly were used as refuges in times of danger. Souterrains are found commonly associated with hut circles, and the entrance to the former frequently was gained from the interior of a hut.

Another indication of this probable preoccupation with self-protection is provided by the *crannóg* (from *crann*, 'tree'), many of which are found in Ireland, and to a lesser extent in western and northern Britain. Crannogs consisted of artificial islands constructed near the shores of lakes and inland rivers from layers of timber, brushwood, stone, clay and peat. Stability was provided by vertical posts which anchored the mass to the subsoil. A strong palisade normally enclosed the flat top of the crannog, on which were erected one or more timber buildings. Although some few large crannogs are known, such as the royal site of Lagore in Co. Meath, most appear to have been individual homesteads. The labour of construction and maintenance, and the discomfort of living in such damp conditions, could surely have been justified only by a real desire for protection. Artifacts found in the smaller crannogs rarely provide evidence of warlike proclivities on the part of their dwellers.

The nearest approach in the Celtic world generally to an urban type of settlement could have been found in certain tribal capitals. These might be hill-forts (*oppida*) or large fortified settlements situated on lower ground. The simplicity of their buildings, the architecture of which differed little from that of rural houses, however, must have offered a contrast to the sophisticated public and private buildings of contemporary classical cities in the Mediterranean. Yet these embryonic towns of the Celtic world may have possessed a sort of barbaric vigour which the mere remains of foundations fail to indicate today. The most developed settlements not unnaturally are those found closest to the Mediterranean, as in the south of France and Iberia, for the idea of urban life as such appears to have been both foreign and repugnant to the Celts. This may be seen, for example, in Roman Britain, where the towns appear to have been accepted reluctantly by the native Britons, whereas the Romanized farmstead and country house, the *villa*, appears to have been readily accepted and enjoyed by farmer and aristocrat alike. In France the Gallo-Roman town was more successful and, again in contrast with Britain, frequently preserved some continuity of settlement into the Middle Ages. This success may have been conditioned to a certain extent by the adoption, in southern France and Celtic Iberia at least, of a form of urban settlement prior to the Roman conquest.

Mediterranean borrowings may be identified in southern parts of Europe in stone building, although mainly still of dry-stone construction, in defensive walls and sometimes in bastions. Yet the regular arrangement of buildings in relation to an intra-mural system of roads found in such settlements was sometimes adopted further north where timber buildings were more common. The large areas occupied by some *oppida* in temperate Europe, some of which exceed those of medieval cities, makes it difficult today to excavate such sites in their entirety. It is probable that only part of the area protected by the outer defensive perimeter was built upon. The remaining space would have provided temporary grazing in time of siege. It cannot be assumed, however, that all hill-forts and low-lying nucleated settlements were occupied by large populations. Some of the hill-forts may have been unoccupied except in times of emergency, while others may have been permanently occupied only by small numbers of people, perhaps for the maintenance of defences. Although the initial impetus which prompted the construction of the majority of hill-forts may have been largely conditioned by military considerations, there is evidence to suggest that in some *oppida* there was a certain amount of movement towards the development of truly urban communities. This is seen most clearly in parts of France which were increasingly influenced by contact with the Roman world in the decades immediately preceding the conquest. In some such *oppida* there is evidence of what may convincingly be interpreted as shops, and even certain areas within the settlement as a whole which were occupied by groups of specialized craftsmen. Even in south-eastern Britain, but again at a time prior to the occupation when Roman influence was strong, mints for the production of local Celtic coinage were established in some tribal capitals, the abbreviated name of which in some instances appeared on the coins. Such a development away from simple barter towards a truly monetary economy and possible economic specialization was foreign to earlier Celtic tradition.

In contrast with the Continent and the southern part of Britain, Ireland remained free of large-scale Roman influence, even during the Roman occupation of Britain. Such contact as may have been made in the course of trade and raids had little effect on the settlement pattern, which was maintained until the emergence of Celtic monasticism. Even in early Christian Ireland the largest centres of population were not true towns. Although the population of some monastic 'cities' (cf. below, p. 214) may have been counted in several hundreds and included craftsmen, these were specialized religious and not secular communities. There are relatively few hill-forts in Ireland, none of which compares in size and complexity with the larger continental and British examples. Literary sources refer to royal

1A. Pillar from Pfalzfeld, found at Saint-Goar on the Rhine. La Tène or Carolingian?

1B. Typical Celtic head in sandstone from Heidelberg, 200 B.C.

2A. Bust of a Celtic hero from Mšecke Žehrovice, Czechoslovakia. End of second or beginning of first century B.C.

2B. The Dying Gaul in the Museum of the Capitol at Rome. A Roman marble copy of a bronze original, the original forming an element of a group raised by Attalos of Pergamum commemorating his victory over the Galatians.

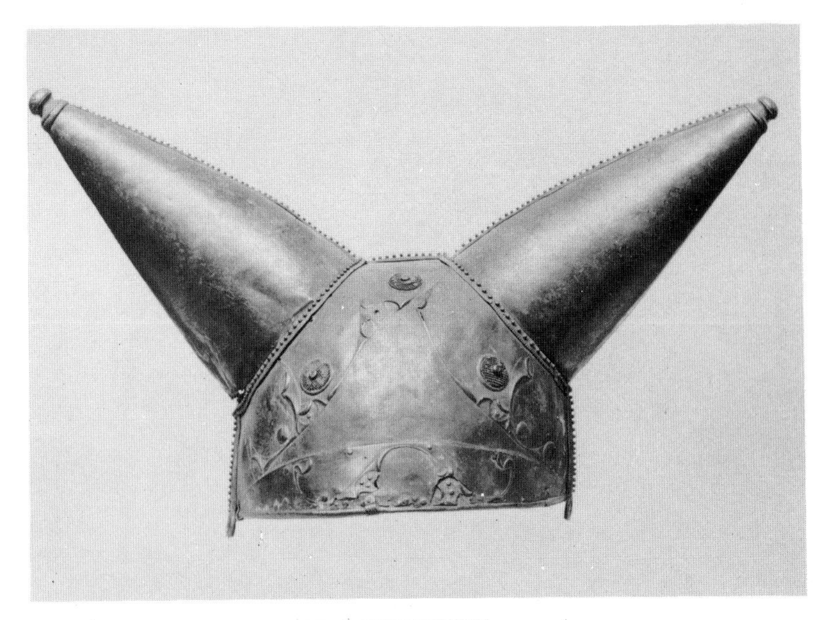

3A. Bronze helmet from the River Thames near Waterloo Bridge, London. First century A.D.

3B. The Desborough Mirror, from Desborough in Northamptonshire. First century A.D.

4. (*opposite*) The Battersea Shield, from the Thames at Battersea, London. About the time of the birth of Christ.

5A. The Athlone Plaque. Bronze ornament of a book cover, from Athlone. Eighth century A.D.

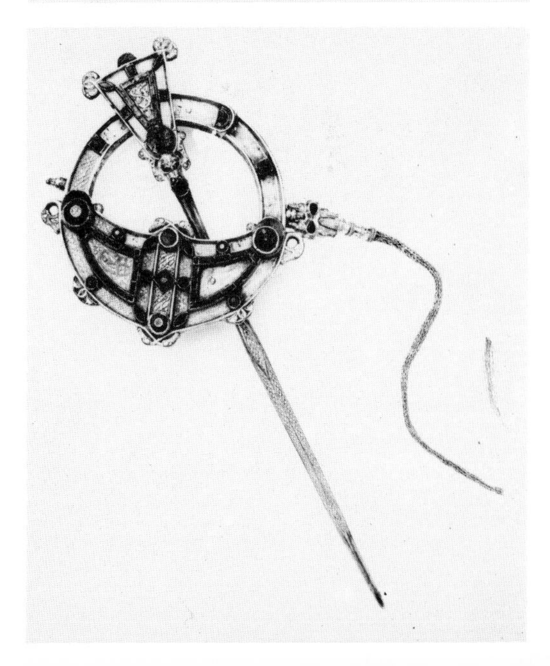

5B. The Tara Brooch, found in a wooden box, together with Viking objects, near the mouth of the Boyne, Ireland. Eighth century A.D.

6. Page from the Book of Kells, from Iona or Kells, found in Kells. Eighth century A.D.

7. (*opposite*) Page from the Book of Durrow, from the library of Trinity College, Dublin. Seventh century A.D.

8A. Muiredach's Cross, Co. Louth, Ireland. Tenth century A.D.

8B. Skellig Michael, Co. Kerry.

seats, rather than tribal capitals, and it would seem that in Ireland there was little stimulus towards even embryonic urban centres.

One of the most widespread field monuments of Irish antiquity is the ring-fort, many thousands of which survive in varying stages of preservation. They were enclosures, normally circular in plan, and surrounded either by a stone-built wall (cashel) or earthen banks and ditches with a timber palisade (raths). Within the enclosure there were one or more buildings, usually a dwelling and associated farm buildings. Most appear to have been in use in Ireland during the pre-Christian Iron Age and the early Celtic period. There is some variation in size, but the majority are small and may be considered to have been individual farmsteads defended by a single wall or bank and ditch. The larger ones, which may have had a diameter as great as two hundred feet, and particularly those with multiple banks and ditches, were probably the seats of kings and princelings. A notable example is the Grianán of Ailech, Co. Donegal, an important centre in north-western Ulster.

With a few exceptions dating from a time shortly before the Roman conquest in areas close to the Roman world, therefore, the Celts chose not to adopt classical architecture, but retained the building traditions of temperate Europe which had proved adequate, whether in wood or stone, for several millennia. Whenever existing structures proved inadequate, they were modified. This may be seen principally in fortifications. Experience of Roman siege warfare, for example, probably revealed weaknesses in walls or ramparts with internal timber cross-bracing. In order to provide greater internal stability, an arrangement of nailed cross-timbers was devised. This was the *murus gallicus* or 'Gallic wall' referred to by Caesar. The cashels and raths of Ireland, although possibly influenced by somewhat similar structures in Atlantic Europe, appear largely to have been a native Celtic development from the circular hut. Similarly, the duns and the tower-like brochs of western and northern Scotland may be seen to have developed within a purely Celtic context from more simple prototypes, perhaps influenced to a limited extent by structural techniques employed in other contemporary types of defensive structures. In each case the resultant stronghold served its purpose adequately within a context in which there was interplay between social, economic, military and environmental factors.

The widespread and constant preoccupation throughout the Celtic world with defences, whether true forts or the modest protection afforded by homesteads, suggests that fear of attack was a real threat to many levels of society. Yet the extent of warfare should not be exaggerated. There could have been little to compare with the carefully planned and executed campaigns of the professional armies of the Romans. The assumption that inhabitants of individual homesteads felt sufficiently secure behind their relatively feeble defences suggests that they anticipated little more than nuisance raids by small marauding bands. Otherwise this type of settlement, which is typical of Celtic Ireland and many parts of Britain, would surely have been replaced by nucleated settlements in which greater security might have been achieved as a result of communal activity. The individual homestead was suited to the largely pastoral economy of Ireland and northern and western Britain. In those parts of the Celtic world where arable farming perhaps achieved a larger significance within the economy as a whole, and so allowed a surplus of food, there may have been a proportionately greater inducement to more extensive social co-operation, as well as specialization. In such areas the existence of the large hill-fort probably resulted from a more developed form of social organization, for in such a milieu it might be supposed that potential attackers would similarly be better organized, more numerous and more determined in their assaults. This is not to minimize the importance accorded to livestock in such communities, as the large areas frequently enclosed by the defences of the larger hill-forts included provision for the temporary grazing of animals. But even the large hill-forts could hardly have withstood a siege of any duration, even assuming that the attackers possessed the psychological and physical means to invest a fort for any length of time.

There can be little doubt that warfare, in one form or another, was important to the Celtic aristocracy. As the geographer Strabo remarked in the first century A.D., 'The whole nation . . . is war-mad, both high-spirited and ready for battle, but otherwise simple and not uncultured.' A distinction should perhaps be made between what might be considered essential and non-essential fighting. The former would include campaigns, the purpose of which was to win new land for settlement at times when pressure of population in the homeland demanded a search for *Lebensraum*. If this could be won peacefully by the infiltration of small groups of immigrants, fighting was not necessary. Wherever more organized resistance was experienced, usually in response to a threat of a large-scale infiltration of Celts, some form of military engagement or engagements was likely to follow. In this category of 'essential' warfare should also be included armed resistance to the Romans, both before and after the conquest, and battles in Britain between Celts and Anglo-Saxons. Such engagements in the past periodically formed part – and continue to form part – of the life of many communities.

The 'warlike' tendencies of the Celts, which appear to have been thought significant by classical writers, might be better classified as 'non-essential' in that territorial aggrandizement was less frequently involved. This type of warfare had characteristics more akin to those of hunting than to true wars of aggression or defence. This was the world of *Táin Bó Cualnge* (*The Cattle-raid of Cooley*) (cf. below, p. 266), that of Celtic raids in the Balkans and Greece and the employment of Celtic mercenaries in these areas. The activities of the *fianna* of Ireland are also relevant. The *fianna* were organized bands of young warriors who spent part of their life in hunting and fighting away from their own tribal areas. Their existence appears to have been both acceptable and welcome socially, and perhaps was intended to provide some outlet for the excesses of aristocratic adolescence, and perhaps some military training, prior to the assumption of the full responsibilities of manhood. It must be emphasized that this 'non-essential' form of warfare was considered more of a sport than true warfare, despite the very real risk of death for those concerned in it. It was also very much the concern of the aristocracy, and was one of several means by which prestige might be attained. Such prestige was frequently achieved by individual combat with an enemy of comparable status, for which there are many indications in the early Irish literature.

One of the most interesting of these is the combat between Cú Chulainn and Fer Diad in *Táin Bó Cualnge*.

> Fer Diad and Cú Chulainn performed marvellous feats. Cú Chulainn went and leapt into Fer Diad's shield; Fer Diad hurled him from him thrice into the ford; but the one weapon which Fer Diad could not withstand was Cú Chulainn's own special weapon, the *Gae Bolga*.
>
> 'Give heed to the *Gae Bolga*,' said the charioteer who was standing by. He sent it to him along the stream.
>
> Cú Chulainn seized it between his toes and wielded it on Fer Diad into his body's armour. It advances like one spear so that it becomes twenty-four points. Then Fer Diad turned the shield below. Cú Chulainn thrust at him with the spear over the shield, so that it broke the shaft of his ribs and went through Fer Diad's heart.

The archaeological record reveals in the many parade weapons, armour and personal ornaments something of the tangible trappings of military prestige and aspiration. Some impression of the panoply of a Celtic warrior in pre-Roman Gaul, for example, is provided by certain burials, notably those containing chariots. The warrior was laid on his back across the platform of his chariot, his weapons to hand, and accompanied sometimes by helmet and shield, personal ornaments and those trappings which adorned his chariot and horses. It was common for him to have been provided with food and wine and fine vessels appropriate to a feast in the after-life. Fighting and feasting appear to have been two complementary and essential facets of Celtic aristocratic life; fighting during the day and feasting at night when the exploits of the day would be recounted, no doubt embellished and, whenever of particular note, repeated subsequently by the professional bards, eventually to become part of tradition.

There is abundant archaeological evidence for the weapons of the Celts, and this demonstrates that they were in no way inferior to those of their contemporaries. The introduction of iron-working at the beginning of the Hallstatt period allowed the production of high quality weapons in quantities not possible during the Bronze Age. The iron sword underwent a certain development during the Hallstatt and La Tène periods, from relatively short cut-and-thrust weapons to longer slashing swords with blunted tips. For in-fighting daggers were used. Swords and daggers were carried in scabbards and sheaths, often of bronze and sometimes ornamented. Spears were also important, particularly on the Continent. During the Hallstatt period the throwing spear appears to have been preferred to the thrusting spear, although later on, possibly due to contact with the western Mediterranean, the latter was adopted by some of the Celts. The *gae bolga* of Cú Chulainn, although credited with apparently supernatural properties, appears to have been a thrusting spear. The bow does not appear to have been in regular use as relatively few arrowheads have been found, but the sling was used in the west, notably in Britain and Ireland. Shields were long, and either straight-sided with rounded ends, or oval. Functional shields were commonly made of wood and sometimes were bound with iron. An iron boss normally protected the hand-grip. Parade shields, as in the Bronze Age, were made of sheet bronze, and some surviving examples may be counted among the finest products of La Tène craftsmen.

Some idea of the appearance of a Celtic warrior may therefore be provided by a study of both weapons and ornaments, and more particularly from their deposition in graves. There are, in addition, some few contemporary representations of Celtic warriors and their equipment in both classical and Celtic contexts. The statue known as the 'Dying Gaul' and a small bronze figurine, both dating from the late third century B.C., depict naked warriors. The latter clearly represents one of the *gaesatae*, a special class of warrior who, as Polybius described, went into battle naked apart from a *torc*, or neck ornament. His weapon was a heavy spear, the *gae*, the model perhaps for the *gae bolga* of Cú Chulainn. Polybius also refers to the *bracae*, or breeches, worn by other groups of Celts who had crossed the Alps to settle in northern Italy. The Gundestrup bowl, probably of the first century B.C., shows foot-soldiers wearing *bracae* and mounted horsemen. Of greater interest are representations of La Tène weapons, including swords and spears, shields and crested helmets, and the long animal-headed *carnyx*, or war trumpet. Roman and Celtic coins also provide contemporary illustrations of warriors and their accoutrements, including chariots.

In warfare, as in so many other aspects of Celtic life, there appear to have been supernatural overtones, as is suggested by the *gaesatae* who fought naked in obedience to an archaic ritual tradition which apparently taught that nudity afforded some supernatural protection. Among the stories told of Cú Chulainn there are indications which suggest that magic and ritual played some part in the training of a young warrior.

There are at least eight versions of the saga on this subject, which is striking in itself, and is not without echoes in Welsh literature. Cú Chulainn made his way to the famous 'school' of Scáthach in 'Scythia' beyond Alba. He straightway 'took the goal' from the beautiful bright youths playing hurley outside her dwelling, and after many triumphs, including the beheading of Cúán, Scáthach's son, he learnt her 'three feats' which Scáthach had never before disclosed to anyone, and he remained with her for a year. After that he went to the castle of Aife, the most famous woman-warrior in the world, daughter of the king of the Greeks with whom Scáthach was at feud, stayed with her for two years, and had a son by her. Then returning to Scáthach he found a band of Irish youths with her, learning all the advantages he had himself except for the *gae bolga*. He made them promise never to fight with one another, 'for you are in no danger from anyone else in the world unless it comes from yourselves'.

These stories are frankly amoral. Scáthach is also described as a prophetess and a sage, and elsewhere we have a set of gnomic verses attributed to her. It is clear that Cú Chulainn traditionally owes his superiority in arms to Scáthach and Aife, and that the story forms a part of the wider saga of *The Wooing of Emer*. The most remarkable feature of the saga, however, is the way in which it is taken for granted that martial feats should be taught by these women, and that their establishments should exist for the purpose. Aife is said to live in a *daun*. The reference to decapitation is interesting, as head-hunting appears to have been an accepted goal of many engagements, again perhaps with ritual overtones. The band of Irish youths also recalls the *fianna*.

The 'schools' of Scáthach and Aife call to mind an institution in the medieval Welsh story of Peredur which seems to bear some remote relationship to them. The story relates that Peredur came in his wanderings to a castle on a mountain, owned by a fine tall woman who told him that nine witches (*gwiddonot*) of Gloucester, together with their father and mother, had conquered all her dominion and laid it waste, all save that one house, which they were expected to attack that same night. At dawn one of the witches came and attacked a watchman, but when she in her turn was attacked by Peredur she told him that they were destined to suffer at his hands, but that he was destined to obtain a horse and arms from her, and under her charge he would learn to be a knight and to handle his weapons. He went with the witch to the Court (*llys*) of the Witches, and there he stayed three weeks, then chose a horse and arms and left. Later in the story we learn that the Witches of Gloucester had killed Peredur's cousin and burned his uncle, and he was predicted to take vengeance on them. Peredur and Gwalchmai sent to Arthur's household to ask him to come and attack the witches. They began to fight them and eventually Peredur struck a death-blow at a witch who uttered a cry and bade the other witches flee, saying that it was Peredur who had learned knighthood from them and was destined to slay them. Then Arthur and his household struck in among the witches, and the Witches of Gloucester were all slain. A similar encounter took place in *Kulhwch and Olwen* between Arthur and a *gwiddon*, who is also called a hag (*gwrách*). In this encounter Arthur was victorious.

The *gwrách* fights only with her nails, but the *gwiddonot* wear helmets, and apparently other armour, and prophecy and predictions are associated with them. They are amazons who live in a settled house called *Llys of Gwiddonod* ('The Witches' Court') with their father and mother. Rhys reminds us that it was not till the enactment of the law of Adamnán (ninth century, but probably embodying documents of the seventh and eighth centuries) that women warriors were no longer found in Celtic countries. Taking what we are told of Gaulish women warriors by classical writers, together with Boudicca, Cartimandua and Maeve and with these stories, we cannot but wonder whether there was not some such institution among the most ancient Celtic peoples.

There can be little doubt that fighting as a sport, rather than a necessity, formed a vital part of Celtic aristocratic life. In any discussion of the Celts this aspect tends to be emphasized, as literary sources almost exclusively, and a considerable proportion of the archaeological evidence, are concerned more with the lives of the aristocracy than with those of the ordinary people. Were the colour and drama of this aristocratic preoccupation with personal prestige and social position removed, what remained would not differ greatly in essentials from the kind of life lived by any iron-using peasant culture of the past.

The introduction of iron-working to temperate Europe does not appear to have altered to any great extent the pattern of farming which had gradually become established during the later part of the Bronze Age. There were changes, brought about by the availability of heavy iron tools and implements, which allowed a start to be made in clearing and draining some of the low-lying more heavily forested areas. The lighter plough remained in use, however, and lighter, frequently upland soils remained under cultivation. Fields of the Iron Age in Britain are sometimes referred to as 'Celtic fields', although it is now known that this type of field had already been established during the Bronze Age. The fields were small, generally between one quarter of an acre and two acres in area, and often square in plan. In south-eastern Britain, which has provided most evidence, large areas of light soils in the pre-Roman period were covered by a network of field-systems, linked by trackways. Individual farmsteads and occasional small villages were scattered among the fields. In certain areas it seems probable that a hill-fort may have served as a focus of social organization. The fact that corn was exported from Britain suggests that this arable farming was capable of producing more than was necessary for feeding the farmers themselves and the aristocracy.

Excavation has revealed details of some Celtic farms and their equipment. Within a palisade or enclosing wall there were husking and winnowing places, granaries for seed corn, drying racks for corn or hay, underground storage pits for grain, and perhaps one or more small buildings ancillary to the farmhouse. There might be one or more enclosures for livestock, for even in areas of intensive arable farming animal bones recovered during excavation attest the presence of cattle and sheep. In some more highland areas, cattle corrals and enclosures of varied types may be recognized, and in such regions available evidence suggests that crop-raising was proportionately less important. The shares of some ploughs were iron-shod, and iron sickles and bill-hooks were in common use. Iron was also used for a variety of wood-working tools, many of which resemble in essentials the design of comparable present-day tools. It must be remembered that the wheeled vehicles of the Celts would have demanded in their manufacture tools capable of detailed and precise wood-working. Corn was ground on small stone rotary-querns, an improvement on earlier prehistoric saddle-querns. There is some evidence of domestic crafts such as cheese-making, weaving and the making of pottery, although in some areas of Celtic Europe mass-produced pottery was coming into use. In most aspects of daily life the Celtic peasantry in the pre-Roman period was economically self-sufficient. Trade and the gradual adoption of coinage were more the concern of the aristocracy who increasingly became aware of, and eventually came to emulate, the economic and social attitudes of the Romans.

Celtic institutions and the Celtic way of life were largely destroyed by Roman occupation. The aristocracy was encouraged to adopt Roman manners and education, and in so doing diminished the personal ties of loyalty which had formed the basis of barbarian Celtic society. Although some of the ordinary people, particularly in areas where Romanization was slight, retained something of their material culture, even this was modified by a monetary economy and the acquisition of the minor products of Romanized mass-production, such as pottery, tools and trinkets. But beyond the frontiers of the Empire, surviving Celtic communities in northern Britain and in Ireland retained until the coming of Christianity a way of life little altered from that of four centuries earlier. Apart from the obvious changes in belief and ritual, Celtic society for some time afterwards preserved most of its pre-Christian characteristics. Although the Church naturally attempted to discourage fighting, feuding and raiding, these essential features of Celtic aristocratic life could not be completely eradicated. There is evidence, indeed, that some Celtic monasteries in Ireland, prompted by a variety of pretexts, raided each other. The monasteries, however, appear to have initiated one significant economic change in their encouragement of arable farming. Literary and archaeological evidence together suggest that from the seventh and eighth centuries onwards land, including some of the heavier soils, was enclosed for crop-raising. Cattle-raising, however, remained important, and it seems probable that successful selective breeding was practised, as the ancestors of many modern breeds of cattle may be identified among the numerous animal bones found in many excavated sites of the early Christian period.

To balance the somewhat grim impression of Celtic life which might be inferred from the emphasis on fighting among the aristocracy and the humdrum life of the peasantry, a final word may be added on games and entertainment. Some of the games are mentioned frequently in Irish literature. There was *brandub*, for example, sometimes compared with *fidcheall* and *branfad*, something in the nature of chess or draughts. A wooden board with sockets for moveable pegs was found at the crannog of Ballinderry, Co. Westmeath, and may have been used in such a game. Bone dice have also been found at a number of sites, dating from both the pre-Christian and early Christian periods.

Apart from racing, which included horse-racing and may have had ritual implications, the most widespread outdoor game in Ireland appears to have been an early form of the modern hurling. Cú Chulainn's many skills embraced this sport:

> And Cú Chulainn saw the beautiful bright youths playing hurley and games, and though he was fatigued after his march and travel, he went to their hurley, and if one of the youths was exulting, he held no converse with him, until he had taken the ball from him over the border to the goal . . . and he took that goal from them; and he took it thrice, without anyone assisting or helping him.

Archaeological corroboration is provided by a representation of what might be interpreted as a player wielding his hurley or hurling stick on the intaglio from a Romano-British signet ring.

But the most widespread entertainment of the Celts probably was that derived from story-telling and talking, accompanied by feasting and drinking. These pleasures appear to have been enjoyed by all grades of society, whether the drink was the expensive imported wine of the nobility or the native beer and mead of the less wealthy.

CHAPTER 6

Religion and Mythology

THE mythology and religion of the Celts are difficult to interpret. It might be assumed that a certain unity of belief had prevailed throughout the Celtic world, despite the continuing influence of earlier indigenous and localized cults and the effect of contact with the Mediterranean civilizations. Yet when we seek to identify that underlying unity we are initially hindered by apparent inconsistencies in the variety of available sources. Since we know that in Europe prior to the Roman Conquest the Celtic peoples did not commit their ritual lore to writing, the only native sources available for Europe and Britain are those derived from archaeology. These may be supplemented to a limited extent by a study of Romano-Celtic inscriptions, although they are inscribed in Latin and date from the Roman period. On the other hand, in Ireland, where local written evidence, based on earlier oral tradition, is ample, conservative and eloquent, these sources date from after the introduction of Christianity, while archaeological evidence for Celtic cults in pre-Christian Ireland is generally less abundant than that of Gaul and Britain. Early Welsh literature contains a certain amount of relevant material, but its interpretation is more difficult in the context of Celtic mythology in that it was first written down later than the comparable Irish traditions, at a time when Christianity had acquired a stronger influence on learning generally. The early Welsh appear to have retained less affection for their pre-Christian Celtic past than did the early Irish. Some classical writers refer to Celtic cult-practices and beliefs, and this evidence cannot be ignored, although again it is sometimes difficult to interpret, and even more difficult to correlate with the other major sources.

EVIDENCE FROM CLASSICAL AUTHORS

A beginning may be made by reference to classical writers. They sometimes noted isolated facts concerning Celtic religion, but rarely gave any coherent account of beliefs as a whole. Dio Cassius, for example, refers to the sacrifice to the goddess Adraste of the prisoners of the Iceni after Boudicca's revolt. One of the most important surviving classical summaries is that given by Caesar in the middle of the first century B.C. This appears to have been based in part on personal observation and close contact with the Gaulish nobility, including perhaps druids, but also owed something to earlier writers. Caesar refers to the gods most commonly worshipped, presumably by the nobility, but sees them in terms of Roman deities; an example of *interpretatio romana*, by which the attributes of non-Roman gods were identified with those of the Roman pantheon.

> Among the gods they worship Mercury. There are numerous images of him; they declare him the inventor of all arts, the guide for any road and journey, and they deem him to have the greatest influence for all money-making and traffic. After him they set Apollo, Mars, Jupiter and Minerva. Of these deities they have almost the same idea as all other 'nations'. Apollo drives away diseases, Minerva supplies the first principles of arts and crafts, Jupiter holds the empire of heaven, Mars controls wars. To Mars, when they have determined on a decisive battle, they dedicate as a rule whatever spoil they may take. After a victory they sacrifice such living things as they have taken, and all the other effects they gather into one place. In many states heaps of such objects are to be seen piled up in hallowed spots, and it has not often happened that a man, in defiance of religious scruple, has dared to conceal such spoils in his house or to remove them from their place, and the most grievous punishment, with torture, is ordained for such an offence. The Gauls affirm that they are all descended from Dis, a common father, and say that this is the tradition of the Druids.

Attempts have frequently been made to equate the deities

mentioned by Caesar with Celtic gods whose names, and sometimes attributes, may be identified either in Romano-Celtic inscriptions and iconography, or in early Celtic literature. According to Grenier and some modern scholars, for example, Dis Pater was a kind of Pluto, an infernal god, lord of death, but also of life. Inscriptions to this particular deity are so far unknown. In general, such attempts at identification have proved unsatisfactory, for although both classical and Celtic deities may have stemmed from common Indo-European roots, there is no means of identifying any change in emphasis of belief which might have occurred during the later development of those cultures which were to emerge respectively as Roman and Celtic. It seems at least possible that the ordered, legalistic mentality of the Romans would have viewed its deities, and credited them with attributes, in a manner different from that of the Celts. It must be remembered, too, that the Romans derived many of their beliefs and cult-practices from the Greeks and Etruscans, as well as retaining something of their own archaic tradition. The Celts in their turn appear to have retained at least a residuum of pre-Iron Age European ritual observance. Precise identification therefore is not possible, although in both societies devotees might have sought from their deities such benefits as protection in war, succour in distress and guidance in life generally. But this need not imply that the Celts visualized individual gods in terms of specific attributes, in the manner suggested by Caesar's description, particularly that relating to a Celtic god of war.

The problem is further aggravated by some inscriptions of the Roman period from both Gaul and Britain. A single Celtic deity may be linked in invocation in separate dedications with more than one Roman god; the name of one Roman god may be associated with more than one Celtic deity. It is of course unknown to what extent Celtic beliefs may have been influenced or even altered by Roman ideas after the conquest of Gaul and southern Britain. It is interesting to note, for example, that Gallo-Roman dedications to Mercury are especially numerous north of the River Garonne and Lyon, notably in the centre, east and the north of Gaul, but rare in Narbonne and Aquitaine. It adds little to our detailed knowledge of pre-Roman beliefs regarding the deities of that area in pre-Roman times. The distribution pattern of certain inscriptions, such as those to Cocidius and Belatucadrus, whose dedications are known principally from the area of Hadrian's Wall in Britain, suggests that the cult of certain native gods was confined to specific areas, and perhaps originally to individual tribes.

Returning to classical writers, the poet Lucan in the first century A.D. refers in his *Pharsalia* to those people among the Treveri and Ligurians 'who propitiate with horrid victims ruthless Teutates, Esus whose savage shrine makes men shudder, and Taranis whose altar is no more benign than that of Scythian Diana'. These three gods have nothing in common – so Lucan implies – except the barbarity of their sacrifices. The fact that three deities are grouped together may be an example of the widespread Celtic love of triads. Of greater interest is Lucan's use of Celtic names, without any attempt to see them in terms of Roman gods. A scholiast, in his marginal notes on an early medieval manuscript of this poem, however, identifies Taranis with Jupiter, Teutates with Mars and Esus with Mercury, whereas a second scholiast offers different identifications. These seem to be little more than medieval attempts at reconciling Lucan and Caesar, as may be seen in the second scholiast's identification of Dis Pater, allegedly an underworld god, with Taranis, presumably a sky-god, as the name means 'the thunderer'. The name Teutates is cognate with the Irish *tuatha* ('people' or 'tribe'), and perhaps means little more than 'the god of the tribe'. This ritual anonymity may have been deliberate, and recalls the ancient Irish rubric, 'I swear by the gods by whom my people swear.' Lucan's reference to these three deities is of particular interest in that their names also occur on Romano-Celtic inscriptions either in Gaul or Britain, and provides one of the few examples of specific agreement between classical writers and archaeological evidence. Although there are reasonable grounds, arguing from iconography, for associating Esus with Mercury, the iconography dates from the Roman period, and therefore is not necessarily a true guide to Celtic attitudes to Esus in pre-Roman times. In any case, on available evidence the cult of Esus does not appear to have been widespread in Roman Gaul, although as part of the policy of Romanization devotees of his cult may have been encouraged to substitute for it a devotion to Mercury. This in turn may have been facilitated by pro-Roman attitudes among many of the druids of Gaul.

An interesting story told by Lucian (cf. p. 46 above) about an old man resembling Hercules illustrates very well the manner in which Romanized Gauls may have adopted classical religious motifs, particularly those which may have evoked some response from within their native traditions. As he was travelling in Gaul, Lucian encountered a representation of an old man dressed in a (lion?) skin, leading a group of followers by beautiful little gold and amber chains attached to his own tongue. These captives followed him eagerly and praised him. A Greek-speaking Gaul who was standing by explained to him that this old man represented eloquence who is pictured as Hercules in his lion's skin because the Celts believed that eloquence had greater power than physical strength. As we have seen Heracles or Hercules is associated with the Muses in a temple said to have been erected at Augustodunum by Fulvius Nobilior in 189 B.C. because he had learned in Greece that Heracles was a *musagetes*. We may compare the Cauldron of Covetousness in Irish mythology, as described in Cormac's *Glossary* as a *boge*, and the picture in *Táin Bó Cualnge* in which a dark man is pictured carrying seven chains round his neck to the end of which seven heads are attached. And what of the Gaulish gold coins of the Veneti, Osismii, and Nammetes of Armorica, which have on the obverse a human head from the mouth of which issues a cord with a series of human heads attached? We cannot doubt that a common Celtic motif may have inspired these strange conceptions which seem to belong to a milieu which expresses itself symbolically, that is in riddles rather than in literal writing.

But more impressive and convincing among classical references to Celtic religion are those which relate not to the gods, but to their sanctuaries. These were found frequently in sacred woods and near lakes, including, it would seem, what are now bogs and swamps. It has been shown that life in towns or cities was foreign to Celtic tradition, and some of the sanctuaries of the Celts reflect a ritual preoccupation with the natural environment. Lucan tells us in the passage following immediately on that relating to the three Celtic gods (cf. p. 144 above) that the Gaulish druids dwell in *nemora alta* ('deep groves') and *incolitis locis* ('solitary places') and practise *barbaricos ritus* ('barbarous rites') and *moremque sinistrum sacrorum* ('a sinister mode of worship'). One of the scholiasts adds to the passage, 'they worship the gods without making use of temples', and it is probable that when Caesar is credited with destroying *ara* and *fana* of the Gauls the use of such words may be regarded as a general Latin poetical expression.

Later in the same poem Lucan tells of a sacred wood which Caesar felled near Marseilles.

> A grove there was, untouched by men's hands from ancient times, whose interlacing boughs enclosed a space of darkness and cold shade, and banished the sunlight from above. No rural Pan dwelt there, nor Silvanus, ruler of the woods, no Nymphs; but gods were worshipped there with savage rites, the altars were heaped with hideous offerings, and every tree was sprinkled with human gore. On these boughs, if antiquity, reverential of the gods, deserves any credit, birds feared to perch; in those coverts wild beasts would not lie down; no wind ever bore down upon that wood, nor thunderbolt hurled from black clouds; the trees, even when they spread their leaves to no breeze, rustled among themselves. Water also fell there in abundance from dark springs. The images of the gods, grim and rude, were uncouth blocks,

formed of felled tree-trunks. Legend also told that often the subterranean hollows quaked and bellowed, that yew-trees fell down and rose again, that the glare of conflagration came from trees that were not on fire, and that serpents twined and glided round the stems. The people never resorted thither to worship at close quarters, but left the place to the gods. When the sun is in mid-heaven or dark night fills the sky, the priest himself dreads their approach and fears to surprise the lord of the grove (*dominum luci*).

Reference also may be made to the groves on the island of Anglesey which Tacitus relates had been devoted to barbarous superstition, and which were destroyed by Suetonius Paulinus before A.D. 61.

We need not take Lucan too literally, but he leaves us in no doubt that there was a sacred wood near Marseilles felled by Caesar. Caesar's campaign was recent and well-known. The early Celtic word *nemeton*, widely attested in place-names, probably has reference to such sacred groves. We may refer, for example, to Drunemeton, the place of reunion of the Galatian Council in Asia Minor; also to Medionemeton in southern Scotland referred to in the Ravenna cosmography; to Nemetobriga in Spanish Galicia; to *fidnemed* in Ireland (where *fid* is the Irish word for 'wood' although a medieval gloss equates *nemed* with *sacellum* (shrine)), while in Gaul several early place-names recall the word. The eleventh-century Cartulary of Quimperlé in southern Brittany refers to a forest in Finistère '*quam vocant nemet*'. Maximus Tyrius tells us that the Celts worship Zeus, and that the image of Zeus is a lofty oak, though this may be a reference to a sanctuary in an oak forest (cf. Dodona), or to wooden *hermae* like the *simulacra deorum* referred to by classical authors. Our evidence suggests that throughout Celtic lands many sanctuaries were located in woodlands.

Hardly less well-attested is the evidence for sacred lakes and rivers. There were sanctuaries, for example, at the sources of the Marne and the Seine. Recent excavations at the latter, the sanctuary of Sequana, which retained its sanctity from pre-Roman times into the Roman period, have recovered about a hundred and ninety pieces of woodcarving dating apparently from the middle of the first century A.D., and including more than twenty complete statues. Several important bronze sculptures had been found on the site earlier (cf. p. 155 below). The find from Llyn Cerrig Bach in Anglesey in western Britain is somewhat different. Here in 1943 a great hoard was recovered from what had been part of a lake. Unlike the deposit at the source of the Seine, the offerings consisted of many weapons, chariot furniture, slave chains with collars attached, cauldrons, and fragments of bronze decorated with La Tène designs. The whole is believed to consist of sacrificial offerings made from the mid second century B.C. to the middle of the first century A.D., at which time ritual activity probably ceased with the storming of Anglesey by Roman troops in A.D. 61.

These are only two of the best documented of many Celtic votive offerings in water which have been recovered by excavation. There is corroboration in classical literature. Strabo, for example, tells of a votive treasure of the Volcae Tectosages, consisting largely of unworked gold and silver, which had been pillaged from their sanctuary at Tolosa (Toulouse) by the Roman general, Caepio, in 106 B.C. Part of it had been stored in sacred enclosures (*ἐν σηκοῖς ἀποκεσμένα*) and put in sacred lakes (*ἐν λιμεναις ἱεραῖς*). Strabo adds that there was widespread treasure in Celtica, but it was chiefly the lakes which made this treasure inviolable, because the Celts let down into them quantities of silver and gold. Strabo is speaking more particularly of the neighbourhood of Toulouse, for he adds further that there was a 'temple' (*ἵερον ἅγιον*), much honoured throughout the countryside, which contained great treasure 'for many had dedicated them and no one dared lay hands on them'. This recalls the votive offering of the great silver bowl from Gundestrup.

One further example may be cited of offering in water, but

from the Roman period – the spring near the Roman fort of Brocolitia (Carrawburgh) on Hadrian's Wall. This is of interest as the name of the tutelary goddess, Coventina, is known from inscriptions. She is also pictured in bas-relief as a water-nymph reclining on a leaf. A second bas-relief shows three water-nymphs, perhaps an example of Celtic triplication, each holding a vessel from which pours a stream of water. These reliefs betray classical influence, but the cult was unmistakably Celtic, based originally on a spring, which, similar to the sacred site of Sequana at the source of the Seine, may have been enclosed within a Celtic temple. Coventina's shrine contained a well or basin, and throughout the Roman period an extraordinary quantity of money offerings had been thrown into it. Altars and sculptured tablets, which were also found thrown into the well, represent late desecration of the shrine, perhaps the work of zealous early Christians in the area. Twelve miles west of Brocolitia is the fort at Great Chesters, the ancient Aesica, which had a conduit six miles long, bringing water from the Cow Burn. The name may have derived from the Celtic word for water (old Irish *esc*, modern Irish *easc*).

Before considering archaeological evidence in more detail, reference may be made to the druids, the pre-Christian 'priests' of the Celts, and their teaching. Despite the very considerable body of literature devoted to their study published since the Renaissance, the druids remain obscure. This is understandable, for they apparently, in common with many early priesthoods, attempted to keep secret all things concerned with their activities. Although literate, they favoured oral transmission of their teaching. It is principally for this reason, of course, that so little is known today of the beliefs of the pre-Christian Celts generally. The activities of the druids are unlikely to be reconstructed, except very indirectly, from archaeological evidence. In view of their own reticence, present knowledge must necessarily rely almost entirely on classical writings, and to a lesser extent on references in native Celtic literature, which in its earliest surviving form dates from after the decline of their influence in Britain and Ireland.

Caesar gives an account of what appeared to him to be significant in relation to the role of the druids in Celtic society, although by the first century B.C. a generalized knowledge of the druids appears to have been widespread among educated Greeks and Romans. The druids seem to have been concerned with education and law. Their most powerful sanction was excommunication, which implied virtual outlawry. A significant comment by Caesar refers to the belief that druidic teaching had originated in Britain, and that in Caesar's time Britain remained pre-eminent in the conservation and teaching of druidic lore. This agrees with Tacitus' statement that the Celts of Britain during the first century A.D. had beliefs very similar to those of Gaul, and underlines the possibility, suggested at the beginning of this chapter, that there had been a certain unity of belief throughout the Celtic world prior to its contact with Rome.

Caesar states that the core of druidic teaching was that the soul did not die, but passed into another body, and that on this account there was little fear of death. It has sometimes been suggested that the Celts believed in metempsychosis, the expiation of sin in other bodies after death, but there is little evidence of any kind that the Celts believed in sin and punishment. There can be little doubt, however, that there was a strong belief in an after-life. This is borne out both by archaeological evidence – particularly that from graves richly furnished with this world's wealth – and early Celtic literature. All this supports Caesar's contention that the Celts had little fear of death.

Finally, Caesar refers to human sacrifice by the druids, sometimes by burning in huge wickerwork images. Popular imagination has seized on this apparently gruesome aspect of Celtic ritual, and perhaps has exaggerated it. There can be little doubt that human sacrifice was practised, but it was unlikely to have been a common feature of day-to-day ritual. There may have been an increase in the number of sacrifices in time of war, when prisoners might be available as victims, as in the time of Boudicca's revolt in Britain. The quotation from Lucan given on page 146 speaks of 'human gore', and his references to the victims offered in propitiation to Teutates cannot entirely be dismissed as poetic imagination, but they may be suspected of a certain amount of poetic licence, perhaps even of deliberate sensationalism. It is not without interest that the Romans themselves had abolished human sacrifice not long before Caesar's time, and references to the practice among various barbarian peoples have certain overtones of self-righteousness. There is little direct archaeological evidence relevant to Celtic sacrifice, apart from head-hunting and a possible cult of the head, referred to on page 157, although beyond the boundaries of the Celtic world proper, Denmark has provided some contemporary evidence of human sacrifice in bodies found in bogs. At the beginning of the present era the areas occupied by present-day bogs would have been covered by isolated woods. The bog body found at Tollund was that of a man who had either been hanged or strangled, and it has been suggested that he had been sacrificed. Sacrifice by drowning is apparently represented on the bowl from Gundestrup, a method of sacrifice which, according to one of Lucan's scholiasts, was dedicated to Teutates. The much more plentiful archaeological evidence, corroborated by classical literary references to various offerings of inanimate objects, often of considerable value, in rivers, lakes, sacred groves and the like, and the possibility of animal sacrifice, suggest that human sacrifice among the Celts, although of great ritual significance, may have been practised more commonly at times of communal danger or stress, rather than as part of regular ritual observance.

ARCHAEOLOGICAL EVIDENCE

It has been shown that dedications were made, usually in the form of inscribed altars of Roman type, during the Roman period on the Continent and in Britain, and that Roman deities were not infrequently invoked alongside Celtic gods. The greatest value of such dedications is that they provide the names of Celtic gods and goddesses, few of whom may be identified in written sources, either classical or Celtic, and who therefore would otherwise remain unknown. These inscriptions from both the Continent and Britain provide some four hundred or so names or appellations of male and female deities, most of which occur only once. Moreover, names attested on more than one inscription appear to recur chiefly within one area, and few individual dedications seem to be distributed widely. Dedications to Belenus are relatively common and widespread in parts of Celtic Europe. On the other hand there is little evidence of a god common to all the Celtic peoples. Lugh was certainly known on the Continent, in Britain and in Ireland, but he is quite exceptional. On the Continent and in Britain his name occurs only as an element in place-names, and is unknown on inscriptions.

The majority of dedications to Celtic deities are neither identified nor associated with Roman gods or goddesses. Where the name alone survives on an inscription it is difficult to determine the attributes of that deity, although some indication may be provided from a philological interpretation of the name itself. Some inscriptions, however, are accompanied by representations of the deity, and comparable representations also survive in a number of instances without dedications, and on objects other than Romano-Celtic altars. The full ritual implications of such representations are not always apparent. There is, for example, on one face of an altar found in Paris an inscription, 'Tarvos Trigaranus' ('bull with three cranes' or 'egrets') accompanying a relief depicting a bull against the background of a tree with spreading branches. Two of the birds are perched on the bull's back, and the third on its head. Here surely is part of the rich symbolism associated with some myth. Taking this relief and inscription as a starting point, it would be possible, and has sometimes been attempted, to search for parallels and near-parallels in the plentiful iconography of Roman Gaul and Britain, and to seek guidance in early Irish literature. It is a fascinating intellectual exercise, involving, *inter alia*, links with Esus, but it does not bring the seeker any closer to understanding the meaning of these tableaux. There is one certainty – the important ritual significance of the bull, its sacred aspect sometimes emphasized by attributing to it three horns. The bull also figures prominently in *Táin Bó Cualnge* and elsewhere in Irish literature. As a symbol of strength and virility, of course, the bull is widespread, and not restricted to the Celts.

The bull also appears on the Gundestrup bowl, and also of considerable interest is the representation among others on this vessel of the horned, but otherwise human, squatting god. It is assumed by most scholars that this is Cernunnos, whose name has been translated variously as 'the horned one' or 'the god with the head of the deer'. This latter version would be appropriate as far as the Gundestrup bowl is concerned, for the antlers on the head of the god are paralleled precisely by those of the deer which stands on his right. Other representations of horned gods are known, however, on which the horns are those of animals other than deer. The name Cernunnos occurs on a single inscription only, on an altar from Paris, although representations of horned gods without inscriptions are more numerous. Associated with this deity on the Gundestrup bowl and elsewhere is a curious creature, a serpent with a ram's head. The study of Cernunnos or the horned god, like that of Tarvos Trigaranus, has many ramifications, and again provides links with Esus. On another face of the altar on which the name Cernunnos occurs, there is part of a relief of the god named Smertrios who is pictured about to strike a serpent with a club.

It is unfortunate that the head of the serpent is missing, for it would be interesting to know whether or not it had a ram's head.

There are many dedications to and representations of goddesses. A widespread cult was that of Epona, a name which signifies a horse- (*epo*-) goddess, and which is borne out by representations of her seated on a mare, and sometimes accompanied by a foal. She appears to have been the only Celtic divinity actually honoured in Rome. Her attributes, unlike those of many Celtic deities, seem never to have varied. More widespread and numerous are dedications to the mother goddesses, referred to simply as *Matres* or *Matronae*. They are pictured normally as a triad, and frequently carry infants, cornucopiae and baskets of fruit. Clearly they represent a Romanized Celtic interpretation of the mother-goddess, whose cult may be traced as far back in time as the Upper Palaeolithic period. In Roman Gaul they are not invoked by personal names, but are sometimes given epithets derived from towns in which they were held in special reverence, and for which towns presumably they were credited with particular tutelary powers. Such were the Matres Nemausicae at Nîmes and the Matres Glanicae at Glanum. The protection of the Matres was naturally not restricted to towns, as a Romano-British inscription to Matres Campestres shows. Some goddesses appear as consorts of gods, such as Rosmerta, who is often associated with Mercury, especially in eastern Gaul, and sometimes is shown, like Mercury, carrying the *caduceus*. Nantosuelta accompanies the god Sucellos on a number of monuments, and is pictured holding a cornucopia.

The multiplicity of names, amply vouched for by inscriptions and other archaeological finds, poses many problems of interpretation. It seems possible that each tribe, perhaps each family and even individual locations, had its own particular tutelary deities, whose worship however does not seem to have excluded that of other divinities. All attempts at interpretation, and particularly those which seek identification of function and attributes between Celtic and Roman gods, suggest that the Celts did not visualize their deities as exercising exclusive functions. The evidence from the Roman period does not reveal a Celtic Mars, a Celtic Mercury, a Celtic Minerva, but rather gods and goddesses who possessed several attributes which sometimes perhaps were even all-embracing. In any discussion of Romano-Celtic inscriptions and iconography the influence on the Celts of Roman ritual thought and practice must never be under-estimated.

Archaeological evidence relating to Celtic cults in the pre-Roman period is also difficult of interpretation. Some of the evidence is valuable, particularly that derived from burials which emphasizes the strong Celtic belief in an after-life. Fewer representations of deities are known from the pre-Roman period. This may have resulted simply from the fact that at this time the Celts did not produce much stone statuary, as this was not part of their own artistic tradition. It was under classical influence that the Celtic gods were carved in stone in the human image and, as has been shown, inscriptions dedicated to them. On the other hand, we have a certain number of wooden images from Celtic sanctuaries, and it is probable that wooden figures generally were more common than present evidence would suggest. In the Musée de Besançon, for example, there is a head wearing a hood and a torque from the healing shrine of Souscez Pré-Saint-Martin, Luxeuil. Wooden figures were apparently fairly numerous in the La Tène period. In the sacred well of the Gallic temple precincts of Montbouy (Loiret) a wooden figure 58 cm. high, and the head of another 22 cm. high, have been found – roughly executed work from the Gallo-Roman period. Reference has been made to the sanctuary at the source of the Seine where Professor Roland Martin has excavated a whole series of wooden sculpture, varying from crude limbless figures wrapped in cloaks to more naturalistic figures, men and women, with hair and features realistically modelled.

They seem to date from the beginning of the Christian era, and to continue into the Gallo-Roman period. Wooden carvings such as these would seem to offer archaeological corroboration of Lucan's admittedly poetic descriptions of *simulacraque moesta deorum arte carent, caesisque exstant informia truncis* (cf. above, p. 146).

The greatest development in stone sculpture in pre-Roman Gaul occurred in the south, especially in the neighbourhood of Marseilles at the mouth of the River Rhône. There the wealth of native stone, combined with influences and contacts derived from centuries of trading and colonization from Greece and from Etruria in the east, and from Spain in the west, introduced sculpture and architecture from these regions over a comparatively wide area of the Celtic world. It had affected Glanum as early as the Hallstatt period, and places even farther into the Celtic hinterland. At Hirschlanden, near Stuttgart, a life-size stele of a naked ithyphallic warrior apparently stood on top of a burial mound. Influences such as these may have contributed to the later development of purely Celtic stone-carving in Gaul. The Gaulish littoral had been occupied by Ligurian people in the sixth century B.C., and in the fifth century B.C. the Rhône had become the eastern limit of Spanish influence; but in the third century B.C. Rome expanded to the west of the people of the left bank. Entremont, to the north of Aix, appears to be an important early site, to judge by the quantity of its statuary and the situation of its *oppidum*.

During the latter part of the fourth century B.C. stone-built temples became widespread throughout this area. The technique is classical, but the purpose is Gallo-Iberian, and may not be compared with true Romano-Celtic temples (cf. below, p. 165). The porticos are of monumental structure, 'veritable propylaea' of Hellenic conception, and they are ornamented with paintings and reliefs. Their roofs were of basket-work of branches and reeds overspread with clay and lime, as Vitrurius describes the Gaulish tradition. Certain pre-Roman temples –

notably those of Roquepertuse, of Entremont and Glanum – were decorated with severed heads (*têtes coupées*) enclosed in the pillars, or by plastic representations of the masks of the dead with closed eyes, which were substituted for them.

In the Celto-Ligurian oppidum of the Salii (or Salurii) at Entremont, referred to by Strabo as a πολις, a sanctuary of the third century B.C. destroyed by the Romans in 124 B.C., a long path, bordered by statues of warriors, led upwards to the highest ground where stood the sanctuary, built at two different periods. Here a number of carvings of human heads have been found. One which later formed the threshold to the 'Hall of the Heads', the earlier Celto-Ligurian sanctuary, originally consisted of twelve heads carved on a single vertical pillar. These heads are very primitive, consisting only of eyebrows and nose, and occasionally a slit-like mouth; other similar groups of heads on a single stone are to be found elsewhere. The 'Hall of the Heads' was contemporary with the last period of the *oppidum*, shortly before its destruction. The later sanctuary, built in part from stones of the oppidum, yielded a much more sophisticated body of free-standing statuary. It comprised a number of *têtes coupées*, and also a child's head, men's heads with curly hair, a woman's head complete with veils and earrings, and a whole company of armed warriors, some statues being almost complete. The wealth of naturalistic human statuary in this hall is remarkable, and must have greatly impressed Celts to the north who may have come into contact with this southern culture.

Similarly, the sanctuary at Roquepertuse (Bouches-du-Rhône), dating from La Tène II times, was divided into two superimposed terraces (to which access was gained by five steps). It was decorated by a portico of quadruple stone pillars containing niches to hold and display human skulls or *têtes coupées*, and on the cross beam which joined the pillars was perched a stone bird over half a metre in height, about to take flight. There was also a double human head with the beak of a bird of prey between the two heads. The pillars, pierced with sockets in the shape of skulls, had been painted with geometric designs, and with living beings such as fish, flying birds and horses, comparable, perhaps, with the decoration of Etruscan tombs. There are anthropomorphic statues wearing a torc and an armlet, and another with a belted tunic, also with polychrome decoration, and seated in the Buddha-like attitude. It is clear that there were local schools of sculpture which were to influence the development of Celtic statuary farther north. The famous statue of the Monster of Noves is a figure 112 cm. in height in the act of devouring a human being, with its two fore-paws resting on the *têtes coupées* of two bearded men. The sanctuaries at the mouth of the Rhône reveal, indeed, besides a classical building technique, a definite cult of the human head. In addition to stone heads, real human heads appear. Some of these seem to have been cut off shortly after death, others have been found scattered in the debris of the road, mingled with the debris of the earlier edifices, perhaps destroyed in the course of an earlier occupation. We have in these excavations an early expression of naturalistic art, developed in the La Tène period under a Graeco-Roman influence, but we have also evidence of a developing style of stone-carving, depicting the human frame from the stiff archaic form to the completely naturalistic. At Roquepertuse, in particular, the plastic form grows in naturalism. There is thus a fusion of an alien stone architecture with a native cult. We are reminded of Strabo's report from Posidonius who had travelled in Gaul in the second century B.C. that it was the custom of the Gauls to cut off the heads of their enemies and nail them on the door-post of their houses. In the Celto-Iberian *oppidum* of Puig Castelar near Barcelona human skulls were found with the nails from which they were hung.

There is also some evidence of the cult of the head in Britain and Ireland. At Stanwick, in Yorkshire, for example, a skull had been pierced for suspension, and human heads were displayed over the gateway to the hill-fort on Bredon Hill in Worcestershire. A number of stone heads are known, dating from both pre-Roman and Roman times, including the tricephalic carving from Corleck in Co. Cavan. The custom of collecting the decapitated heads of the slain as war trophies is described in the Irish sagas *Echtrae Nerai* and *Mac Da Thó's Pig*. Here we deal simply with war trophies. But in the Welsh *Mabinogi of Branwen, Daughter of Llyr*, the decapitation of Bendigeid Vran is something very different. The head possesses some kind of magical quality. We are told of his companions that they took the head, and with it

> ... at the close of the seventh year they went to Gwales in Penvro. And there they remained four score years, unconscious of having ever spent a time more joyous and mirthful. And they were not more weary than when first they came, neither did they, any of them, know the time they had been there. And it was not more irksome to them having the head with them than if Bendigeid Vran had been with them himself. And because of these fourscore years it was called the entertaining of the noble head.

It might be argued that a truly Celtic feeling for pre-Christian ritual imagery long survived the introduction of Christianity in Britain and Ireland. Stone heads form part of the decoration of a number of Irish Romanesque churches. Two examples may be cited; the west doorway at Killeshin in Co. Laios, which has a single head, and St Brendan's Cathedral at Clonfert in Co. Galway, where the richly decorated west doorway incorporates more than twenty heads, including ten set in triangular niches, an arrangement not unlike that found in southern Gaul in pre-Roman times. Both these churches were built on the sites of early monasteries. In Britain one of the most remarkable suggestions of continuity is that provided by the medieval tricephalic carving in Llandaff Cathedral, South Wales.

As might be anticipated, there are fewer stone figures, as opposed to heads, in these islands. The most significant are those from Ireland, although there is still debate as to their precise age. There is an interesting group of presumably pre-Christian carvings on three of the islands in Lower Lough Erne in Co. Fermanagh. The back-to-back arrangement of the Janus-faced figure at Caldragh on Boa Island may be compared with that of the tall, austere stone figure from Holzgerlingen in Württemburg. The manner in which the right forearm extends across the body to grasp the left arm on each face of the latter is paralleled on a carving apparently found near Newry, Co. Down, and now in the Chapter House of the Anglican Cathedral at Armagh. The Newry figure is not janiform, neither does the style of carving closely resemble that of the Holzgerlingen figure, although both have horn-like protuberances, but it is not unreasonable to suggest that there was some connexion between the underlying motives responsible for these carvings in Ireland and Germany. There are other imperfectly understood, but presumably pre-Christian, stone figures in Ireland, including what has been interpreted as a relief of a horned god on a stone pillar at Tara. Among the carvings housed in Armagh Cathedral are some animal figures, which also may be pre-Christian. The unique, ithyphallic hill-figure at Cerne Abbas in Dorset is probably Celtic, but whether of Iron Age or Romano-British date is uncertain. The fact that he wields a large club has frequently suggested an identification with Hercules. It seems more reasonable to regard this as a representation of a purely Celtic god, perhaps the Dagdá (cf. below, p. 170).

As it is difficult, if not impossible, to draw really meaningful conclusions concerning the Celts' view of their gods and goddesses portrayed in human form, so is it difficult to determine their attitude towards deities worshipped in animal form. There can be little doubt that certain animals – and these would include birds – were sacred to the Celts. The dedication to Tarvos Trigaranus and the very name Epona alone suggest this. Many instances may be cited from the whole corpus of Celtic art to suggest that some of the animals represented were portrayed from motives of cult symbolism. The bull has been mentioned and is figured frequently, as is the boar. The small stone figure from Euffigneix, Haute Marne, is of interest as the identification of an anthropomorphic deity with the boar appears to be implied by the naturalistic carving of a boar on the actual body of the human figure. The juxtaposition of the human horned god with the stag on the Gundestrup bowl perhaps had a similar intention. The human deity and the name Cernunnos ('the horned one') are interesting in that the god is portrayed as having retained, or perhaps having acquired, certain animal characteristics. Whether this implies that some of the Celts were in the process of transferring older zoomorphic deities into human form is uncertain, but would seem unlikely in view of human representations known from pre-Hallstatt times. It is possible that shape-shifting or transformation is involved, as these occur in early Celtic literature. Such hypotheses, however, involve wider considerations best interpreted against a general background study of primitive religion, which cannot be pursued here.

Some animals may have been regarded as totems, or at least as symbolic of certain groups. This is suggested by the use of boar figurines, for example, as crests on helmets, and the representation of this animal on other pieces of military equipment. The hill-figure of the horse at Uffington in Berkshire may represent Epona, who not unreasonably might be considered to be the tutelary divinity of the neighbouring hill-fort. An apparent taboo among the Britons against eating hares, fowl and geese, mentioned by Caesar, has been interpreted as a possible instance of totemism, but these animals are portrayed infrequently in specifically ritual contexts. Water birds, however, are figured, sometimes holding chains in their beaks, or otherwise attached to them. Symbolism involving both birds and chains occurs on a number of occasions in early Celtic literature, sometimes associated with descriptions of shape-shifting or transformation.

Before referring to archaeological evidence for Celtic ritual structures, decorated stones may be mentioned. These may have served as foci of ritual, much in the way it is thought individual free-standing stones or *menhirs* were used during the Bronze Age in parts of temperate Europe. A squat, baetyl-like stone at Turoe, Co. Galway, is one of three in Ireland decorated with La Tène motifs, all of which presumably had some cult significance. The technique of relief carving, although not the motifs, of the Turoe stone may be compared with that of the four-sided carved stone pillar from Pfalzfeld in the Rhineland. A head with a 'leaf-crown' forms part of the decoration on each face of the Pfalzfeld pillar, again lending support to the probability that it had some cult significance. A closer parallel may be drawn between the Turoe stone and the decorated stone baetyls in Brittany, particularly that of Kermaria in Finistère.

For some time it was believed that the Celts, other than those of southern Gaul, had adopted the idea of a formal shrine or temple only after the Roman conquest, even although the typical Romano-Celtic temple obviously owed little or nothing to classical patterns. This attitude was understandable at a time when there appeared to be little archaeological evidence for pre-Roman ritual structures among the Celts, and any lacuna, were it felt necessary to justify it, could be filled by reference to classical authors' descriptions of sacred groves and the like. On the other hand, it would have seemed strange had the Celts rejected entirely the use of artificial settings for their ritual observances, for ritual structures were in use earlier in temperate Europe. The only exception to this apparent lack of Celtic ritual structures in pre-Roman Britain, for example, appeared to be somewhat ambiguous traces of Iron Age 'shrines', themselves sometimes suggestive of pre-Celtic pattern, found beneath some Romano-Celtic temples. During the 1939–45 war, however, remains of a wooden 'temple', apparently dating from the third century B.C., were found on the site of London Airport at Heathrow in Middlesex. The plan of this structure is such that it may convincingly be interpreted as a somewhat rustic prototype of the architecturally more sophisticated Romano-Celtic temple.

Recent excavation and study suggest that some ritual was conducted in Celtic Europe during the pre-Roman period in settings more formal than woodland groves and water-sides. The square plan, common to the majority of Romano-Celtic temples, is known from Yorkshire and from the Continent in La Tène contexts in the form of square-ditched enclosures. Some of these earthworks enclosed one or more burials, including an occasional chariot-burial, some have traces of ritual settings of posts, including perhaps carved wooden images, and some appear to have been used for cult practices other than funerary. This last type of earthwork may also have enclosed one or more wooden posts, but some of these *viereckschanzen*, as they are termed in southern Germany, contain deep shafts. A tall wooden post was found in one of these pits; this post presumably had originally stood upright on the ground surface. There can be little doubt that offerings of various types of artifacts, and possibly food, were deposited in shafts of this type, whether or not enclosed within a *viereckschanze*. The Romano-Celtic well and shrine dedicated to Coventina would seem therefore to have been a more formalized variant of pre-Roman ritual practice. Another type of ditched enclosure, again containing burials and timber uprights, is known in Celtic Europe. This type, however, is long and rectangular on plan rather than square, and may be more than three hundred feet long. A massive wooden post, the height of which has been estimated as some forty feet, was the central feature of a large circular earthwork in the Rhineland, known as the Goloring, and dates from late Hallstatt times. It is possible, but cannot be proved, that a post such as this may have been topped by some cult figure or object. Had this been so, it might have been the prototype of tall stone columns surmounted by Romanized figures, but recognizably Celtic in inspiration, found in Roman Gaul.

Although the area of the Goloring compares with that of some of the smaller hill-forts, it was not a defensive earthwork as the ditch was inside the bank. Its closest parallels in a Celtic context outside the Rhineland are earthworks in Ireland, traditionally associated with the Celts, and including those of such important centres as Tara and Emain Macha. Earthworks consisting of an outer bank and inner ditch, and enclosing settings of posts, upright stones or even pits, are known from the late third–early second millennia in Britain. These ritual sites are termed 'henge-monuments', and include Avebury and Stonehenge. This point is emphasized, as it is in agreement with the proposition offered in chapter 1 that any appreciation of Celtic culture is to be gained most adequately from a recognition of continuity extending from the pre-Iron Age past. This would seem to be relevant to any consideration of Celtic cult-practices, for not only may earlier analogues for cult centres such as the Goloring be cited, but there is also comparable evidence to suggest that some of the other types of pre-Roman Celtic ritual centres developed from Bronze Age, and perhaps even Neolithic, prototypes. It is not without interest that some Neolithic chambered tombs, such as Newgrange, are mentioned frequently in early Irish literature (cf. below, p. 173). It is of course difficult to estimate accurately both the extent to which pre-Celtic (meaning pre-Iron Age) ritual practices were retained from the Hallstatt period onwards by the Celtic aristocracy, and how many of these apparent survivals represent a continued tradition practised solely by the descendants of earlier peoples, and not by the incoming aristocracy. What is known and may be inferred of Celtic religion naturally centres on the aristocracy. The people of lesser social status may have continued earlier practices, yet the retention of earlier forms of ritual structure suggest that the aristocracy itself did not remain aloof from cult-practices which, by the time of Celtic expansion in the Hallstatt and La Tène periods, may already have seemed archaic when they were encountered anew. In considering evidence from Britain – and perhaps from Ireland – it is tempting to speculate that insular conservatism retained older traditions which later were to appeal strongly to newcomers. Caesar's reference to the importance of Britain as a centre of druidic teaching is perhaps apposite. It may also be relevant to consider the stone settings of Bronze Age Britain; circles and alignments which appear to have been erected, in part at least, for calendrical observation, and based apparently on more than an elementary knowledge of astronomy.

Some appreciation of this archaeological evidence is of value in interpreting the ritual content of early Irish literature, but before turning to this material it is convenient to examine briefly the survival of Celtic cult-practices under Roman occupation, and particularly the evidence from Romano-Celtic temples. It has been shown that many inscriptions to Celtic deities survive from this period. Although it is difficult to determine to what extent Celtic attitudes to their own deities were modified or changed by contact with the Roman pantheon, this corpus of inscriptions amply demonstrates that Celtic cults continued to flourish throughout the Roman period. In Britain particularly there is evidence of a revival of Celtic cults during the latter part of the fourth century A.D. at a time when the established Romanized way of life was threatened, even although Christianity was then the established religion. Something of the attraction of Celtic cults may be seen from dedications to native deities offered by officers and men of the Roman army stationed in the north of England. In the military zones of Britain, however, there appear to have been fewer temples than in the civil zone and in Gaul.

The plan of the typical Romano-Celtic stone-built temple in Britain resembles that of Gaul. The inner part was a square box-like room, the *cella* or sanctuary, sometimes raised, and surrounded by a portico or verandah. The *cella* was small and entered by a single door and lighted probably by small windows high up in a clerestory, the whole temple sometimes enclosed by a square precinct wall or *temenos*. The *cella* was not always square in plan, and some were circular or polygonal. In a typical Romano-Celtic temple in the district of Bermkastel, dating from the second century A.D., one of the *cellae* contained a spring. The temple at Sanxay near Poitiers contained a pit thought probably to have been the tomb of a hero. Certain circular pits are believed to have been tombs, and one contained the skeletons of two men thought to have been thrown in alive. Romano-Celtic temples were built both in the countryside and in towns, and the latter in particular were frequently embellished with fine carving and the use of marble and other imported stones. Temples were normally built singly, but sometimes in pairs, and even three or more temples may have stood together, as at Trier, generally within a *temenos*. Temples sometimes formed part of a complex of buildings which might also include theatres, baths and springs. In particular, medicinal springs possessed their associated temples. There can be little doubt that periodic celebrations were accompanied in Roman, as in pre-Roman times, by more secular festivities, and would also have provided opportunities for commerce in the form of fairs.

In Britain Romano-Celtic temples persisted throughout the Roman period. At Silchester all the temples are of Celtic form, and there was one of the rectangular box-like pattern at Verulamium. Many temples in Gaul are connected with Roman gods, but dedications to native gods are also common, and at times later Roman structures and even Roman dedications have been superimposed on earlier Celtic ones. At Gosbecks Farm near Colchester a Romano-Celtic temple of the second century A.D., which was associated with a theatre, stood in the corner of a square enclosure surrounded by a ditch which contained pre-Roman material remains; but a bronze statue of Mercury proves the later Roman use. At Frilford in Berkshire a circular Romano-Celtic shrine had been built over the razed remains of an earlier circular earthwork enclosure which had enclosed six large posts. These may have been part of an open-sided but roofed shrine, comparable with some believed to have been built in pre-Roman Gaul. Excavation revealed, from the recovery of pre-Roman artifacts including brooches, that ritual activity began at least as early as the use of La Tène brooches in southern Britain and that, after reconstruction and architectural embellishment, the site remained in use throughout the Romano-British period, apparently until the fifth century A.D. Sir Ian Richmond noted its resemblance to the forest sanctuaries of Roman Gaul. Of particular interest is the iron ploughshare placed as a foundation deposit under the central post of the front row. It may be mentioned that the famous Celtic head with a torc from Mšecké Žehrovice in Bohemia (cf. p. 227 below) was found in a pit within a rectangular area of 200 by 105 metres, evidently a sacred enclosure.

Perhaps the most outstanding native dedication of a Romano-Celtic temple, either in Britain or Gaul, is that at Lydney on the steep bank of the Severn in Gloucestershire, for here Romano-Celtic archaeology, epigraphy and early Celtic literature meet in harmony. Its dedication is to Nodens, Nodons or Nudens, who may be identified with the Irish god Nuadu Argatlám, 'Nuada of the silver hand'. The name is known in Welsh tradition as Lludd Llaw Ereint ('Lludd of the silver hand'), the father of Shakespeare's Cordelia and of the Irish Gwyn ap Nudd. The site at Lydney had a long history. An Iron Age camp was succeeded by a Roman iron mine, succeeded in its turn by a temple to Nodons in about 364–7, remodelled and reinforced by a precinct wall within a few years, and the whole settlement flourished during the last quarter of the fourth century. The temple differs from the normal Romano-Celtic form, for it is of basilican plan, and was almost certainly a temple of healing with associated offices; a guest-house or inn, baths for visiting worshippers, and an *abaton* or a healing centre, where invalids were visited by the god or one of his sacred dogs of healing in their sleep. The site perhaps had more in common with the cult of Asclepius than with other commoner Celtic temples, but Nodons is undoubtedly Celtic. The coins and the other votive offerings suggest that it was an establishment for wealthy patrons, which, in common with other native cults, continued in use into the fifth century.

EVIDENCE FROM CELTIC LITERATURE

Little is known in detail of pre-Christian sanctuaries in Ireland, although ritual centres undoubtedly existed. Owing to the conservation of oral tradition in Ireland, however, a rich corpus of mythology survived to be written down in the early Christian period. The remarkable affection of the Celts in Ireland for their pre-Christian past allowed them, without compromising their newly won faith, to preserve something of their pagan tradition. Some of the individuals who figure in the myths were undoubtedly gods, although Christian ethics did not permit them to be represented as such. It is possible to establish correlations between certain details relating to places and things, and even aspects of behaviour, as recounted in the literature, and archaeological material, particularly that of the continental and insular Celts of the La Tène period. A close study of these correlations and their interpretation is difficult and, if uncritical, may be misleading. Much remains to be done, but such a study is essential in any attempt to understand the beliefs of the pre-Christian Celts.

Turning to the literature itself, there are, for example, traces of the triad of Gaulish divinities in three goddesses concerned with battle and death who occur in Irish stories, although here the goddesses do not occur as a triad, but individually. These are the Mórrígan, 'the great Queen', and Macha and Badb. Badb is the essential goddess of battle, and frequently appears as a crow or a raven. The Mórrígan is thought to be the forerunner of Morgan la Fée in the medieval Arthurian Cycle. But she was an unpleasant person. An ancient elegy tells of a Leinster prince who was drowned in his little curagh, and of the 'hateful laugh' of the woman (the Mórrígan) who 'has flung her white mane [the breakers] against Coning in his curagh'. Of Macha we hear comparatively little. Brigantia also is attested by inscriptions in both Gaul and Britain. According to Cormac's *Glossary* she is the daughter of the Dagdá and the patron of poets, but she forms a triad with her two sisters who are the goddesses of smiths and laws, an odd association. She is believed to have been Christianized as St Brigid.

With the pious intention of elucidating the history of the earlier population of Ireland, the learned Irish of early Christian times schematized the arrival of the earlier inhabitants and their gods into a series of invasions, the latest provided with biblical respectability. A similar concept is found in early Welsh literature, and was drawn on by Nennius, so it must be at least as old as the early ninth century. A comparable tradition continued in Irish literature until well into the later medieval period. In Ireland the tradition is formalized under the heading *Lebor Gabála* (*The Book of Invasions*). First comes an invasion from Spain led by Partholón, all of whose members perished of a plague. The second invasion was led by Nemed mac Agnomain, who after some years returned to Spain, being hard pressed by other invaders, the Fomori; but eventually they returned to Ireland and colonized it. Later came the Fir Bolg, a race of agriculturalists from Greece, together with the Fir Gálioin and Fir Domnann. These names respectively are cognate with the Belgae, the Gauls and the Damnonii (or Dumnonii), and may refer to the arrival of specific tribal groups. Then came the Tuatha Dé Danann, 'the tribes of the goddess Danu', led by their poet Amargin, who landed on Irish soil and conquered first the Fir Bolg and later the Fomori in two battles fought at Moytura. In the second Battle of Moytura the Fomori were finally banished overseas, leaving the Tuatha Dé Danann in possession. In this last battle Lugh came from overseas to lead them, for he possessed 'all the arts' and so was accepted as the leader.

The last to arrive were the Milesians, the sons of Mil. This was a late, and probably spurious tradition, presumably intended to confer Christian respectability on the immediate forebears of the Celts in Ireland. For the Tuatha Dé Danann were the gods of the Celts, and the purpose underlying the introduction of the Milesians was to allow them to displace the by then embarrassing Tuatha and to cover up the implications of their pre-Christian ritual and beliefs. The *Lebor Gabála*, presumably the official version, has it that the Tuatha were banished from Ireland, but other widespread and perhaps more popular traditions, sympathetic to and nostalgic of the past, allowed them to remain. Henceforth their magical world was that of the *sídh*, the prehistoric burial mounds of Ireland. And therein lie the origins of later and contemporary folk-tradition centred on the fairies.

The Irish gods do not emerge as gods in the usual meaning of the term. They are neither worshipped nor sacrificed to. They are supernatural beings with magical powers. This, of course, is the result of Christian censorship. The greatest of all the gods is the Dagdá, 'the good god', not good in a moral sense but 'good at everything' (*ruad ro-fhessa* or 'lord of perfect knowledge'), an excellent god, also called *Eochaid Ollathair* ('father of all'). He had powers of wizardry, and led the Tuatha Dé Danann into Ireland against the Fir Bolg. In this the first Battle of Moytura the high king Nuada (the Nodons of Lydney – cf. above, p. 167) lost his right arm, and was borne from the field. The Fir Bolg made a compact with the Tuatha Dé Danann and the Fomori, and henceforth occupied Connaught and the outer islands.

The Dagdá was the father of Brigid, *banfile* ('female poet'), and of the Mac Óc ('the young god'). His club was so weighty that it had to be borne on wheels, and it slew nine men at one stroke. He had also a harp which could play three airs – the sleep strain, the laughter strain, and the grief strain. He had a cauldron of abundance which no one could leave without being satisfied. The bronze cauldron is a distinctive artifact of the Late Bronze Age in Ireland. The Dagdá's cauldron was made the subject of satire in the *Second Battle of Moytura*, where the Fomori, the enemies of the Tuatha Dé Danann, prepare for him a stupendous porridge in his cauldron (another tradition has it that the porridge was to be eaten from a huge hole in the ground), with its vast ladle, and the Dagdá is invited to eat it all on pain of death; but having swallowed it all he even scrapes the bowl with his fingers. His attributes are typical of many Celtic deities in that they were not restricted to any one particular aspect of life. He was a true father-figure. His coarse appearance and his archaic club strongly suggest that here is an echo of a cult of an earlier god whose worship and affection had been strong enough to survive the arrival of more sophisticated incomers.

The text of the *Second Battle of Moytura* is believed to be older than that of the *First Battle*. It has only been preserved in a manuscript of as late as the sixteenth century; but the language is early, probably as early as the ninth century, and the tradition is pre-Christian. By way of introduction we are told that the Tuatha Dé Danann had learned magic and wizardry in the Northern Isles, and thence they had brought the spear of Lugh, which was all-conquering, and the sword of Nuada, which was an infallible weapon, and the Dagdá's magic cauldron. In the *Second Battle of Moytura* all the gods are assembled together to fight for the reclamation of Ireland from the older gods, the Fomori, who had ruled it before the Tuatha Dé Danann. Their king is Bres, son of Elatha, whose father was a Fomor, but whose mother is of the Tuatha Dé Danann – an interesting hint both of earlier matrilinear succession and of conflict and accommodation between conflicting cults. Bres, however, is not a good king. Under him the Irish are heavily oppressed by the Fomori, and he has allowed the Tuatha to do menial service for them. Moreover, he neglects the poets, and he is stingy, and when guests come to him he does not grease their knives, and their breaths do not smell of ale. Finally the Tuatha demand his abdication. The Fomori depart to the isles and both sides prepare for war.

The god Lugh comes to the court of the Tuatha Dé Danann and demands entrance. The door-keeper asks him first to name his qualifications, 'for no one enters Tara without an art'. Lugh claims, in turn, that he is a carpenter, a smith, a champion, a harper, and other things. Finally, he is put to the test in a game of chess, and when he is victorious Nuada admits him and entrusts him with the defence of Ireland, for he himself is disqualified by the loss of his arm. Lugh sends the Dagdá to the Fomori to ask for a truce, to which they agree, but they make the Dagdá look ridiculous by forcing him to eat an immense meal of porridge (cf. p. 171 above). While the preparations for the battle are going forward the story-teller skilfully introduces us to all the gods of the Tuatha Dé Danann by enumerating their contributions to the fight. Goibniu the smith can offer weapons which shall never fail; Diancécht the physician, who has already made an all-purpose arm of silver for Nuada (hence his epithet *Argatlám*), will cure every wounded man on the day following so that he shall be made whole; Credne the brazier will supply rivets for the spears, hilts for the swords, and bosses and rims for the shields. The Dagdá adds the climax by promising that the bones of the Fomori under his club shall be as hailstones under the feet of herds of horses. In the battle which follows, Lugh succeeds in casting a stone from his sling which knocks out the evil eye of their king Balor through the back of his head, slaying thereby twenty-seven of the Fomori, and the rest flee to their ships. The slain are as many as the stars of heaven, the sands of the sea, the flakes of snow, the drops of dew upon the grass, and crested waves of storms. The Fomori flee to their islands, and henceforth Ireland belongs solely to the Tuatha Dé Danann. This story owes much to the fact that it introduces us to practically all the Tuatha Dé Danann, and tells us also of their individual prowess.

Of the purely native Irish gods who are not known outside Ireland, it is natural to think first of the chthonic gods, especially as they occur most often in the heroic sagas. These are most commonly associated with the great prehistoric tombs of the Neolithic period such as the tumuli of the ancient dead in the valley of the Boyne, known as Brugh na Bóinne, unless the name may be taken to refer specifically to Newgrange, one of the most imposing tombs of the group. Brugh na Bóinne was the home of the Mac Óc or Aengus Óc, the Dagdá's son by the wife of Elcmar. The Dagdá himself had no local habitation. He was ubiquitous, and the nearest thing the Irish have to a universal god, though he was often subordinate to Lugh. The association with mounds is widely attested. We have the god Midir whose dwelling was at Brí Léith in Co. Longford, and the Bodb whose *sídh* (or supernatural dwelling) is beyond Feimhin in Co. Tipperary in Munster. But association with springs is also attested. The source of all wisdom and knowledge is the well of Segais, at the source of the Boyne; those who ate of the hazel-nuts which grew beside it, or drank the *imbas* ('inspiration') from them became inspired with the seer's gift of poetry and prophecy.

We have an early story in which Aengus, the Mac Óc, in his dwelling at the Brugh has a dream of a lovely girl, and falls into a wasting sickness for love of her. His father and mother, the Dagdá and Boann (the goddess of the Boyne itself), make inquiries on all hands for the girl, but in vain. At last they inquire of Bodb, 'the king of the *sídh* of Munster', and he ultimately finds her. She is Caer, the daughter of Ethal Anbhuail from the *sídh* in Connaught. The Dagdá and his companions set out with three chariots to Connaught where they spend a full week as the guests of Alill and Maeve, who ask them why they have come, and Ethal Anbhuail is forced to come out of his *sídh* and reveal how his daughter may be ensnared. She is on Loch Bél Dragon in the shape of a bird, with three times fifty swans round her with silver chains and curls of gold about their heads.

Aengus was in human shape on the brink of the lake. He called the girl to him. 'Come to speak to me, Caer!' 'Who calls me?' said Caer. 'Aengus calls you.' 'I will go if you will undertake on your honour that I may come back to the lake again.' 'I pledge your protection,' said he. She went to him. He cast his arms about her. They fell asleep in the form of two swans, and went round the lake three times, so that his promise might not be broken. They went in the form of two white birds till they came to the Brugh of Aengus Mac Óc. ... The girl stayed with him after that.

Among the oldest of the stories of the Irish gods are stories of rebirth. These are all concerned with the god Manannán mac Lir who does not appear to be directly connected with the Dagdá or the gods of his circle, but is pictured as approaching Ireland from overseas or across a lake. His name is commemorated in that of the Isle of Man, but no ancient stories survive from this island. Beliefs connected with Manannán were still sufficiently tenacious in the seventh century A.D. for a claim to be put forward that Mongán, an Ulster princeling, was his son. Manannán is, moreover, generally identified with Manawydan fab Llyr of the Welsh *Mabinogion*, so we must associate him with the Irish Sea. Lir is an Irish god who dwelt on the cliffs of Co. Antrim, and his children, three sons and a daughter, are told of in a later Irish saga of the fifteenth century known as *The Fate of the Children of Lir*.

One of the most beautiful of all the stories of rebirth connected with Manannán tells of Étain, the wife of Eochaid (or Eochu) Airem, king of Tara, and of her relationship with Midir, Manannán's fosterling, and the owner of the *sídh* of Brí Léith, Co. Longford. Étain had been the wife of Midir, but she was changed by his former wife, Fuamnach, out of jealousy, into a butterfly 'that finds its delight among the flowers', and she flew about the world until she finally came to the house of Midir's fosterling, Aengus mac Óc. He makes a glass bower for Étain, and carries it about with him wherever he goes, and there each night she sleeps beside him, and she becomes fair of form 'for the bower was filled with marvellously sweet-scented shrubs, and it was upon these that she thrived, upon the odour and blossom of the best of precious herbs'. But the jealousy of Fuamnach lures Aengus from his dwelling, and then she blows a blast which carries Étain out of her bower over Ireland until finally she falls through the smoke-hole of the roof of the house of Étar the Warrior, and into the cup of his wife, who swallows her and bears her as a human daughter, Étain. And Étar nourishes her as his own daughter.

A certain king, Eochaid Airem, is seeking a wife, and he sends his messengers throughout Ireland upon that quest. One day Étain, the daughter of Étar, sees a horseman approaching

> Green, long and flowing was the cloak that was about him, his shirt was embroidered with embroidery of red gold and a great brooch of gold in his throat reached to his shoulder on either side. Upon the back of that man was a silver shield with a golden rim; the handle for the shield was silver, and a gold boss was in the midst of the shield; he held in his hand a fine-pointed spear with rings of gold about it from the haft to the hand. The hair that was above his forehead was yellow and fair, and upon his brow was a circlet of gold.

(A description such as this recalls not only the observation of Ammianus Marcellinus that the Gauls have always been very particular about their appearance, but also the plentiful archaeological evidence of personal adornment.) The king falls in love with the maiden and he seeks speech with her: 'Whence art thou sprung, O maiden,' says Eochaid, 'and whence is it that thou hast come?' 'It is easy to answer that,' says the maiden. 'Étain is my name, the daughter of the king of Echrach; out of the *sídh* am I.' The king pays her bride-price and brings her to Tara, where a fair and hearty welcome is accorded to her.

Eochaid's brother Alill subsequently falls in love with Étain, and falls into a wasting sickness for her; but in shame he tells no one the source of his illness. It is necessary that as king, Eochaid should go for a year on a circuit of Ireland, and he leaves Étain in charge of his brother, Alill. At last Étain divines the cause of his sickness, and to relieve him makes a tryst with him, but for three successive nights Alill sleeps instead of keeping the tryst. In his place comes a strange man in Alill's likeness, but Étain realizes that he is not Alill. Then the man confesses that he is in reality Midir of Brí Léith whose wife Étain had been long ago, though later separated by the jealousy of Fuamnach. But Étain refuses to go with him unless Eochaid allows it. Eochaid finally returns, Midir comes too, steals Étain and hides her in his *sídh* of Brí Léith. Eochaid and his men march there, destroy it and rescue Étain. She returns to Eochaid, 'and then she had all the worship that a king of Ireland can bestow, fair wedded love and affection such as was her due from Eochaid Airem.' A picturesque account tells how Midir got possession of Étain, although Eochaid took all possible precautions to prevent his access. One night in the banqueting hall Midir was seen standing before the company in the centre of the palace.

'Thou hast promised Étain's very self to me,' said Midir;
'I myself told thee,' said Étain, 'that until Eochaid shall resign me to thee I would grant thee nothing.'
'But I will not resign thee!' said Eochaid.
'Nevertheless he shall take thee in his arms upon the floor of this house as thou art.'
'It shall be done,' said Midir.

He puts his weapons into his left hand, the woman beneath his right shoulder and he carries her off through an opening in the roof. When the company stand up around the king, they see two swans circling around Tara. In this way Midir and Étain escape.

The supernatural world which forms the setting of many

tales, such as that of Étain, is rarely varied, but it is not described in detail. It is always a land of perpetual youth, where no one ever grows old or sick or dies; where flowers are always in bloom in a meadow, where young lambs frolic, and peace and goodwill reign perpetually. At times it is connected with truth-telling, but this is a specialized form. When Manannán mac Lir meets Bran in mid-ocean (cf. p. 281, below) he makes, by his magic, the sea appear as a flowery plain, and the fish become lambs. Even when we pass some time in this supernatural realm, as in the saga of the *Sick-Bed of Cú Chulainn*, the description is quite general and does not really change. This is Manannán's world, the land of the 'ever young', Tír na n-Óc, which may be compared with the Odaínsakr ('the land of immortality') of Old Norse mythology; Manannán's people, like Guthmandr in the Old Norse sagas, 'do not die, but live from generation to generation'. In this land of youth, perhaps, we are given a glimpse of Celtic beliefs and hopes regarding the afterlife.

In one early cycle of sagas we get a more intimate glimpse of the supernatural world. The earliest story occurs in the cycle of the 'high king', Conn Cétchathach ('of one hundred battles'), the grandfather of Cormac mac Airt, and probably dates from the eighth century. As Conn stands at dawn on the ramparts of Tara with his three druids and his *fili*, they are surrounded by a mist from which a horseman emerges. The horseman greets Conn and invites him and his entourage to go with him to his dwelling. They come eventually to a plain where there is a golden tree and a house with a golden ridge-pole. Inside is a girl seated on a crystal chair and wearing a gold crown. Close to her are a silver vat, a vessel of gold and a golden cup. Lugh himself is there, seated on his throne. He tells them that he has come back 'after death' to tell Conn the length of his reign and of all his successors. The girl is the 'Sovereignty of Ireland', and as she serves Conn with meat and ale she asks Lugh the name of every one in turn, and his *fili* writes them down in *ogam* on staves of yew. Then the *scál* (Lugh) and his house disappear, but the vat and the vessel and the staves of yew remain with Conn.

The experiences of Conn and his family are all connected with the supernatural world. His son, Conla, is enticed away from him by a supernatural maiden and goes with her to the supernatural land for ever; but we are not told anything more about it. Conla's brother, Art Aenfer ('Art the Solitary'), is also beloved of a woman of the Tuatha Dé Danann, but there is no ancient version of this tale. The *Echtrae Conli*, however, relates a story of Cormac, Conn's grandson, which has much in common with that of Conn's.

The story opens, like Conn's, with a picture of the king alone one May dawn on the ramparts of Tara when he sees a warrior approach. He is finely dressed, like all Irish supernatural beings, and he carries on his shoulder a branch with three golden apples, which when shaken give forth delightful music, such as might put the sick and wounded to sleep. Cormac asks him whence he has come. The reply is characteristic: 'From a land where there is only truth,' said he, 'and there is no old age, nor decay, nor sadness, nor envy, nor jealousy, nor hatred, nor arrogance.' They swear friendship together, and the warrior gives the branch to Cormac in exchange for three wishes, which are to be granted at Tara. Cormac returns to the palace and all admire the sleep-inducing branch, but after a year the warrior comes and takes away as his three wishes Cormac's son and daughter and wife. Cormac pursues him and a great mist falls, and Cormac finds himself alone in the midst of a wide plain, where he sees a fort with defences of bronze. Passing through a series of enclosures he enters a beautiful palace with a shining spring surrounded by hazel trees, and salmon in the spring are eating the hazel nuts as they fall from the trees. We are here at the Spring of Inspiration.

Within the palace a handsome warrior and a beautiful girl welcome him, and the pig for the evening meal is duly cooked.

Then Cormac tells how his family has been taken from him, and the warrior chants a lullaby so that Cormac sleeps. On awaking his retinue and his reunited family stand around him. A beautiful gold cup is brought to the warrior which has the quality of breaking into three parts when three lies are told over it, but of becoming whole again when three truths are told. The cup is made whole when the warrior says that Cormac's son has not seen a woman, neither has his wife nor daughter seen a man since leaving Tara. For the warrior then reveals that he is Manannán mac Lir who has brought Cormac to see the Land of Promise. When Cormac wakes next morning he finds himself with his family on the grass at Tara with the branch and the cup.

It will be seen that an early Irish tradition or traditional ritual connected with the high kings of Tara, from Conn Cétchathach onwards for several generations, has been utilized by later saga tellers as a framework for various purposes – for history as told by the poetic inspiration in the case of Conn himself, for the moral purpose in the case of Cormac, Lugh and Manannán are interchangeable, but the identity of the general framework will be recognized. It is interesting to note also how both here and in the other stories of this family the woman is always the means by which the god of rebirth, the *scál*, expresses himself.

It would be unreasonable to seek within the whole corpus of early Irish literature a coherent summary of the beliefs of the Celts as such. Nothing even remotely comparable with the modern concept of 'theology' emerges, nor should one be expected, particularly when one considers the circumstances in which these oral traditions were first written down. Yet when read critically, this often beautiful literature may reveal much that is relevant to a modern appreciation of early Celtic religion. Concessions to Christianity were slight, and in the main consisted in obscuring where necessary the divinity of the principal characters in the myths. The supernatural, however, is everywhere evident, particularly in that pertaining to the Tuatha Dé Danann. For these surely were the gods of the Celts in Ireland. Most peoples create their gods according to their own mortal needs, ideals and aspirations, and in the Tuatha may be glimpsed something of the manner in which La Tène Celts in Ireland may have pictured the ideal life. Celtic society and particularly its social obligations, such as delight in hospitality, are here transferred to the idealized world of the supernatural. The superior powers of the Tuatha were perhaps thought to have been available to their devotees.

There can be no certainty that whatever attitudes towards religion may be revealed in the early Irish literature of the Celts in Ireland were necessarily shared by continental Celts. Yet the appearance of Lugh in the literature and his commemoration, perhaps as a tutelary deity, in Celtic place-names from Lyons to Carlisle, hint at that elusive element of underlying unity of belief referred to at the beginning of this chapter. What may be deduced of Celtic gods as they appear in the literature, however, tends to confirm the inference derived from a study of archaeological evidence and comments by classical authors that these gods and goddesses neither possessed restricted attributes, nor exercised circumscribed powers. One of Lugh's epithets, for example, was *Samíldánach* ('many-skilled' – cf. above, p. 172), and the Dagdá was *Ruad Ro-fhessa* ('lord of perfect knowledge'). Few of the presumptive deities of Irish literature may be identified either in Romano-Celtic inscriptions or in classical authors, but this serves to emphasize that the Celts in their individualistic fashion chose to worship local divinities.

Irish literature is, not unnaturally, obscure as to ritual observances as such, although there are references to what may be interpreted as various activities including ritual races, ordeals (sometimes preceding the inauguration of kings) and sacrifice. The persistent recurrence in the literature of certain days in the year on which particularly important events took place makes it possible to identify the four major peaks of the Celtic ritual calendar. This is reinforced by later folk-tradition, particularly that concerning *Lugnasadh*, and Christian attempts to efface pagan practice by adopting and adapting to Christian usage well-established cult-practices, as in the case of *Imbolc. Samhain* (1 November) was the beginning of the Celtic year, at which time any barriers between man and the supernatural were lowered. *Imbolc* followed on 1 February. This appears to have been involved primarily with fertility ritual, traditionally associated with the lactation of ewes. Christianity, in an attempt to reconcile the strong attraction of this feast with its own teaching and ritual, made it the feast of St Brigid, who in Irish Christian tradition was made the midwife of the Virgin Mary. St Brigid herself, if she ever existed, appears to have taken over the functions of a Celtic goddess of the same name and comparable attributes. *Beltine* (or *Beltaine*) was celebrated on 1 May, a spring-time festival of optimism. Fertility ritual again was important, in part perhaps connecting with the waxing power of the sun, symbolized by the lighting of fires through which livestock were driven, and around which the people danced in a sunwise direction. 1 August was *Lugnasadh*, the festival of the ubiquitous Lugh, more than a strong echo of which survives even today in Ireland and other parts of the earlier Celtic world. Emphasis on stock-rearing, appropriate to what is known of Celtic economy in Ireland, is apparent in these celebrations, which seemingly took little account of a solar calendar centred on solstices and equinoxes.

In concluding this survey of Irish mythology, I would call attention to the naturalness with which men, women and the gods meet and pass in and out of the natural and the supernatural spheres. In many circumstances there does not seem to have been any barrier. At times a 'druidical' mist surrounds the hero and heralds the approach of the god; at others the god appears from across the sea and perhaps a lake; sometimes a human being enters a *sídh* or burial mound, either as a human being or as a bird; but normally the two-way traffic between the natural and the supernatural is open. In general, however, though by no means invariably, return to the land of mortals is difficult and sometimes impossible for mortals who have visited the abode of the dead.

A beautiful dignity hangs over Irish mythology, an orderliness, a sense of fitness. All the gods are beautifully dressed and most are of startlingly beautiful appearance. It is only by contrast with other mythologies that we realize that the 'land of promise' contains little that is ugly. There is no sin and no punishment. There are few monsters, nothing to cause alarm, not even extremes of climate. There is no serious warfare, no lasting strife. Those who die, or who are lured away to the Land of Promise, the land of the young, leave for an idealized existence, amid beauty, perpetual youth, and goodwill. The heathen Irish erected a spirituality – a spiritual loveliness which comes close to an ideal spiritual existence.

It is much easier to speak with confidence of Irish mythology than of Welsh, for Irish stories of mythological beings are among the oldest recorded stories which we possess, and have reached us in a finished and coherent form. Nothing of this kind can be claimed for Welsh mythology. Our only coherent stories are contained in the *Mabinogion*, which were not recorded in written form till many centuries had elapsed since the first writing down of the Irish stories. The Irish stories belong to the heroic age; the Welsh ones have come to us in a medieval dress, they are a product of the Christian Middle Ages. Nevertheless such is the conservatism of the Welsh literary world that despite the obvious English and Norman influences which we can sometimes discern in them, they have remained essentially Celtic. We can recognize much that they have retained of the early Irish features, particularly when we compare their mythological features with those of other peoples. The absence of a sense of sin and of punishment is here, as in Irish mythology, very notable. Monsters and demons are rare, and tend to grow comic rather than terrifying, like Yspaddadyn Penkawr, the 'chief giant', in *Kulhwch and Olwen.* Above all, we find in these Welsh tales the same absence of a clearly demarcated line between the natural and the supernatural, and again the men and women pass unconsciously and unconcernedly from the natural world to the supernatural, and supernatural beings appear equally unconcernedly in the world of men, following this Celtic two-way traffic with equal naturalness.

As example we may refer to the first and third stories in the *Mabinogion*, the stories of *Pwyll, Prince of Dyfed*, and *Manawydan the Son of Llyr*. In both these stories the hero enters quite naturally into the supernatural world, following the lead or the invitation of a supernatural being, in the former case that of a lady, in the latter that of a 'pure white' boar, white being the colour of supernatural animals in Welsh tradition. The story of Pwyll resembles in some degree the early Irish *baile* stories for both have a formal setting (see p. 177 above). In the story of Pwyll, the hero deliberately mounts the *gorsedd*, or mound in the midst of Arberth in Dyfed, in order to experience a supernatural vision, and the supernatural lady leaves her home in the supernatural region in Annwn, and invites Pwyll to follow her thither. In both the story of Pwyll and the *baile* of Conn Cétchathach the main motif which follows takes place in the supernatural world, and in both the heroes ultimately and quite naturally resume their normal human form.

There is however a subtle difference between the Irish and the Welsh stories. In the former the transition of the natural to the supernatural, and vice-versa, takes place quite naturally, and we pass from the one element to the other without any special preparation or technique. In Welsh, though this simple transition also occurs, we sometimes, on the other hand, encounter the element of professionalism, or magic. The story of *Math the Son of Mathonwy* is a story of a dynasty of magicians. It is by magic that Gwydion changes the horses of Pryderi, the son of Pwyll, into pigs: 'He betook himself to his arts and began to work a charm.' In the combat between Gwydion and Pryderi which follows, Pryderi is slain partly by the strength and fierceness of Gwydion, but partly by the magic and charms. When eventually Gwydion and his brother Gilvaethwy throw themselves at the mercy of their elder brother Math, Math 'took his magic wand, and struck Gilvaethwy, so that he became a deer, and he seized upon the other hastily lest he should escape from him, and he struck him with the same magic wand, and he became a deer also'. This process he repeats three times with his 'magic wand'. Later it is by means of the same magic wand that Dylan is born of Arianrod, while Gwydion changes sedges and sea-weed into a boat, and makes Cordovan leather out of dry sticks and sedges, and while being entertained by Arianrod 'he called unto him his magic and his power', and behold he had created a hostile army around her castle! And so the tale continues.

There are no very obvious reasons for this difference in the treatment of the supernatural between Irish and Welsh, but other differences are also noticeable. We have, for example, no early gods from Wales except those which have already been noticed, chief of which are Nodens or Nodons and Manawydan fab Llyr, both from the west, and both quite probably influenced directly from Ireland if not imported by immigrants. The sparsity of our Welsh sources makes it extremely difficult to account for these differences, but we may reflect that in Irish stories we have seen that in several cases Britain is represented as the home of specialized training in supernatural accomplishment; this appears to be the special *métier* of women in both these Irish stories and in the Welsh story of Peredur and perhaps in the story of St Samson from Brittany, itself probably of Breton origin. Other forms of the supernatural are also found in Welsh which play little part in Irish, such as for example dreams, which are prominent in *The Dream of Macsen Wledig* and *The Dream of Rhonabwy*; but it is not easy to be sure whether the wider scope of the supernatural in Welsh is due to foreign and later influence, or to the conservatism which we have noted elsewhere in Welsh tradition but which has left but sparse remains in the literature.

CHAPTER 7

Christianity

CHRISTIANITY IN ROMAN GAUL

CHRISTIANITY came to Gaul at a time when a number of other Eastern cults were flourishing, perhaps at the end of the first century. The most ancient Christian inscriptions are believed to belong to Marseilles, but the earliest attested Christian communities are those of Vienne and Lyons, and the earliest Christians appear to have been Greek and Oriental, to judge by their names. A Greek inscription shows that in the third century there was another community at Autun. The conversion was gradual and partial. The community at Lyons maintained close relations with the churches of Asia, and after their persecution under Marcus Aurelius they told of their sufferings to their Asiatic brethren. The Christians, so it would seem, were something of a faction in the empire, refusing to associate themselves with the Imperial cult. Their numbers were so small in the second century that the serious persecution under Marcus Aurelius is best explained by a suspicion that they were proselytizing or causing dissension in the empire.

The great bishop of Lyons in the third century was Irenaeus, a Greek by origin, and a writer of some importance, and under him Christianity made considerable progress. We soon hear of communities at Dijon, Langres, Besançon. Reims and Trier seem to have had communities before the fourth century and under Constantine, early in that century, measures were taken to give some civil status to the Christians. The precise date of Constantine's conversion remains problematical although it is generally thought to have been about A.D. 312. It is perhaps difficult to explain, other than from genuine belief in the religion, the interest of Constantine in western Christianity if Christians were not becoming influential, particularly as so many of his subjects remained pagan, and more especially as his army, on whom he depended, was attached to Eastern religions, especially Mithraism; and also why he should, after 313, heap presents and riches on the churches of Africa and Rome, from year to year. Here we have, as Professor Lot observes,* not tolerance but partiality.

Christian life in Gaul gained from the favourable conditions, and from this period each city contained a community directed by a bishop. In each provincial capital the metropolitan bishop enjoyed an ill-defined pre-eminence over the provincial bishops, though the primacy of the metropolitan was not definitely affirmed before the Council of Turin in 398. The organization of the Church was taking place. The bishop was assisted by priests, deacons, and sub-deacons, and by the inferior orders – lector, acolyte, exorcist, porter. Most of the faithful worshipped out of doors, and before the Peace of the Church in 313 they did not venture, for the most part, within the city. About the fifth century, however, churches (*église*, *ecclesia*) were built, which however did not as yet constitute a parish, for the city was still the only parish. Meanwhile, the church income and finances were of the poorest. The clergy were poor, and for a livelihood had to ply a trade. The bishops depended on gifts from the faithful, though they inherited the old responsibilities of hospitality, even supporting hostelries for travellers (*xenodochia*), and purchasing the release of captives from the barbarians. Hilary of Arles even sold the sacred vessels for this purpose. All these and many other responsibilities were sustained by the bishops who accordingly had to be elected by the *paruchia* (diocese), which in practice consisted of the notable of the 'city'.

What Sulpicius Severus tells us of his hero St Martin may safely be taken as a picture of what was taking place towards the close of the fourth century. Martin is generally regarded as the true apostle of Gaul. As yet the Church had not penetrated into

*Ferdinand Lot, *La Gaule*, p. 436.

the country districts, and the people of the countryside, the *pagani* (*paysans*), remained 'pagan'. In 371, however, Martin was elected bishop of Tours and held the episcopate for twenty-six years. He lived at first as a recluse, but later founded the monastery of Marmoutier (*magnum monasterium*) near Tours, which rapidly gained great prestige. Martin took seriously his episcopal visitations and his round of country visits even beyond his own episcopate. He destroyed heathen temples, sanctuaries, and idols, erecting churches in their places. We are not entirely dependent for our information on Sulpicius Severus, who might be regarded as biased, for Gregory of Tours mentions parishes in Touraine which Martin founded. Moreover, it has been noted that in the series of pagan temples of this area there are none of later date than Gratian (A.D. 375–383), and many cases are known of heathen temples of which the sculptures are badly mutilated and deliberately destroyed. Something similar is also noticed by Simplicius of Autun, and in Normandy, where the conversion was brought about at roughly the same time by Victicius, the bishop of Rouen.

We may ask why the conversions received so strong an impetus at this period. Valentinian was a Christian, but merely a tolerant one. Gratian had been a pupil of Ausonius, but he was also a disciple of St Ambrose, and it is natural to suppose that in his reign missionary effort was at its height. First of all many of the Gallo-Roman aristocracy were converted, and a number of the monks in the entourage of St Martin came from the best families in Gaul. Moreover, the years 350–80 are decisive for the conversion of the populace as a whole. This is most noticeable in the foundation of parishes, which in the country districts served as outposts to the civil episcopal seat. Brice founded five parishes, Eustochius four, Perpetuus five.

The form of Christianity favoured by St Martin was monastic and to some extent eremetical. As he came from Bythinia it was natural that this should be so, for it was the form of Christianity in vogue in the Egyptian desert and indeed throughout the East. It was, however, completely alien to the Christianity which was gradually establishing itself throughout Gaul, which was essentially episcopal in character, and which from the beginning was bound up with the function of the bishops as officials of the chief towns of their districts. They very naturally objected strongly to the *peregrini et extranei* who now to some extent usurped their episcopal functions, and they resented the election of such people to vacant sees over the heads of local men who had spent their lives among the people, had worked among them already, and who had a right to expect preferment where they were well known. Martin had many enemies among the bishops of Gaul, and his victory was not easily won.

Monasticism, however, had come to stay, though not necessarily in the eremetical form which Martin had introduced. In fact, though he began as a recluse at Ligugé at Marmoutier, he had already in his own lifetime established an episcopate and a vigorous community life with a large number of monks. Moreover, early in the fifth century the cenobitic life was introduced into the south of Gaul, first by the foundation of the monastery of Lerins by St Honoratus on the little group of islands off the Riviera, and almost immediately afterwards that of a monastery near Marseilles by John Cassian. That of Cassian was largely a contemplative institution and its founder had received his inspiration from his travels among the Desert Fathers in Egypt. Cassian had written two famous books, the *De Institutis Coenobiorum* and the *Collationes*; but the founder of Lerins had been trained in Greece, and his monastery was a highly intellectual institution. Both these monasteries were destined later to play an important part in British Christianity. It became the fashion among hagiographers to say that a saint had been trained on the island of Lerins. The works of Cassian gave a rule to cenobitic monasticism which was the most influential till the rule of St Benedict.

Meanwhile, Christianity had spread and integrated itself

among the ruling classes of Gaul, in both town and country. As such it played an ever-increasing role as the civil administration decayed. Excellently educated under the Roman educational system, and accustomed to rule their own great estates, the Gaulish aristocracy were increasingly inclined to enter the episcopate and to take a responsible part in the running of the country. The Gauls themselves realized the special qualifications of a great nobleman like Sidonius Apollinaris for administering justice and effectively protecting them in the lawless conditions of the fifth century, as well as recognizing his learning and spiritual powers. A man like Bishop Patiens of Lyons was willing to rob his own granaries for the poor in time of famine, and at his own expense to convey food-stuffs into the needy areas. By their profession of Christianity such men laid their great country estates and their town bishoprics at the disposal of their country in its greatest need, and helped to establish Christianity as the future hope of Gaul.

It is obvious that neither Martin nor the rest of the missionaries could have fulfilled their mission without the support of the emperors. In Gaul Gratian initiated a series of measures which, in fact, banished paganism from the state, and his policy survived him. In 388 Arcadius in the East had the heathen temples destroyed, and Honorius in the West confiscated the temple revenues. In the fifth century paganism was deprived of all its rights. Deprived of sanctuaries and resources, and finally of its clergy, it gradually gave way to Christianity.

CHRISTIANITY IN ROMAN BRITAIN

We do not know the date at which Christianity came to Britain, but it may have been approximately contemporary with its arrival in Gaul. It may be presumed that early Christianity in the more Romanized parts of the province would have been influenced by that of Gaul. Tertullian, writing in about 200, states that the Gospel was preached in parts of the island which the arms of Rome had not yet penetrated, and Origen, *c.* 240, alludes to the Christian faith as a unifying force among the Britons, although he also tells us that many of the Britons had not yet heard the Gospel. This suggests that by about 200 the existence of Christianity in Britain was known in the Empire as a whole, for both Tertullian and Origen were writing from far away. The traditions of the earliest British martyrs, St Alban of Verulamium and Aaron and Julian of Caerleon, certainly seem to be early, though we cannot say precisely under which persecution they perished. It looks as though Christianity was firmly established before the Peace of the Church, and this supposition is supported by the well-known word-square, or acrostic, scratched on a fragment of red wall-plaster from a house at Cirencester, which has been arranged as a cross composed of the words *Pater Noster* – in fact as a Christian cryptogram. Its appearance seems to attest the presence of Christians in the Romano-British city of Corinium in the third, or even in the second century.

The events of the fourth and fifth centuries may be briefly summarized. Constantine's measure giving peace to the Christian Church, and the so-called 'Edict of Milan' of A.D. 313, mark a change which made Christianity everywhere a *religio licita*; but the presence of three British bishops at the Council of Arles in 314 shows that the British church was already firmly established on the same lines as that of Gaul, for one of them is described as the bishop of York, one of London and the other was perhaps from Colchester. We are comparatively well-off for evidence from the fourth and fifth centuries. In 325 we learn from St Athanasius that the Church of Britain accepted the findings of the Council of Nicaea, and in 347 they accepted his own acquittal. In 359 British bishops attended the Council of Rimini, and Pelagius, whose heretical doctrines were closely associated with Britain, was born before 380.

There is also some archaeological evidence for the practice of Christianity during the fourth century, such as the furnishing of a Christian chapel in the villa at Lullingstone in Kent, with its Christian symbols and monogram. Although this particular villa was destroyed more than two centuries before the coming of St Augustine to Canterbury, it is just possible that this corner of England, always in close touch with Gaul, may have retained some elements of Christianity throughout the immediate post-Roman period. More recently the mosaic discovered in 1963 at Hinton St Mary further to the west in Dorset has been credibly identified by Professor Jocelyn Toynbee as representing a fourth-century portrait of Christ, with a chi-rho monograph behind his head. The little archaeological evidence for Christianity in Roman Britain is in fact associated largely with the villas, whether in the form of Christian symbolism on wall plaster or mosaic floors, or as inscriptions on table-ware or signet rings. It has been suggested that a small basilica in the Romano-British town of Silchester in Berkshire may have been Christian, but this is not certain. If it was Christian, its small size would seem to indicate a very small congregation. Bede refers to a church built during the Roman period at Canterbury, and later known to be dedicated to St Martin (see below, p. 195). All this suggests that practising Christians were few, and were perhaps confined to the more Romanized elements of society, and particularly the upper classes. The resurgence of native Celtic cults in the latter half of the fourth century further suggests that Christianity remained a minority religion in the civil zone of Roman Britain.

Beyond the civil zone, in Cornwall, Christianity had certainly been introduced by the fifth century, if not already during the fourth, but paganism lingered on into the sixth. The Celtic form of the chi-rho monograph and certain sculptures on the Irish crosses similar to those of southern Gaul suggest this, and may be connected by trade with those parts of Gaul with which Cornwall had been in touch for centuries before the conquest of Britain by the Romans. The geographical distribution of the early inscriptions is further confirmation, for they are grouped along the road which crossed the central Cornish plain from the north to the south coast. The earliest memorial stones are our greatest guide here, being commonly in early days rough upright slabs like menhirs, and bearing inscriptions in the oldest form of the chi-rho monogram, and the very early Latin lettering of the Continent.

In the British kingdom of Strathclyde the conversion was traditionally even earlier. Bede tells us that 'long before' the coming of Columba to Iona in the sixth century St Ninian, who died in about A.D. 432, had converted the southern Picts, and eventually become bishop of Whithorn in southern Galloway. The traditional date for the foundation of Ninian's *Candida Casa* at Whithorn is A.D. 397. Bede adds that he had been 'regularly' instructed in Rome, and that he had established the cathedral and the see called after St Martin the bishop, and that his remains and those of many other saints rested there. Bede's information is clearly derived from Pecthelm, a friend of himself and of Bishop Aldhelm of Malmesbury, and was obtained from the newly created bishopric of Whithorn. It relates to Roman times, but must be regarded as tradition rather than history; hence the stress on the Roman elements in the story, which are doubtless due to Pecthelm and to Bede's pro-Roman prejudices. Little on which we can rely is known of Ninian, but his memory is deeply embedded in the tradition and place-names of Whithorn which date from the sixth century onwards.

CHRISTIANITY IN POST-ROMAN BRITAIN

There can be no doubt therefore that in the fifth century Christianity was firmly established in these islands. Between 420 and 430 a certain Fastidius, a British bishop, addressed a book *On the Christian Life* to Fatalis, a British widow. Patrick's work in Ireland certainly belonged to the fifth century and his early education was almost certainly British and not continental. It would seem likely on the whole that Christianity lingered on sporadically in certain parts of the more Romanized areas of Britain from the Roman period. The real inspiration of the Celtic churches, however, in both Britain and Ireland, was the missionary effort inspired by the monastic ideals of fifth-century Gaul.

The earliest surviving remains of post Romano-British Christianity are the inscribed memorial tombstones of the fifth, sixth and seventh centuries. These are found chiefly in Cornwall, Devon and Somerset, and in Wales, and in smaller numbers in the Isle of Man and the western parts of north Britain, especially in Strathclyde, but appear to be unknown in the lands beyond the Forth–Clyde isthmus. These British inscriptions are normally in Latin, those of Ireland are in ogam letters, while bilingual inscriptions in the two alphabets are not uncommon in Britain. In Britain the native tongue remained in daily use, while in Ireland the native language remained till the Church imposed Latin. In general inscriptions in late classical capitals in horizontal lines belong to the late fifth century, but at the end of the century debased forms become normal, and the lines run down the face of the stone vertically. About 600 semi-uncial hands were introduced from Gaul where the script was in use *c.* A.D. 500.

The settlement of the heathen Anglo-Saxons in Britain did not affect the north and west, where Christianity seems to have lingered from Roman times. It was however Celtic Christianity, and although completely orthodox, not only in matters of ritual, but also in much more fundamental questions of organization and outlook, it gradually acquired a more conservative character than that of Gaul, as we shall see. While eastern Britain during the Anglo-Saxon invasions became heathen for a time, and then under Pope Gregory, suddenly became Christian of the most orthodox kind, the people of the west carried on quietly with the customs which they had learnt from their ancestors. Long before we hear from Bede of the conversion of Ethelbert, the king of Kent, and of the Gaulish (and

Roman) Christianity of his Frankish wife Bertha, we know that Wales was Christian. Gildas in the early sixth century reproaches the Welsh princes not with heathenism, far from it, but with lukewarm Christianity. The Christianity of Argyll and of the Irish settlers was the continuation of the work of the Irishman St Columba, who died in 597.

Something of a coherent narrative of British Christianity, however, is not available until the writings of Bede, who died in 735. He clearly had access to earlier reliable documents at Canterbury. He tells us that there was a church just outside the eastern wall of this city 'built while the Romans were still in the island', which was assigned to Ethelbert's queen, Bertha, who was a Christian, and who had brought with her to England Bishop Liudhard, who used this ancient building as a chapel in which he said mass. It was probably dedicated by Bertha and Liudhard, so Bede tells us, to St Martin of Tours, who died in about 397, and whose cult, as we have seen, was especially flourishing on the Continent about this time. St Martin's, Bede adds, was the church in which St Augustine and his monks and converts 'began to meet, to sing, to pray, and to say mass, to preach and to baptize, until the king, being converted to the faith, allowed them to preach openly and build or repair churches in all places'.

Augustine died some time between 604 and 609. His episcopate was therefore a brief one. His task was clear. He had to convert the Anglo-Saxons to Christianity, and he had also to try to reconcile the older Christianity which he found established here with the more up-to-date form which he brought from Rome. This was not an easy task. British Christianity now had an honourable history and this was the sixth century, the age of the saints, the age which produced Gildas, Paulinus and David. The Britons were, moreover, impeccably orthodox but, owing to their remote position, largely cut off from easy and regular communication with Rome. They had fallen behind, and were unaware of many of the changes and reforms in ceremonial and practice which had taken place on the Continent. The British Celtic people were disinclined to change their old time-honoured customs, which had produced such satisfactory results. Bede records an ecclesiastical saga – the story is quite unacceptable as history – which narrates two visits of St Augustine to the Welsh bishops to try to induce them to recognize his archiepiscopate, and to join 'with him' in converting the Anglo-Saxons. The Welsh bishops, after due deliberation, refused and continued in their isolation for another century and a half, first resisting the Romanization of the Saxons from the east, and later, when the south of Ireland had conformed to Roman influence in the Easter controversy, being cut off equally from Roman pressure from the west. They were, in fact, the last elements of the Celtic Church in the British Isles to come under the influence of Rome, and it is doubtless for this reason that they became subjects of Bede's inexorable censure throughout his *Ecclesiastical History*.

During the hundred and fifty years of peace which ensued for Wales the Celtic order appears to have continued unchanged. In 603, the year commonly assigned for St Augustine's second visit, seven bishops were present at the meeting, and it would seem that roughly speaking the chief territories into which Wales was organized in the Dark Ages were so represented: Bangor in Gwynedd, St Asaph in the north-west, Powys on the English border, Menevia in Dyfed and Llandaff in Gwent. These were based on the chief monasteries of their territories, which were under the immediate control of the bishop, who was generally the same person as the abbot. It will be seen that the life of the Celtic Church in Wales continued until well into the seventh century, and Gildas may be said to be the chief spokesman of the monastic life, which was closely connected with that of the anchorite. But as Zimmer puts it,* this isolation of the Welsh Church prevented its intellectual growth, and the scholars of even the eighth century can com-

* *The Celtic Church in Britain and Ireland*, p. 62.

pare ill with those of the Roman Church in England – with Aldhelm, Bede, Alcuin. Wales was left behind. In 665 the Saxon bishop Ceadda was consecrated bishop of York by Wini, bishop of Essex, assisted by two Celtic bishops, so hostilities cannot have been altogether consistent at this period. Indeed, early in the seventh century Aldhelm, the bishop of Sherborne, wrote to King Geraint of Dumnonia, urging him to adopt the Roman usage in regard to Easter, but apparently without success. In fact affairs between the two Churches remained comparatively quiet during the eighth century. About 926, however, King Athelstan established the English diocese of Cornwall, making clear the final victory of the Saxon over the Celtic Church in this part of Celtic Britain.

Meanwhile in England the controversy between the two Churches proceeded rapidly. In the north of England the Celtic Church was chiefly represented by Ireland, and between the English and the Irish good relations had prevailed ever since the conversion of the Northumbrians from St Columba's Iona. On the death of Ethelbert of Kent in 616 a short heathen period intervened in Kent and Essex, but the marriage of a daughter of Ethelbert to Edwin, king of Northumbria, brought the two forms of Christianity into close contact. The bride brought with her to the north Paulinus, a member of the Canterbury Church, consecrated bishop in Canterbury in 625, and he consecrated Edwin at York in 627, and carried out an extensive missionary tour from Northumberland to Lincoln. As a result of this Pope Honorius created a second archbishopric at York, installing Paulinus as bishop; but the death of Edwin brought about a pagan reaction in Northumbria, and Paulinus fled to Canterbury with the royal family. When Oswald ascended the Northumbrian throne he sent to Iona, where he had spent his exile, and in 635 Aidan came from Iona to Lindisfarne – the beginning of the Celtic Church in northern and eastern Britain – and they succeeded by their missionary efforts in converting the whole of Northumbria. At this period many

Irish missionaries and recluses took an active part in the conversion, for we gather from the pages of Bede that the best of terms existed between the Irish and the English scholars, and Bede gives a major share of the credit to the Irish, who welcomed large numbers of students from England, and gladly entertained and taught them free of charge. It is not surprising to hear that almost all the Celtic missionaries working in England were either Irish or Scots from Iona at this time.

Indeed, the Irish and Scottish missionaries were prominent in the conversion throughout the seventh century and Wales continued to take no part. Malmesbury and Glastonbury are ancient Irish foundations. The former was founded by a recluse, Maeldubh, and became famous later under the great Aldhelm. Sir Frank Stenton has rightly said, 'There is little profit in trying to assess the relative importance of the Irish and the Continental influences in the conversion of the English.... The spheres of Irish and Continental enterprise cannot be clearly defined',* and he calls to mind the Irish Fursa and Bishop Dagan in East Anglia and Kent. He continues: 'The strands of Irish and Continental influence were interwoven in every kingdom and at every stage of the process by which England became Christian.'

In 663, however, the fundamental difference between the Celtic and the Roman Churches came to a head. Bede tells the picturesque story of how this came about by relating the difference over the date of the celebration of Easter, the king of Northumbria and his court feasting because they retained the old Irish date, while the queen was still engaged in her Lenten fast, in accordance with the revised date of the continental Church. This was, of course, only a superficial cause of trouble. The real cause lay deeper, and in the old struggle between the ancient conservatism of the Celtic Church and the newer customs of Rome. At the Council of Whitby, however, held in 664, Oswiu, now king of Northumbria, gave his decision in

*F. M. Stenton, *Anglo-Saxon England*, p. 124.

favour of Rome. The meeting was not in itself of great importance, but it resulted in a long struggle, the outcome of which was to bring the British Church, and ultimately the Churches of Ireland, Scotland, Brittany and finally even Wales, into conformity with Rome. But this is looking ahead. A long and serious struggle was to intervene.

CHRISTIANITY IN IRELAND

The precise date at which Christianity was first introduced into Ireland is unknown. It is usual to attribute this to St Patrick in the fifth century, partly on the grounds of entries in the *Book of Armagh*, the *Annals of Ulster*, the *Annals of Inisfallen*, etc., and partly on the grounds of his own writings, on the fact that writing seems to have been introduced at that time, and because his great prestige in later times seems to make this a natural assumption, despite linguistic evidence to which we have referred already (p. 86 above). His prestige was chiefly known and most of his authentic career was passed in the north, however, and within the growing power of the Uí Néill. The south on the other hand, apart from some traditional associations with the saint, which can be explained as due to a desire to stake a claim in his fame, has always been in much closer contact with the Continent, and this contact continued uninterrupted throughout the Patrician period. The south is the home of the ogam inscriptions, and apparently was under much continental literary influence, especially in verse. Writing had already begun in Munster in the sixth century. Although the convent of Lismore has disappeared, leaving no visible trace, we know it to have been in close touch with continental thought during its lifetime. The Irish themselves had a tradition that Christianity began first in the south, which deserves careful consideration. Owing to the prestige of the Uí Néill in the north Patrick became the hero of a northern 'epic'; but he is never mentioned by Prosper, Constantius, Bede or Gildas. Kenney has shown* a large number of traditions associated with the south of Ireland of saints who are represented as teaching the Christian religion before Patrick: Declan of Ardmore; Ailbe of Emly, to whom was dedicated the chief Church of ancient Munster; Ciarán of Saighir in the old kingdom of Osraie; Abbán of Moyarney and Killabban among the Leinstermen; Ibar of Beg-Eire, the island in Wexford Harbour.

The earliest reliable notice of Christianity in Ireland which has come down to us is from the chronicle of Prosper of Aquitaine, who wrote in the south of Gaul before becoming *notarius* to Pope Celestine in Rome, and is a contemporary witness of first-class authority. He tells us that in the year 431 a certain Palladius was sent 'as the first bishop to the Irish believing in Christ'. There were, therefore, some Christians in Ireland before 431. Who Palladius was we are not told. We have several references to a later Palladius but the name is a common one, and we know nothing of his subsequent career beyond conjecture. In the following year the *Annals of Ulster*, which records the notice from Prosper, mentions the arrival of St Patrick. Is there any relationship between these two entries? Again we do not know; but it is significant that Prosper does not mention Patrick, and the mission would have been almost contemporary with that of St Germanus to Britain in 437 – a time when Christian Rome first became interested in Britain.

Whichever of these two dates we take to give the true record, St Patrick's episcopacy comes within the fifth century, and although we have no contemporary notice of him, from either Britain or Ireland, the interval before records appear is only a relatively short one. Our earliest document giving an account of his life is in the *Memoir* by Tírechán, who had been a disciple of Bishop Ultán of Ard-m-Brecdin in Meath, and who died in 657. It is written in the interests of the *paruchia Patricii* ('the diocese of Patrick's communities') of which Armagh already claimed to be the head, and is mainly concerned with his work

* *Sources for the Early History of Ireland*, Vol. I, p. 310.

in Connaught. It represents the saint as making a journey through Meath, Connaught and Ulster. About the same time, or only a little later, we have a life of the saint by Muirchú moccu Macthéni who lived in North Leinster. He dedicated his book to Bishop Aed of Slébte in Co. Carlow. Aed died in 700 according to the *Annals of Ulster*, and both Muirchú and Aed attended Adamnán's Synod (*A.U.* 697). The traditions of both these writers go back therefore to the early seventh century. Both, however, are strongly coloured by the controversies of the day. Bishop Aed of Slébte is known to have favoured Armagh and to have joined with the north of Ireland in favouring the union with Rome in the controversy, and we may take it that it was under Aed's influence that the correct keeping of Easter figures so largely in Muirchú's *Life of St Patrick*. Moreover, Muirchú, though he himself belongs to south-eastern Ireland, does not mention traditions connecting Patrick with this part. He places Patrick's active life entirely in Armagh and Ulster. We may take it, therefore, that the two earliest *Lives* of Patrick were composed in traditions which were wholly in favour of Armagh. In other words, Muirchú's account is concentrated on Patrick's relations with the Tara kingship and the foundation of Armagh, and the claim of Armagh to primacy was similarly dependent on the 'high kingship'. Only two miles from Emain Macha, it must have been selected as the principal Patrician sanctuary before the fall of Emain Macha to the Uí Néill. Tírechán sought to draw up an inventory of the churches which constituted the regional *paruchia Patricii*, and the church of Armagh was undoubtedly intimately connected with Patrick. We do not know the date either of the founding of Armagh or of the razing of Emain, but Patrick must have founded Armagh before the destruction of the neighbouring fortress.

There is good reason, as we have seen, to believe that Christianity was established in at least the south of Ireland before St Patrick's day and that his original *paruchia* was small.

We can also believe that he had carried the Gospel beyond the well-known boundaries, and that Tírechán's list is that of the seventh century, or at least the sixth. It would seem that Patrick's sphere of influence has grown with his fame. It carried with it a Church largely episcopal in organization and, in general, modelled on the Church of Gaul – the Roman continental Church – of Patrick's own day. Yet after his death we find Irish Christianity figuring in the Irish and the continental life of the time as largely monastic and discrete, by no means under a single, still less under a Patrician, organization. How is this to be accounted for?

In the first place the Christianity of Ireland was by no means confined to the fifth century. Zimmer has shown that the religious vocabulary, and indeed the language generally, and especially that part which appertained to Church services, had been borrowed in a British form already by the fourth, or early fifth century. The first stratum of Latin loan-words was just enough to provide a skeleton service of Christian terminology, containing 'all the words necessary for a nascent community with an elementary organization'. But there was no word for 'bishop'. All this seems to suggest that the first stratum of Christian loan-words was already established when the first bishop was sent by Pope Celestine 'to the Irish believing in Christ'. Moreover, there is a rigid silence about the 'national apostle' in some of the principal Hiberno-Saxon writings of the sixth and seventh centuries – in the *Penitentials* of Finnian and Cuimíne Fota for instance. There is no word of him in the *Life of St Brigid* by Cogitosus, nor in St Columbanus's writings, though the latter states definitely that his country had first received the faith from the Romans. The earliest organization of the Irish Church, as introduced by Patrick and his predecessors, was almost certainly diocesan, modelled on that which obtained throughout western Europe; but within a comparatively short time in Celtic Britain and Ireland this system proved incapable of adaptation to a tribal system of society. Its place was therefore taken in the sixth and seventh centuries by the 'Celtic' Church, in which the diocese gave way to the federation of monastic communities, each with its *paruchia* under the supreme jurisdiction of the 'heir' (*conarb*) of the founder-saint. As early as the fifth century, indeed, Armagh had reorganized itself on monastic lines, but compared with the 'families' of Columcille and Ciarán the 'heir' of Patrick held spiritual authority over a very restricted area, for the saint's *paruchia* was largely confined to the Argialla tribes. Within this area the cult of Patrick as the *erlam* or patron saint was zealously maintained and, no doubt, often asserted against the expansion of more recent communities, whose founders, however great their individual merits, had reaped where Patrick had sown. The extension of the cult of Patrick to much wider areas, and eventually to the whole country, is clearly bound up with the Easter controversy which convulsed the Irish Church all through the seventh century. When, and why, did the diocesan framework make way for the monastic organization which later prevailed in Ireland for a considerable time?

While the north was progressing towards the future Patrician Ireland with which we are familiar, the south, and indeed the east and west also, were developing, not on continental lines, but on lines much more in conformity with Ireland's older history. As the Romans had not occupied Ireland, she had continued to develop her pastoral economy uninterrupted. There were no towns to speak of, and therefore a diocesan episcopacy was unsuitable. The religious centres of population tended to be concentrated in monasteries under their abbots, and sometimes the bishops lived in the monasteries. When this occurred their functions were, of course, quite distinct from those of the abbot. The bishops' and also the deacons' functions were ritual and liturgical, the abbots' were practical, and the entire management of the monastery devolved on the latter's shoulders.

At the dawn of the sixth century Irish Christianity, like

Welsh, and in fact like Celtic Christianity throughout the British Isles, was wholly monastic. It consisted of a number of independent monasteries each founded from a mother-house, and other foundations owing obedience to her, sometimes cenobitic, sometimes consisting of small cells of solitaries. The masses and order of the services were not uniform. While fundamentally at one with the Catholic Church, and completely orthodox, the Irish enjoyed considerable freedom in regard to practical details. Among the most outstanding of the early monasteries in Ireland were Kildare, traditionally founded by St Brigid; Clonfert, perhaps founded by St Brendan; Bangor in Co. Down founded by St Comgall, an important historical seminary; Lismore on the Blackwater in south-east Munster, founded by St Carthach or St Mo-Chuta; and a number of others less famous in the south; above all Clonmacnoise on the Shannon, founded by St Ciarán, was a great house of learning and the place where the *Annals of Tigernach* were written. Columcille is said to have founded Derry, Durrow and Iona. Columbanus left the school of Bangor in Co. Down for the Continent where, before he died in 615, he had founded Annegray, Luxeuil and Bobbio. But these and the similar organizations of Wales, however great their local fame, were wholly independent. There was no central unity in the country, and it was this absence of a central common practice which in the end brought about the defeat of the Irish 'Church' by the central organization of the Roman Church in the British Isles generally.

One of the most striking and original features of Irish Christianity is the love of wandering, *peregrinatio*, which was interpreted in both its literal and its figurative sense. A convenient but somewhat misleading document known as the *Catalogus Sanctorum Hiberniae* (*Catalogue of the Saints of Ireland*) arranges the early Irish saints into three classes. The First Order, which is described as 'most holy' consists of those who receive their *missa*, that is their order of services, from St Patrick. The

Second Order, which is here only said to be 'very holy', consists mainly of presbyters. The bishops are said to be very few. They had various liturgies and various monastic rules, and they received their Order (*missa*) from the holy men of Britain, Saints David, Gildas and Docus. The Third Order is described as merely 'holy', and as dwelling in desert places, living on herbs and water and alms, and having nothing of their own. In certain manuscripts these three Orders are arranged chronologically, but the basis of the document is clearly in favour of St Patrick, and the late Rev. Paul Grosjohn has shown that in spite of its popularity in modern times, the document is not earlier than the ninth or even the tenth century and that it shows an imperfect knowledge of the Third Order, while the three Orders are a purely artificial arrangement. This 'Second Order' of Irish Christianity differentiates it from the Patrician Church, and is the fundamental element of the 'age of the saints' in the sixth century, characterized by the names and acts of a number of saintly founders, the most famous of whom was St Finnian of Clonard.

It is not always easy to draw a clear distinction between this Second Order and the movement of the Anchorites or the Culdees (from *Céli Dé*, 'Companion of God'), who became prominent during the first half of the eighth century, and who seem to be a continuation of the more ascetic side of the so-called 'age of the saints', but have developed into an organized body by the eighth century. By this time they had developed some important leaders at the head of their chief monasteries, such as those of Tamlachta (modern Tallaght) and Finglas to the north and south of the Liffey, and Terryglas on the Shannon. Máelrúain of Tallaght seems to have been the most important of these, and the tutor (*aite*) of Oengus 'the Culdee', the most important literary man of the time; and it was, like that of the Desert Fathers of Egypt, a highly intellectual order. But despite the undoubted asceticism of Máelrúain and his followers, the Irish scribe knew well how to season his learning with the lighter side of life, in particular with a close and humorous watch on animals and wild things of all kinds. The Leinster St Moling had in his solitude both a fox and a wren, and 'a little fly that used to buzz to him when he came in from Matins'. Between the various kinds of *peregrinatio* in the age of the saints a sharp distinction was made. Their special ideal was defined as 'seeking the place of one's resurrection', which is the kind of motive Adamnán had in mind when he tells us that St Columba left Ireland for Britain: '*pro Christo peregrinari volens enavigavit*'. This form of permanent peregrination from one's home and kindred to pass one's life in solitude is one of the important features of early Irish asceticism, commonly known as anchoritism. It is quite divorced from mission work, to which in fact there is no ground for supposing the early Irish were ever prone. Although in later years we find the Irish widespread over the Continent, this was not connected with missions to the heathen. There were *papas* in Iceland, but no mission or missionary activity. They went to communities which were already Christian, and it was a very natural outlet for Irish scholars, in the Viking Age and before, to seek asylum and also a natural market for their talents and training in continental centres.

St Columcille (Columba) of the northern Uí Néill in Ireland sailed in about A.D. 563 for the British colony in Dálriada established in the west of Scotland, and on neighbouring islands such as Hinba. Scotland was already in part Christian. The conversion of the southern Picts is attributed by Bede on somewhat insecure grounds, as we have seen, to St Ninian, 'long before'. The conversion of Strathclyde is attributed traditionally to St Kentigenn (St Mungo) during the reign of the British king Rhydderch Hen during the sixth or early seventh century. About 565 St Columba founded in Iona a flourishing settlement of the Irish Church which in the following century under St Aidan was to convert the north of England, and to compete in importance with the Celtic Church in Ireland. St Columba never became a bishop, but remained the head of the Irish Church in Iona till his death in 597. The monastery grew and flourished, and when his *Life* was written by his collateral descendant St Adamnán towards the end of the seventh century, it was still in flourishing relations with Northumbria, and it remained loyal to the Irish Church throughout the Easter controversy, even after King Nechtan of the southern Picts had banished the Iona monks from his kingdom in 716 (cf. p. 208, below).

Meanwhile in Ireland the Easter controversy had taken a serious form. In the south we learn from a letter of Cummian, thought to have been bishop of Durrow, to Segine, the bishop of Iona (623–52), that by 629 a considerable body in the south-east of Ireland were in favour of full conformity with the continental Easter reckoning, and had already celebrated Easter according to the Roman practice. The letter is thought to have been written about 632–3, and claims that at a synod of Mag-Léna in Co. Offaly the new order had been accepted, but Cummian adds that a reaction had set in which claimed to adhere to the old dating. The pro-Roman party was sent to Rome for guidance, and returned with added authority, and in 636 the south of Ireland joined 'the new order which had lately come from Rome'. The direct communication with Rome at this period is noteworthy.

The north of Ireland was as yet showing no signs of conformity. A letter from Pope John in 640, while he was still pope-elect, was addressed to Tommene mac Ronain, abbot and bishop of Armagh, Columbanus, abbot and bishop of Clonard, and others, but without success. The development of the cult of St Patrick and the see of Armagh, however, worked gradually towards unity, and the *Life* of St Patrick by Muirchú and Tírechán's *Memoir*, both composed towards the end of the seventh century, are important documents of this process. Muirchú specially stresses unity and gives prominence to Patrick's first celebration of Easter, and Tírechán's *Memoir*, as we have seen, claims to make a proud inventory of the parishes of the see of Armagh. It is also possible that particular influence was exercised by the Roman Church through the abbey of Whithorn and its abbot Pecthelm towards the end of the seventh century. Pecthelm had been trained by Abbot Aldhelm of Malmesbury, a devoted disciple of the Canterbury School, and was a friend and correspondent of Bede.

The strongest pressure on the north of Ireland, however, seems to have been exercised from Northumbria direct. The Northumbrian monk Ecgberct had become the chief advocate of the Roman computation of Easter in the north of Ireland since the Synod of Whitby in 664, and had spent much of his life in working for the Anglo-Roman party in Ireland. Towards the close of the century he was joined in this work by Adamnán, the abbot of Iona, who had become convinced of the rightness of this course during his stay in 686 and the two following years at the Northumbrian court. He was, however, unable to persuade the community of Iona to this way of thinking, and he accordingly sailed to Ireland and there, as Bede assures us, 'brought almost all that were not under the organization of Iona into Catholic unity'. The Synod of Birr, 'Adamnán's synod', as it was called, which was held in 696, is regarded as the official acceptance of the Roman order in the north of Ireland. Adamnán returned to Iona and died before he could win over his own community, but in 713 was the famous mission from Nechtan IV, king of the southern Picts, to Abbot Ceolfrith of Wearmouth and Jarrow, and as a result in 716 'the clergy of Iona were expelled by King Nechtan across Druim Alban'. There they found that the English monk, Ecgberct, had gone over to Iona after the Synod of Birr, and two years later Iona celebrated Easter according to Roman dating. But the end of Iona's prestige was in sight. The first triumph of the Northumbrian Church, together with repeated Viking raids, brought the famous monastery to a close. Henceforth the supremacy of the Irish Church rested in

Armagh, and the chief authority of the Columban confederation passed to Dunkeld in Scotland and to Kells in Ireland. To Bede Iona was already a thing of the past.

I have discussed the Irish Church in what may seem unnecessary detail, because our documents are here much fuller than those from Wales. Moreover, the coming of Patrick aroused much controversy there, and, in fact, the Irish Church during the seventh century was keenly alive. In Wales, on the other hand, we have few documents for the period, and everything goes to suggest that she remained quietly in the organization of the Celtic Church. However, late in the eighth century (in 768 according to the *Annales Cambriae*), the Church suddenly enters the Cambrian Annals with the announcement that Bishop Elbodug of Bangor successfully introduced the calculation of Easter according to the Roman Church (though the *Chronicle of the Princes* records the date as 755, and places it in the north as late as 777). The controversy was taken up in Wales, for the same source mentions that in 809, on the death of Elbodug 'a great dispute arose among the clerics because of Easter, the bishops of Llandaff and Menevia refusing to submit to the archbishop of Gwynedd, themselves claiming to be archbishops of older standing'. This was virtually the end of the Celtic Church in Wales, for hitherto no archbishop had been known in Wales since the fourth century. From now onwards, however, the Welsh princes sought the protection of the English kings against oppression from fellow-princes and also from the Norsemen. The education of the Welsh clergy also improved. At the end of the tenth century and the beginning of the eleventh the consecration of the bishops of Llandaff by the archbishop of Canterbury seems to have been customary, and the influence of Lanfranc and Anselm in Welsh affairs in the eleventh and twelfth centuries becomes regular.

In Devon and Cornwall the change from Celtic practices to those of Rome did not come until the tenth century, as a result of Athelstan's conquest of Cornwall. The Continent was naturally ahead of Britain. Spanish Galicia had already accepted the reformed Easter at the Council of Toledo in 633, and in many monastic foundations in Central Europe the change had largely come about by the eighth century. Louis the Pious, learning from Matmonoch, abbot of Landévennec in Brittany, that they still continued to keep the old order, commanded the abandonment of Celtic practice and the adoption of the Roman tonsure and the Rule of St Benedict; but Celtic practice died hard and continued till very late. The change was generally a gradual one.

The Easter controversy had been a dignified one, carried on without heat and without persecution. It was natural that Rome, and with Rome Canterbury, should wish to include all the west in the *Unitas Catholica*, and it was equally natural that the west, after a long and wholly creditable period of Christianity, should see no reason to change its time-honoured system for one founded quite recently by an alien and unloved race. The result was a sudden and extensive output of literature in Ireland. Whereas in earlier times, before the Roman challenge, she had been content to carry on her traditions orally, she now apparently felt it necessary to state her position clearly in writing, both for the sake of the Irish themselves, and as an answer to the Roman arguments. Oral tradition was now reinforced by literature. The Celtic Church became articulate, not only to justify itself, but also in order to allow it to take its place in the European scene.

As the doctrine of Celtic Christianity had never been called in question, and the controversy turned on details of practice, it was natural that the Irish writings should be primarily of a personal character, rather than deeply concerned with theology or religious speculation, for which, indeed, their facilities may have been limited. Temperament and pre-Christian tradition may also have been significant. These writings consisted chiefly of martyrologies, rules and penitentials and saints *Lives*. The

Felire (Martyrology) of Oengus the Culdee was evidently connected with Tallaght. Most of the saints mentioned in it are Irish. The earliest *Rule* preserved is the original Irish text of a prose work on *The Rule of Columcille*, but it is believed to be a prose paraphrase of a verse rule by Máelrúain, and it breathes the very spirit of the anchorites, for whom monastic regulations are unnecessary. Here we feel ourselves very near to John Cassian and the Desert Fathers. The *Penitentials* are extremely rigorous if we interpret them literally, but a certain amount of abstract schematizing is to be suspected, for the contemporary *Lives* of the saints present us with a more human and natural picture. The most outstanding feature of these Irish penitentials is the prominence of private penance as opposed to the public act of penance of the ancient continental Church. In the Celtic Church private penance was imposed by a confessor, and this was a natural development in a Church which was not an urban institution, and in which eremitism was an important feature.

The influence of the Eastern Church is perhaps most clearly to be seen in the liturgical and hagiographical works. The earliest liturgical work of the Irish Church is the *Antiphonary of Bangor*, which is believed to have been compiled in the seventh century, and which is said to contain hymns of the fifth and sixth centuries. The most widespread literary development of the period however is the *vita*, the narrative form of a saint's *Life*, and this was also shared by Iona and Wales. In Iona, Adamnán's *Life of St Columba*, written in the late seventh century in the form of *acta* in three sections, was already in an old-fashioned framework when it was composed; and despite the great reputation for education of St Illtyd's monastery in Wales few writings have survived from this period except those of Gildas, and much later *vitae*.

The *vitae* were indeed the greatest literary development of the Celtic Church from the seventh century onwards. This narrative form had been introduced into western Europe by the literary masterpiece, the *Life of St Antony* by St Athanasius, the great pioneer of Egyptian monasticism. It was quickly followed in Gaul by Sulpicius Severus' *Life of St Martin*, which became popular in Ireland as we can see from the number of manuscripts in which it is preserved. One copy was included in the Book of Armagh alongside Muirchú's *Life of St Patrick*, in the early ninth century. Towards the middle of the seventh century we have the *Life of Columbanus* by his disciple Jonas; but already towards the close of the seventh century Muirchú is claiming in his Preface to the *Life of St Patrick* that he is composing in a new style which had been introduced by his 'father' Cogitosus, who is known to have written the extant narrative *vita* of St Brigid of Kildare (in the middle of the seventh century). We also have a *vita* of Monenna or Darerca of Killelvey near Armagh, derived from a lost *vita* of the first half of the seventh century, and the literary phraseology of Muirchú's *Life of St Patrick*, Cogitosus' *Life of St Brigid* and the *Life of St Samson* from Brittany are said to show impressive resemblances, possibly derived from Cassian's *Collationes*. Incidentally, the *Vita Anonyma* of St Cuthbert of Lindisfarne was composed by a Lindisfarne monk towards the close of the seventh century. The narrative *vita* was now, in fact, the most popular form of literature of the Celtic Church. It spread from Wales to Brittany, where we have a number of examples from the ninth century.

THE ARCHAEOLOGY OF CELTIC CHRISTIANITY

The distinctive nature of Celtic Christianity is also reflected in its material remains. It might be argued that, even without the surviving literary evidence, these remains would indicate archaeologically at the very least an element of individuality, distinct from the main tradition of continental Christianity, as represented by its archaeology. A deeper study of these remains, however, would reveal that Ireland and western Britain during the immediate post-Roman period and into the early Middle Ages were not isolated entirely from Europe and the Mediterranean. As in their pre-Christian past, the insular Celts at this time were able to adapt new ideas to their own use. This is demonstrated most forcibly in metal-work, stone-carving and illuminated manuscripts, such as the Ardagh chalice, Muiredach's cross and the *Book of Kells.* These may more appropriately be discussed under the heading of Art in chapter 8, and in this section brief reference is made only to structural remains.

It has been shown that in the more Romanized areas of Britain there is little evidence of Christian architecture. It follows that there would therefore have been little opportunity for the more traditionally Celtic areas of Britain, and for Ireland, to have learned anything from this source of church building. Furthermore, any emulation of the continental architecture which was contemporary with the early Christian period in Britain and Ireland would have been beyond the resources and experience of the insular Celts. The material culture of the Celts in Ireland and western Britain was similar to that of their pre-Roman forebears on the Continent, but it lacked initially the experience of erecting in stone anything other than simple dry-stone structures.

When Christians in the western Empire were allowed to build churches, they adopted the classical basilica as a model. Similarly, traditional structural forms were adopted in Ireland for ecclesiastical use. There is little archaeological evidence for the earliest monasteries, as wood was probably used wherever suitable timber was available. Even after excavation, however, it is not always possible to distinguish between a religious and a secular site, unless there is definite evidence of religious activity, such as Christian burials, inscriptions or carvings. The typical monastery appears to have been enclosed within a bank of earth or stone, and so to have resembled a secular ring-fort. Indeed, there is evidence to suggest that existing ring-forts were sometimes converted to religious use. The size probably varied considerably from small monasteries comprising a handful of buildings to more extensive religious settlements. It is believed that the monastery at Clonard accommodated more than a thousand individuals. In the early Christian period in Ireland monasteries of this size were the only really nucleated settlements, and although they are sometimes termed 'cities', they were essentially specialized communities. A monastery such as Clonard was also a centre of learning, and in addition to the monastic brethren, there would have been a variable number of students. It is tempting to interpret this close relationship between religion and learning as a legacy of pre-Christian times. The enclosure wall may also have served a function comparable with that of pre-Christian ritual sites, that of delimiting the 'sacred' area. On the other hand, in some instances a defensive wall was desirable, as there is literary evidence even from pre-Norse times of the raiding of one monastery by another.

Whether an early Celtic monastery was comparable in extent with that at Clonard or comprised a small number of buildings, such as that on Church Island, Co. Kerry, or as in the first phase on Ardwall Island off the coast of Galloway, the internal wooden structures would probably have been simple. Excavation reveals only the ground plan, but this may be supplemented by representations in illuminated manuscripts and on high crosses, by metal reliquaries in the shape of churches, and by stone structures which retain traces of their derivation from wooden prototypes.

The principal building was a rectangular wooden church or oratory with a thatched roof, although there is evidence to suggest that some were roofed with shingles. The walls were either of wattle-and-daub or sawn planks. In order to accommodate an expanding congregation additional oratories were built, a reflection perhaps of their inability to construct large buildings. A description of the seventh-century church in St Brigid's monastery at Kildare, however, suggests that larger churches were sometimes built. Other buildings included a refectory, a scriptorium or school, a guest-house – emphasizing the traditional Celtic obligation of hospitality – and a number of cells or huts for the monks. In some monasteries there may have been workshops for skilled craftsmen. There would also have been farm buildings associated with some of the larger monasteries. Important economic advantages of Christianity included not only a reduction in unnecessary fighting and cattle-raiding, but also the encouragement by the Church of arable farming.

The oldest surviving remains are those which were built in more isolated parts of Ireland, particularly on islands. The most perfect example of an early stone-built church is the oratory at Gallerus in the Dingle peninsula of Co. Kerry. It is quite small, being a little over fifteen feet long internally. Although some mortar was used in the core of the stone-work, it is largely of dry-stone construction with a corbelled and gabled roof. A more sophisticated church of comparable size is that on St Mac Dara's island, Co. Galway, in which some of the details of the massive masonry appear to have been derived from plank-built wooden churches. It is possible, in fact, that this structure had an internal timber bracing to support the heavy, steeply ridged stone roof.

The finest example of an early Celtic monastery is on Skellig Michael, a rock pinnacle lying eight miles offshore from Bolus Head in Co. Kerry. Its isolated and almost inaccessible position and the absence of frost have contributed to its preservation. The monastic settlement is enclosed by stone walls. Within the enclosure are two oratories, each smaller than that at Gallerus, but of similar construction. The monks' cells are dry-stone built corbelled huts (*clocháin*), a stone-built variant of the wattle-and-daub huts of parts of the mainland. Despite its isolation the community may have been largely self-supporting in its food supply. Fish and sea-birds would have been available in plenty, goats may have been kept, and it has been suggested that herbs and possibly a few vegetables may have been grown in small plots protected by stone walls on the sheltered eastern side of the rock. It is not known when this monastery was founded, but a reference in the *Book of Leinster* to the abduction from Skellig Michael of Etgal by Norse raiders in 824 shows that it was in existence at the beginning of the ninth century. Its origins may therefore date from the previous century, or even earlier. In 882 the *Annals of Inisfallen* record the death of Flann, son of Cellach, abbot of Skellig, and the Four Masters mention the death of Blathmhac of Skellig in 950. In 1044 the same annals record the death of Aedh of Skellig Michael, whom the *Annals of Inisfallen* call 'the chief of the Gael in piety'. The monastery evidently survived throughout this period, and indeed many isolated sanctuaries continued to serve throughout the Middle Ages as places of pilgrimage.

It seems possible that by the sixth century islands off the coasts of Ireland and Britain were being chosen as sites for monasteries, as is clear from the choice of Iona off the west of Scotland by Columba, Lindisfarne off Northumbria by Aidan and Inishbofin off Co. Mayo by Colman. Already in 617 St Donnan and his disciples had been massacred on the island of Eigg in the Inner Hebrides. Adamnán tells us that one of Cormac's voyages, undertaken to find a *deserta*, failed because he had taken with him a certain monk who had not obtained permission from his abbot to sail with him. A movement to island sanctuaries would therefore appear to have begun at this time and reached its peak during the seventh and eighth centuries. Dicuil, who was probably a monk of Iona under Abbot Suibhne, and who in 814 was at the court of Charlemagne, and who was still living in 825, refers to Iceland, of which he had received an account from certain ascetics who had lived there in 795. He also speaks of anchorites who had lived on islands around Britain and Ireland and on the Faeroes for nearly a century previously, but who had been driven out by the Vikings. We learn from Adamnán that Brude Mac Maelchon, the Pictish king, commanded a *subregulus* from the Orkneys to give protection to Cormac ó Liatháin, driven out of his course in the northern ocean. It seems most likely that the isolation enjoyed by island sanctuaries in the seventh and eighth centuries was destroyed by the Vikings.

None of the islands mentioned is so severe in its isolation as Skellig Michael. Later building has obscured earlier structures on many islands, as on the mainland. The remains on Inishmurray, some four miles off the coast of Co. Sligo, may however be regarded as perhaps more typical of an early monastic island settlement than Skellig Michael. On Inishmurray the enclosure wall survives in places to a height of thirteen feet. Within the enclosure, which measures 175 feet by 135 feet, there are the remains of oratories and monks' cells. Also preserved are several early decorated stones, some suggesting contact with the Eastern Church.

It was in such modest and simple monastic centres that the illuminated manuscripts, and perhaps much of the fine liturgical metal-work, were produced. Yet the very simplicity of the stone buildings is another example of the manner in which the insular Celts were able to retain what was relevant of their past tradition and adapt it to new needs. What survive of monastic buildings, of course, are simply the shells. There is no surviving evidence of any interior decoration, but it is not difficult to imagine, and perhaps it is not too fanciful to suppose, that the interior of the oratories at least may have been decorated in some manner. But perhaps treasures such as the Ardagh chalice and the *Book of Kells* needed no back-cloth other than the bare walls of a church. On the other hand the description of St Brigid's church does refer to paintings and hangings of linen.

The most distinctive and widespread architectural monument of Celtic monasticism is the round tower, and dates from the time of the Norse invasions, when the 'Golden Age' of Celtic Christianity was passed. Remains of some eighty examples are known in Ireland, and there are two in eastern Scotland, at Abernethy in Perthshire and Brechin in Angus. The towers, tall and slender, vary in height from about seventy to about a hundred and twenty feet, and intact structures retain a distinctive conical roof. The single door is set some distance above ground level, and could have been reached only by a moveable ladder. This underlines one of their functions, that of serving as a refuge during Norse raids. They also served as belfries and watch-towers, the latter function being aided by their height. Although the Irish round tower was probably derived from continental types at the beginning of the tenth century, they underwent insular development, and demonstrate that by that time Celtic monks were able, when it was necessary, to build competently in stone.

The disappearance of the idiosyncratic Christianity of the Celtic Church was inevitable, owing to the absence of central organization; but it is impossible to reach the end without a feeling of regret. A Christianity so pure and serene as that of the age of the saints could hardly be equalled and never repeated. It had carried much of the spirit of the Desert Fathers to 'the edge of the habitable world'. Then, under the pressure of 'civilization' from the Continent, it had begun that habit of wandering which is one of the most remarkable features of Celtic religion, and of which the island sanctuaries are the most unique and remarkable testimony. No one can visit Inishmurray or the Skelligs without being overawed and overwhelmed by the devotion that could choose these bare rocks as a habitation, nothing to look out upon save sea and sky and the distant hills. This is the true spirituality of the Celtic Church.

The Celtic love of wandering was not confined to the outer islands. The journeys of the Irish monks and scholars to the Continent and the contribution of their scholarship and their expertise in the penmanship of the great monastic libraries are even better known. From Landévennec on the west of Brittany to Kiev on the Dneiper they have left their name and their work in colophon, marginalia and other forms of testimony to their work, to say nothing of the written notices of their work by their contemporaries. This continental activity is often attributed to the Viking raids on Ireland, which, no doubt, contributed largely to it; but it began long before the Vikings, when Columbanus left Bangor to found monasteries at Annegray and Luxeuil in France, at Bregenz in Switzerland and at Bobbio in Italy, from the time of his arrival on the Continent in 591 to his death in 615.

The Christianity of the Celts has a marked spirituality of its own. Having no towns, no currency, no large-scale industries, it had little temptation to material and worldly ideals. It retained to the end a serene inner life which could never be repeated in a rapidly changing world, and it could convey this spirit in its poetry at home and abroad to after ages in its work as in its religious devotions:

A hedge of trees surrounds me,
A blackbird's lay sings to me;
Above my lined booklet
The trilling birds chant to me.

In a grey mantle from the top of bushes
The cuckoo sings:
Verily – may the Lord shield me –
Well do I write under the greenwood.

CHAPTER 8

Celtic Art

ART IN CONTINENTAL EUROPE

THE term 'Celtic art' is commonly used in a restricted sense to mean the art of the La Tène culture. This is justified, not because Celts other than those of this culture were without artistic expression, but because the singularly propitious atmosphere of the La Tène period, brought about by a combination of cultural, social and economic circumstances, was the stimulus which prompted the sudden emergence and flowering of this art. It might be considered the first truly indigenous art of temperate Europe, although it derived most of its initial inspiration from outside that area. In so doing it was conforming to a pattern comparable with those which had engendered most cultural developments in Europe from the sixth millennium onwards.

It is recognized that La Tène art drew on three principal sources. First, there was the native tradition, particularly that of metal-working, both beaten and cast, seen in the Urnfield and Hallstatt cultures. Second was a classical or Graeco-Etruscan influence, and the third was derived from eastern sources. The circumstances which allowed local craftsmen to choose and combine ideas derived from seemingly disparate origins were social in that these craftsmen were fulfilling commissions from patrons who wished to display their wealth and personal status by suitable ostentation. The circumstances were economic in that these patrons were wealthy on account of their control of important raw materials which enabled them to trade with areas beyond those which they controlled. In return they received objects and commodities from areas outside temperate Europe. Among the more important in the present context were wine and the appurtenances associated with civilized wine-drinking, common in the Mediterranean. These included pottery and metal vessels of various types; the potential of their decoration, and less commonly that of their shape, were soon to be appreciated by Celtic artists. It is more difficult to isolate the specific contribution of eastern influences, for by this time Greek and Etruscan art had also come under oriental influence in decoration. But in addition to this, there can be little doubt that the Celts became aware of eastern decoration, the origins of which may be sought both in the art of older civilizations as far distant as Persia and in less distant barbarian cultures in the steppe-lands of southern Eurasia. Contact with this last source would have been possible at a time when there were many movements of people in and out of this region.

It is possible perhaps to visualize the satisfaction with which a Celtic chieftain would have displayed those of his festive possessions brought from the classical world of the south. He may not have pondered long on any incongruity felt in dispensing and drinking wine from vessels in an architectural setting so different from those of the civilized town and country houses of the Mediterranean lands. He may have felt both pride and humility in that he was able to savour, far from their source, the same kind of wine and vessels enjoyed in the classical world. It is impossible to say to what extent the finer points of classical decoration were appreciated for their own sake among the Celtic nobility, but the fact that trade of this kind continued after the emergence of Celtic art shows at least that classical artifacts themselves were prized as being socially desirable. But it was undoubtedly on the artists that the greatest impact was made.

In continental Europe La Tène art was already in decline by the time of the Roman conquest, but it continued to develop and flourish in Britain until the first century A.D. In Ireland, which did not come under Roman rule, it also continued to develop during the early centuries A.D. After the introduction of Christianity the tradition of La Tène art still remained sufficiently strong to contribute a vital and not inconsiderable element to the art of early Christian Ireland, so distinctive in the tangible remains of Celtic monasticism. Before discussing Celtic art generally in Britain and Ireland, we may review briefly some aspects of the continental background.

Turning first to the Hallstatt culture we find that its art is in a sense very much less distinctive than that of La Tène. The art of the Hallstatt Celts may be said to succeed the largely geometrical style which for some time previously had been prevalent throughout temperate Europe. It retains something of this geometrical style, for although it also embraces living creatures, such as horses and water-birds, these are generally arranged in parallel bands of identical figures around the decorated surface. It is something of a stereotyped art, and there is little evidence of individual taste or initiative.

During the fifth century the stimuli already mentioned began to influence Celtic craftsmen. There is, for example, a sudden and keen awareness on the part of the artists of the plant and animal life around them. With these the human head is sometimes curiously blended. Sometimes a mask, animal or human, appears, Oriental fashion, amidst the foliage. These motifs are in no sense realities. It is only rarely that we could give a name to the animal or vegetable depicted. The plants in part are derived from, and certainly influenced by, the palmette motifs of Greek art, and these are combined with motifs reminiscent of the strands of honeysuckle, and of unopened buds. The animals often do not have realistic limbs, but contort, and twist, and sometimes turn into more than one species. The heads are not *têtes coupées* and owe nothing to the Celto-Ligurian art of the south. They are not, and never were, living heads, but appear and disappear amid the foliage with startling suddenness yet with complete naturalness. They form part of the design, and have nothing to do with scientific reality. They are a part of unnatural natural history. In this, of course, there may be much ritual symbolism.

These characteristics are certainly not entirely derived directly from classical Greece. Comparable arrangement of motifs and patterns may be seen in Etruscan art, particularly the provincial art of Este and Venetia. A link other than trade, for example, between the Celtic and Etruscan worlds is suggested by an iron and bronze sword-sheath from Hallstatt, dated to the fifth century, which is thought to be the work of an Italian from Este who was in the employment of an Etruscan chief and dressed his people in Celtic garments. Plant and zoomorphic design – the lions, serpents, etc., which appear at this time – seem to have more in common with the art of South Central Asia. The polychrome decoration, use of coral and, later, red enamel, must surely come originally from Iran, perhaps through the Caucasus. These are some of the eastern elements already hinted at. La Tène art, as we have seen, seems to be a combination of all these.

When it comes to examining specific motifs, it is often difficult to locate the source. Whence come the masks, for example, like that from Schwarzwald in Germany, the human heads, with twin lobes at their ears, the arms raised from the elbow, the snaky coils on the decoration of the armlet, the ubiquitous torcs, as on the plaque from Waldalgesheim (in Germany)? Often the style from the south (Etruria) and the east are unmistakably found on the same object; but no imported object from the east has ever been found in a grave with a Celtic object showing this imported style. How did this eastern influence come to the Celts since there was no direct connexion? What are the intermediaries?

This characteristic La Tène art may be said to have burst upon Central Europe in the middle of the fifth century, and to be found wherever the Celtic war-lords established themselves. It is an aristocratic art, chiefly found in the graves of chieftains, and consists largely of luxury articles such as weapons, jewellery, table-service and horse and chariot trappings. One of its many strange features is that it has no obvious period of gestation, and appears from the start as a fully mature art. Though it is known in north-west France, Bohemia, Bavaria and western Austria at different times, it is most richly represented in the regions of the Middle Rhine, especially in the group of barrows known as the Middle Rhenish chieftains' graves. Most of these are lavishly furnished with imports from the south, such as Italian metal table-services and Greek pottery. Its features are love of decoration and ornament, repetition of motif, *horror vacui* and extreme skill in adapting its pattern to the space to be filled. Its masterpieces are of relatively small size.

The early La Tène style is believed to have developed in the wealthier chieftains' dwellings, mainly in the area of the Moselle, the Saar and the Rhine, where it was imported from the south and south-east in the first half of the fifth century. To judge from known finds it would seem that fine handicrafts rather than architecture and sculpture were the first great contribution of Celtic art to Europe. It is possible that some of this work was originally produced by imported craftsmen, working with fine virtuosity and combining native art motifs with foreign, especially Oriental, models. This may have been the case with those human masks and the twin lobes which have no western European originals and are thought to be of Mediterranean origin. It must be remembered that the skill of native craftsmen was considerable, and it is probable that imported ideas rather than imported craftsmen were more important, even from the beginning. The lyres and palmettes, the tendrils and lotus designs are perhaps from the south, and the spirals of all kinds began early and lasted throughout Celtic art, assuming every possible form of curvilinear design. A minor but curious feature of these curvilinear designs is that they manage to achieve the impression of regularity while in reality following a varied pattern. Sometimes a beaded decoration is added and sometimes a regular circular arrangement appears to give regularity, while the circles are joined by an irregular scroll.

As La Tène art develops the Oriental elements are less marked than the classical. The tendril in all forms becomes prominent, and there can be little doubt that this is now the work of native artists, rather than of imported workers. Moreover, with the spread of the Celts at this stage, the art is more abundant and spread over a wider area than in the first stage. Southern imports to the north almost disappear, as the native Celtic art becomes relatively popular. This is the earliest La Tène art to come to Britain, and is represented, for example, by the horn cap for a chariot found in the Thames at Brentford – a good example of the tendril design.

These very individual designs were applied to various kinds of object. A great many brooches are found decorated with human and animal masks of all stages of realism and fantasy. A princess's grave at Reinheim on the Saar (Germany) has a gold torc with terminal ornaments in the form of human heads and lion masks, and these are not uncommon. The grave also contained a bronze mirror with anthropomorphic handles, and a splendid bronze flagon. Some Celtic flagons are masterpieces of refined workmanship, notably the flagons from Basse-Yutz on the Moselle. Many superb torcs have been found, their terminals decorated with human and animal masks and with floral ornaments. These are sometimes regarded as cult objects. A magnificent Celtic torc with an iron core and terminals formed of realistic animal heads from Trichtingen, Würtemberg, which weighs 6.75 kilograms, is thought to have been too heavy to be intended to be worn, and was most probably hung on a wooden post in a sanctuary, or on an idol.

The mature La Tène style, known as the Waldalgesheim style, dates from the second half of the fourth century B.C., with its centre in the Rhineland and part of Switzerland and France; but artistic gold torcs, and indeed other examples of this phase, are scattered throughout the Celtic world during this, the great era of Celtic expansion. From this time also bronze-work begins to be adorned with enamel; at first red alone, later other colours. This was probably Oriental in origin, perhaps first reaching the Celtic peoples through Caucasia. But in the La Tène and early Gallo-Roman styles it was the contribution of the Belgae which gave the real impetus to enamel work in Britain.

During the third century Celtic art became less aristocratic, and 'industry' to some extent took the place of artistic production. The chieftains still retained the leading role, but the distribution of goods was wider, though fine ornament and good fighting gear continued to be made. In the second century relief forms became common, especially in bracelets. The material of this plastic art was mainly bronze, but gold ornaments were also made. Above all splendid swords and scabbards make their appearance at La Tène in the late second and early first century B.C., with the scabbards decorated with vegetable and animal relief delicately incised. On the whole, however, there was a decline in art production. Cult objects, like bowls, became commoner, but in general there was an increase of cheaper goods and a falling away of artistic inspiration.

Early pottery is mostly black or brown, always perfectly finished and polished, obviously copying bronze, and copying bronze also in its angular forms and elegant curves. Among luxury vessels are those with a white or yellowish groundwork, with ornaments of the same style which we have found on bronze objects – amphorae with volutes and S-design, silhouettes of animals, especially horses, all in superimposed bands. These had begun in the Hallstatt period and continued into La Tène I when we begin to find painted vases more commonly, and these continue to the beginning of the Roman period. Incised pots are found as well as painted ones, especially in Brittany. Armorica and Britain also used relief. But the designs become impoverished in the later period, and some of the finest examples of La Tène pottery occur in Britain.

Celtic stone sculptures are not common. The two chief regions where they have so far been found are Provence and Germany. The sculptures from Provence are largely of classical inspiration, and have already been discussed in connexion with the great sanctuaries of art, Roquepertuse and Entremont, in an earlier chapter. The stone statues from Germany are much more typically Celtic, for we cannot trace any close parallel outside Celtic lands. One of the most remarkable is the four-sided pillar at Pfalzfeld in the Hunsrück in the land of the Treveri, which has already been described. It is an impressive monument, even without the head, which is lost. It tapers upward and its decoration may be seen on all four sides. At the base is a human head with two converging lobes in place of hair, and the pillar itself is decorated with a cable pattern. The whole forms an odd combination of obelisk and column, a product of Celtic fancy, with certain elements recalling Etruscan monuments such as those of Este.

A curious two-headed statue from Holzgerlingen (Württemberg) is interesting partly in view of its size, for it is one and a half times life-size, and partly because it is reminiscent of some of the earliest menhir sculptures in its sparsity of detail. It is, however, entirely Celtic, with its straight eyebrows, its slit-like mouth and triangular nose, while one of the two lobes which adorned the head is still preserved, along with the right arm. From Heidelberg we have another famous head, which when complete must have been about the same size as the Holzgerlingen sculpture. By far the most interesting human sculpture found so far, however, is a human head of a god or hero excavated at Mšecké Žehrovice in Bohemia (cf. p. 167 above). It was found in a pit situated in a rectangular area, which was evidently a sacred enclosure.

Most of the human heads are, however, found on bronze ornaments. All are frontal and ornamented with the leaf-shaped lobes already described. Most are earless and some are bearded. Some are functional in that they may be used as handles. A very common phenomenon is the mask, which is found at all periods, completely naturalistic, but not intended to be worn over the face, though hollow inside. The eyes in one which is preserved were originally of blue and white glass, and the mask was probably intended to be inserted on a pillar or to stand on an altar. Another mask of a Celtic hero from the Pyrenees is incised on bronze sheet and is open at the back and again with holes cut out for the eyes, which are absent, but were made of enamel or stones; the whole was originally fixed on a wooden pillar. One interesting and well-modelled little group of small-sized human-figure sculpture is represented in the late La Tène and early Roman periods by little nude figures, apparently in ritual movement. They were found at Neuvy-en-Sullias (Loiret) and represent female dancers and men walking or carrying large objects. They were found in the neighbourhood of a shrine.

It is claimed that the only large-size animal sculpture of Celtic origin is the goose from Roquepertuse, which cannot be claimed as purely Celtic. Ducks and other birds are commonly used as ornaments, and a duck with coral eyes sits charmingly on the tip of the Basse-Yutz flagon. Man-eating beasts are also very common, and manifestly basically Oriental, though often modified to suit their use. The Basse-Yutz flagon, for example, is basically Persian, but with some Chinese features in the eye-brows, and Scythian and Persian features appear in the enriched spirals on the shoulders and haunches.

LA TÈNE ART IN BRITAIN AND IRELAND

There is a sphere of Celtic art outside Gaul which continued to develop when Gaul was losing its initiative under the growing influence of classical artistic conventions. This was Celtic Britain, in this as in so much else the last stronghold of the Celtic genius, and this British La Tène art flourished at a time when on the Continent it had already entered upon its decline. The early phase of British La Tène can be traced to the middle of the third century B.C. At this period groups of immigrant warriors from the middle Rhinelands established themselves in southern England, living beside the native population in a somewhat backward culture which possessed many Hallstatt characteristics. But they brought with them fully developed La Tène art with many Waldalgesheim characteristics, as seen particularly in swords and scabbards.

Very soon native La Tène schools arose in Britain, and we can speak now of insular La Tène art as a special branch of La Tène. Various styles and workshops have been distinguished, such as the early Torrs style, chiefly noted by the Torrs pony-cap in south-west Scotland, and the drinking-horn mounts, formerly believed to have formed a part of it. This insular style combines relief and linear ornaments, which are chiefly present as tendril scrolls. The tendrils sprout into leaves, and often have bird-headed finials, as in the round shield-boss from the Thames at Wandsworth or the shield from the River Witham, once adorned also with a boar. The Torrs style, however, is clearly combined with a special Irish style seen in the Lisnacrogher scabbard plates from Ulster, and the two areas have been thought to have been combined in a single school.

Perhaps the most distinctive British development of La Tène art is the mirror style, a development perhaps from the incised decoration of scabbards. The British mirrors are of bronze, and have been dated from about 75–50 B.C. to the first century A.D. The most famous examples are the Birdlip mirror from Gloucestershire, the Desborough mirror from Northamptonshire, and the one of unknown provenance in the Mayer Collection, now in Liverpool Museum, the last being perhaps the most beautiful. In these mirrors the background is covered with lightly incised notching which throws into magnificent relief the rhythm of the design formed of earlier plant or scroll patterns arranged with due reserve in the space to be filled.

In the late La Tène and Gallo-Roman period the Belgae considerably influenced the native British La Tène schools. It was the Belgae, for example, who gave the chief impetus to the use of red enamel by the use of the champ-levé technique to cover early ornamental fields. They chiefly affected south-eastern Britain from about 75 B.C., and their artists were probably Gaulish immigrants, because many of the finest works come from the parts where the invaders settled, and are even found in Belgic graves. The Aylesford and Marlborough buckets are notable examples. The Aylesford bucket is dated to *c.* 50 B.C. It was found in a pit-burial believed to be Belgic, which contained, in addition to the bucket, a skillet of frying-pan shape and three brooches inside the bucket, together with fragments of cinerary urns. The grave formed a part of a contemporary cemetery. Around the bucket the topmost band is decorated in relief with a mixed design of the typical Celtic comma leaves, engaged whorls, and two horse-like creatures peaked and horned and with double tails. The bucket itself is ten inches high, and is formed of a framework of three wooden staves bound by thin metal bands attached by rivets. The flagon is of Italo-Greek manufacture. Another vat was found near Marlborough, Wiltshire, but is thought to have been made in Armorica and imported. The sea-horses which occur on the uppermost band are conspicuous on the coins of the Cenomanni (Main) and Redones. The vat is 21½ inches high and decorated with human heads in repoussé work and various fantastic animal- and god-like designs.

To this period belong some of our most superb British La Tène objects. One of the most praised is the bronze horned helmet from the Thames decorated with delicate embossed work and fine relief and red enamel. Another masterpiece is the bronze shield, probably gilded, from the Thames at Battersea, beautifully decorated with simple La Tène designs contained in three circles. The restraint and refinement of the piece are beyond praise. To judge by the central boss and the circular ornaments which remain of the Witham shield this was a piece of still more superb workmanship. It is enriched with embossed curvilinear decoration of Celtic patterns and the Greek palmette, with fine engraving. An elongated figure of a boar, now traceable only by rivet holes and slight discoloration, appears to have formed part of an earlier decoration which was removed to make way for the present one.

To the last pre-Christian century also belongs the Snettisham hoard, Norfolk, unearthed in 1948–50. This is the largest accumulation of precious metal so far recorded from Iron Age Britain. The most spectacular part of the treasure was over fifty gold and electrum torcs, which must have been either the property of a corporation of priests or the regalia of a royal dynasty, perhaps of the Iceni. East Anglia is relatively poor in military accoutrements, but very rich in articles of personal adornment. At Bawsey and North Creake, also in north-west Norfolk, torcs of gold alloyed with silver and copper also indicate that personal belongings of this type were used in the area in the latter part of the first century B.C. A recent find of gold torcs from Ipswich has added appreciably to this inventory of possible Icenian wealth. Other objects for personal use surviving from East Anglia include two disc brooches from the same find, ornamented with a winged griffin and a pony and, found elsewhere, rings of gold alloy for the thumb or toe. The Belgic invasion of about 100 B.C. also introduced coinage into south-eastern England, and the earliest known coins from East Anglia, dating from soon after 100 B.C., were found in the Snettisham Treasure.

The frequency with which objects have come to light from rivers and bogs is very striking. We hear from Caesar, Posidonius and Strabo of the Gaulish custom of consecrating part of the spoils of battle and other treasure in consecrated places, and archaeologists have not unnaturally connected with this custom the finding of weapons and arms in rivers. Accordingly, a magnificent find from Llyn Cerig Bach in Anglesey has been thought to have been such a sacred deposit (cf. p. 148 above). The find consisted mostly of weapons and equipment of war, of chariot metal fittings, and a slave's chain, complete with collars for the prisoners. The Battersea and Witham shields have been thought to be of similar origin, but may equally well have been dropped by chance in crossing the river.

The Roman occupation of southern Britain imposed restraints on the traditional structure and function of Celtic society which allowed little room in which Celtic art could flourish. In the initial enthusiasm of becoming Romanized, the aristocracy may have felt that their art, as part of their previous way of life, had become inferior to that of their flattering conquerors. Having adopted the toga, the villa and the town house, they may have come to sense that much of their previously cherished ideals and conventions were old-fashioned and perhaps bucolic, compared with the novelty of feeling part of a Mediterranean-orientated civilization. There were also the economic effects of imported mass-produced articles to compete with the products of the older craftsmen. But it was the destruction of Celtic society which destroyed Celtic art in southern Britain by the withdrawal of patronage from these craftsmen. The new order allowed no opportunity to commission a shield or helmet, and certainly none to decorate a war-chariot. Although a handful of examples of true Celtic artistry survives from the Roman occupation, little in general remained of the old tradition of ornamental metal-work. It is curious that some of the best features of La Tène artistry survived in the decoration of native-produced pottery, although of course in a very attenuated form.

CELTIC ART IN IRELAND

In Ireland more than anywhere else in Europe we have a country and its art developing practically in isolation. The few imports from Roman Britain may have introduced some new ideas, but they were not sufficiently strong to alter the native development of her art. Art often flourishes best under stable patronage, and the social and political situation in Ireland was little subject to change. Christianity brought the first great flood tide of new motifs and techniques, but even these came slowly. Of the wholesale character of Latin culture Ireland knew nothing. Later Ireland was little concerned in the break-up of the Roman Empire and was unaffected by its devastating effects on Europe. It was untroubled by the effects of the Teutonic invasions everywhere, even those in England, although of these, at least, Ireland could hardly have remained ignorant. Ireland was able to benefit by the break-down of Roman power in Britain to send colonists to that island. She nevertheless carried on in her island security and perfected the old Celtic culture of the Continent, generally ignorant of Mediterranean culture and Mediterranean art, especially the art of human representation. Thus uninterrupted, she developed the elements of her native Celtic art to a degree of perfection which we are only today beginning to understand.

Roman influence had little effect on the La Tène style in Britain for at least a century after Caesar's conquest. We have seen that when continental Celtic art was in decline insular Celtic art continued to flourish and even to develop. In Ireland, similarly, it continued and developed new beauties of its own. Here, for example, the recognition of the value of the blank space for showing up ornament in early Christian times is beautifully illustrated by the Ardagh chalice and in the *Book of Durrow*, and in this respect Ireland had nothing to gain from recourse to external styles. From Ireland, too, we are fortunate in possessing manuscripts which enhance and perfect the La Tène form of ornament with an unsurpassed, indeed a wholly unequalled, intricacy and perfection of design. In Ireland also we have stone sculpture for the first time in any quantity, and this seems to have developed internally from the hesitant experiments of prehistoric times. This contributed, for example, to the combination of Celtic design and biblical motifs on the high crosses which are a distinctive development. Native Irish Celtic art continued under the patronage of Celtic monasticism until the submergence of both with the introduction of continental art styles and developed European monasticism, in the eleventh century.

Ireland is, perhaps, the one part of Europe in which we can ever hope to find a truly Celtic art surviving. Almost untouched by Roman art, it retained its Celtic motifs and developed them into an art world of its own, ornamental, yet never wholly losing touch with the world of reality. But this is a reality unfamiliar to the modern world, akin, as Françoise Henry has said, to the world of magic, which makes use of familiar shapes and ideas in wholly unfamiliar surroundings. It is asymmetrical even while conveying a superficial impression of symmetry. It makes use of a geometrical framework which completely hides itself under a guise of naturalistic dimensions. It combines human and animal motifs with complete disregard of species and anatomy, yet with an air of naturalness which fits perfectly in the phantasmagoria of the whole conception.

This is not to say that foreign importations, ideas and techniques were unknown in Ireland. At the very beginning of the Christian period, the occupants of the rath of Garranes in Co. Cork were using large quantities of Mediterranean pottery which, to judge by the other objects found, seems to have been of the fifth and sixth centuries A.D. Similar pottery has been found in south-western Britain and a few other Irish coastal sites. There are some grounds for thinking that the pottery may have been containers of wine or olive oil. Again, single stone crosses, from engraved boulders to elaborate slabs, are found in practically all early Irish monasteries and are unusual in European Christendom. The inspiration may have been brought to Ireland from Gaul, Italy and the Near East. We may point further to the use of dots on the illumination of manuscripts, which is of Coptic origin, and is found in monasteries of the

Egyptian desert, whence it passed into Byzantine art to occur in Byzantine manuscripts of the sixth century. How these contacts between the very isolated Ireland of the sixth century and the Eastern monasteries came about we do not know, but we know they came directly by way of Gibraltar from the Near East and continued to the end of the sixth century, and may have been interrupted by the Arab invasion of Spain.

Irish art, however, is utterly different from those of any of these Eastern sources. It is, as was continental La Tène art, a distinctive art, quite different from contemporary continental art, quite different from the art of Roman Britain. Mlle Henry claims that it owes some of its elements to native megalithic art, and something of a case can be made out for this in the isolated boulder of the Turoe (Galway) and the Castle Strange (Roscommon) stones, which were decorated over their entire surface with La Tène whorls. The two crude human statues from lower Lough Erne (Fermanagh) and the screaming figure from Armagh, helmeted and with moustache, have something in common with the continental Celtic statue from Holzgerlingen, but nothing in common with a more sophisticated Celto-Ligurian statuary from the mouth of the Rhône. Is this due to very early continental influence? Or can it really be something which has survived in Ireland from the Megalithic period?

It is not easy for us – the products of centuries of classical education and scientific outlook – to realize the naturalness with which the early Irish mind passed from the reality of the known to the realm of fancy. Mlle Henry has aptly compared it to the early voyage literature, the *Voyage of Bran*, in which Bran and his companions pass over the sea in search of the islands of the Blessed, and Bran meets Manannán mac Lir, who tells him that all is not as it appears: that what appears to be his boat, is to Manannán a two-wheeled chariot, and that what to Bran appears as the sea full of fish is in reality a flowery plain peopled by sportive lambs and calves. It is nothing to the Irish artist to end a curvilinear design of interlacing snakes with bird heads, or to decorate the capital monogram at the beginning of St Matthew's Gospel in the Book of Kells with a human head of perfectly natural design. There is nothing inappropriate in the whorl of the capital letter of incredible intricacy at the beginning of the same gospel in the same manuscript, containing a small circle occupied by two cats, quietly watching two rats gnawing a church wafer (cf. p. 250 below). Yet the cats are real cats, their species carefully distinguished as a brindled and a tabby, while the rest of the decoration which fills the entire page is wholly imaginary and flamboyant.

The essential qualities of Irish art are more easily gauged from a study of her metal-work, of which many more examples have survived, partly because of their small size, durability and portability, and partly because metal-work was the most popular and cheap of the media in general use. Perhaps we might begin with the sword scabbards and chapes found at the crannog of Lisnacrogher (Antrim) and in the River Bann at Toome and Coleraine. Fox connects these with the school of south-western Scotland which produced the Torrs pony helmet, but F. Henry is inclined to regard them as a native development from earlier Irish art. These are all beautifully engraved with patterns which are variations of the scabbards from Bugthorpe and Hunsbury in Britain thought to be of second or third century date. It may be that we have to allow a time-lag for Ireland. These scabbards and their chapes have peculiar outlines, and no other scabbards of this type have been found in Ireland. They have to be dated in any case to the last centuries before Christ. They appear to be the product of a workshop where La Tène art was produced at its best and most typical of the continental style.

From an early period, too, enamelling was known in Ireland, as is shown by a little object from Lisnacrogher Crannog of two little bronze ducks on a piece of red enamel, and a small bronze relief and open-work disc from near Ballinareve, dating from the time of Christ or slightly before. Bronze pins and penannular brooches are among the earliest Irish imports, the latter derived from Roman models, and from an early period they were often enamelled. Both are widely distributed throughout our islands, especially, as one might expect, the pins. An interesting enamelled pin comes from Norrie's Law in Fife, which is decorated with Celtic Pictish designs and a tiny cross, and can be dated to the seventh century by the Byzantine coin in the same hoard (cf. p. 234 above). A silver penannular brooch comes from the same hoard, another silver one from Pant-y-Saer in Anglesey, and a bronze one from South Wales.

During the early Christian period the ornamentation on metal-work was greatly increased, not only by the wide use of red enamel, but by the incrustation of semi-precious stones and coloured glass and the use of filigree, and the technique of millefiori was now copied from Roman jewellery. The most outstanding treasures of this enhanced technique are the Ardagh chalice, the belt-shrine from Moylough (Co. Sligo), the so-called Tara brooch from Ireland, and the Hunterston brooch from Ayrshire in Scotland. The Tara brooch is a superb monument of barbaric splendour, but the chalice in its refinement and distinction would more than satisfy the most exacting modern taste. It is made simply of a large cup and spherical foot of beaten silver united by a metal rod, and the edge of the cup is strengthened by a brass roll on which the upper ends of the two handles rest. It is of massive beauty combined with fullness of line and the use of ornament is sparing, but thrown into relief by the large amount of blank space; yet not wholly blank, for there is an inscription engraved lightly on the surface which in no way obtrudes itself. The lovely curves and quiet design are balanced by the gleaming colours and brilliance of the restrained ornament of gold foil, discs of red enamel and glass bosses.

The belt-shrine from Moylough (Sligo) resembles the Ardagh chalice in certain points of technique. It consists of four leather strips richly ornamented with metal-work. It is, in fact, a *cumdach* or cover which expresses externally the nature of the relic which it encloses, just as a crozier-shrine reflects the size and nature of its *bachall* or a bell-shrine the size and form of its bell. Despite its 1,200 years of life the belt-shrine remains a thing of great beauty, both for its craftsmanship and its artistry. One of its most striking features is the occurrence of many die-stamped ornamental panels – a type of decoration comparatively rare in Irish decoration of comparable style and date, though it occurs on the Ardagh chalice and on the secondary silver disc of the St Ninian's Isle hanging bowl from the Shetlands in Scotland. The date assigned is usually seventh or eighth century, but is quite uncertain.

The so-called Tara brooch is a comparatively small object, only 3½ inches in diameter, made with a closed cast-silver ring. It is prepared on both front and back with a series of raised frames made to hold little panels of filigree, the brooch being decorated both in front and at the back. The back is decorated with panels of gilt chip-carvings, two nearly flat discs of enamelled glass like the bosses on the chalice, and sunken spiral patterns of incredible fineness, as well as birds biting one another's legs. When the brooch was fastened on a garment the other side only was seen, and as the brooch is unusually small the work is of delicate quality, consisting of beasts designed by fine and intricate raised bands of amber and gold wire, twisted and coiled. Reptiles of larger size figure on the framework, with two little human heads of moulded dark glass. The contrasting colours of the gilt surface and the amber beads serve to throw a vivid light on this little jewel.

The Hunterston brooch comes from Ayrshire in Scotland opposite the north-east corner of Ireland. It may possibly have come there as loot taken from Ireland by Vikings; but a fragment of another found at Dunbeath (Caithness) has, like the Hunterston brooch, animal decoration in filigree reminiscent of the Tara brooch. Both these Scottish brooches have a little animal covered with gold granulations. The Hunterston brooch is quite simply decorated on the back, but here we find the names of two Vikings, presumably former owners, scratched in the runic characters of the Hebrides in the Viking Age. It is larger than the Tara brooch, measuring 4¾ inches, and the pin, though broken, is 5½ inches long. It is decorated with amber studs and zoomorphic and serpentine designs, and with panels of simple interlace; the elegance of the design is almost equal to the best manuscript illumination.

In addition to these great and deservedly famous works, there is a large series of hardly less well-known works of the eighth and ninth centuries in metal form, many of them chance finds, others found in the Norwegian graves where they had been carried as loot. Indeed it is perhaps in the museums of Bergen and Oslo that one gets the best idea for dating. Examples of such works are the ornaments of chalices, shrines, reliquaries, *cumdachs* or ornamented boxes for manuscripts. We may refer to the *Annals of Ulster*, where the relics of St Conlaed (799) and of St Ronan (800) are said to have been placed 'in a shrine of gold and silver'. These little bronze objects are mostly covered with gilt; glass and amber beads are often inserted, and interlacings, spirals, and animal hatchings are fitted into little panels.

It will be noticed that figurative representations in bronze are relatively scarce at this period. The most famous example is the Athlone plaque which is impressive but completely unrealistic. It consists of a crucifixion group in the usual Byzantine style, with two angels above, and the two human figures, the one with the sponge, the other the lance bearer, below the outstretched arms of Christ. The head of Christ is realistic, with its straight fringe and closed eyes, but His single garment is entirely covered with running spiral ornament, partly incised, partly superimposed in bold relief. The relic had been taken from the binding of a book.

When we turn from metal-work to the stone carvings on the

high crosses we find the human form much commoner. This is not merely because on the crosses the crucifixion is naturally more frequent, for we also find large numbers of narrative scenes from scripture, from the Old Testament, and the lives of saints. The technique of stone carving is really quite independent of that of metal-work, and although the motifs are often interchangeable, they really developed more or less independently, yet in a way on parallel lines. We have seen that stone carving had a lengthy history in Ireland, and although new motifs arrived to transform it, there may have been a native tradition behind it, which is not the case with the really ornate metal-work. Moreover, the stone crosses have affinities in other techniques and share to some extent their designs. Thus the single slab with one or more crosses from simple hermitages, and the larger collection of burial crosses from Clonmacnoise, are at times decorated with devices, both human and geometrical, which we also find on the larger cross slabs and the high crosses.

Early examples of crosses engraved on upright slabs occur at Fahan Mura and at Carndonagh in Donegal. They form, together with other examples in the Inishowen Peninsula, a group or school to themselves. Saint Mura was the patron saint of the chief branch of the northern Uí Néill, whose seat was at the fortress of Ailech on a hill nearby, and the Columban monastery of Derry, which was traditionally connected with St Columba, was also close at hand. The Fahan slab stands nearly nine feet high, and has a triangular summit; the cross engraved on it stands out in bold though shallow relief from the slab, and even extends slightly beyond the limits of the frame. The design on both sides consists of knot and plait work formed of broad ribbons with a double edge, and on one side two little armless square figures occupy the space below the cross. On the north edge of the slab a clear inscription in Greek letters gives the Mozarabic version of the form of the Gloria Patri: 'Glory *and honour* to the Father and to the Son and to the

Holy Ghost.' All the indications suggest that the slab belongs to the sphere of the Columban monasteries at the close of the seventh century.

In the cross of Carndonagh a few miles to the north the cross has shaped the slab to its own design, though the same broad interlacings appear here which we have seen on the cross of Fahan, and which in Carndonagh completely cover one side of this magnificent ten-foot cross with its closely interwoven ribbons. On the other side plaited and knotted ribbons form a cross, below which are two little groups of birds arranged in triquetras. The body of the cross is occupied by an extremely simplified version of the crucifixion, the head of Christ being much enlarged, while four little armless figures occupy the spaces above and below His outstretched arms. Three more equally simplified little figures occupy the lowest panel and the whole of the carving is very light. Beside the cross are two little pillars carved in the same style which have been interpreted as Old Testament figures, but the relationship of the pillars to the slab is far from clear. In the churchyard at Carndonagh nearby is another cross which, though much cruder, belongs to the same group.

These crosses in Donegal are in some measure in a class by themselves and may owe something to prehistoric technique; but their ornamentation is certainly Christian Irish, though essentially different from that of the other Irish high crosses. During the early Middle Ages the only countries of western Europe where stone crosses covered with ornaments and figures are to be found are in Britain and Ireland, where they occur from the eighth to the twelfth centuries, probably beginning at about 750. The English crosses, notably Ruthwell and Bewcastle, seem to be roughly contemporaneous but follow a different tradition, with their monumental stone figures of Christ, and their love of foliage and naturalistic representation of the vinescroll. The symbol stones of Scotland, especially the earliest ones, again follow a completely separate tradition. The early

Christian Near East had monumental stone crosses, the Copts favouring flat slabs carved in low relief, the Armenians wrought crosses covered with ornaments and figures; but how influences from these areas reached our islands is quite unknown. Their arrival may be connected to some extent with the disruption which followed the Arab invasion of the Near East and Spain (cf. p. 235 above).

From about the middle of the eighth century elaborately carved high crosses may be said to be the chief static ornaments of the monasteries, in contrast with the simplicity of their architecture. A plan of the monastery of St Mullins preserved in the eighth-century *Book of Mulling* shows a round enclosure, with crosses dedicated to the four evangelists and to four prophets guarding it, as it were, outside. Inside the enclosure were other crosses dedicated to the Holy Spirit, 'Angels from above', Christ and His Apostles, etc. A similar arrangement seems to have prevailed in St Kieran's churchyard near Kells, and possibly in Iona. Most of the crosses are between ten and fifteen feet high, and made of white or cream sandstone.

Most of the surviving eighth-century crosses are near the middle of the Shannon and Clonmacnoise is an obvious centre, for here evidence of a sculptor's workshop can be traced from the numerous monumental stone slabs on a small scale which still survive; it was also, of course, a great religious centre. But despite the disappearance of the monastery of Lismore in Munster, I am strongly inclined to regard these valleys of the Blackwater and Suir throughout the eighth century as the centre and perhaps the origin of the high crosses which include the well-known crosses of Ahenny, Kilkieran, Killamory, Kilrea. Lismore was a very important monastery in the early eighth century, and always in close touch with the Continent. A small school of figured crosses occurs at the foot of the Wicklow Hills in the east, of which the strange Cross of Moone is an outstanding and unique example. A date for the Clonmacnoise group is suggested by the inscription on the Bealin

Cross, which would place it in the last decade or so of the eighth century; the group north of Lismore would seem to be datable to about 750 at the latest.

Dividing the crosses into groups we note that the first group such as Ahenny (Tipperary) and Kilkina (Kilkenny), both near Carrick-on-Suir, have close similarities: figured ornament consisting of spirals and interlacings predominates and only on the bases are figured scenes carved. The bases of the crosses, however, are covered with ornaments, all carved in low relief. The emphasis on the carving is all reserved for the interlace and knobs of the actual cross, which are strongly reminiscent of metal-work. The group of crosses generally associated with Clonmacnoise, including the Bealin Cross which has probably been moved from there, are covered throughout with animal decoration which has taken the place of spirals. Hunting scenes of a fanciful kind are prominent – horsemen riding amongst dragons or stag-hunting – but no figured scenes of current Christian iconographical type appear.

Passing now to the east of Ireland, a group to the west of the Wicklow Mountains and further south in the valley of the Barrow are all carved in granite, and are therefore simple in detail, and show lack of deep relief and a complete absence of bosses. The most remarkable example of the group is the Moone Cross (Kildare), about seventeen feet high but very narrow, with a very high pyramidal base and a slender stem and rather small head. It is carved throughout with little figures, each in its separate superimposed frame, all very squat and mostly devoid of arms but with large heads. The crucifixion, which is small, is placed very low, between the shaft and the base, which consists of twelve tiny identical armless figures, presumably the twelve apostles. The cross is unique, but strangely impressive.

At Kells there is a group of four crosses, of which one is comparatively small and beautifully carved, near the round tower. A second is unfinished, and figured scenes are very prominent on the other two, standing out boldly and almost giving the impression of free-standing sculpture in the round. All the crosses are completely covered with figured scenes, and here for the first time the knots and interlacing animals are completely relegated to a subordinate position. All the crosses are ringed. With this splendid group we may class the Cross of Muiredach and the west Cross at Monasterboice, the Cross of the Scriptures at Clonmacnoise and the Cross of Durrow. The Cross of Muiredach bears an inscription asking for a prayer for him, and the cross is generally attributed to the second Muiredach who died in 923. It is a massive erection, the two main panels carved with figured scenes and panels of ornament. On the crossing and arms are depicted the crucifixion and the Last Judgement, in the smaller panels below the former are scenes from the New Testament, and below the latter scenes from the Old Testament. The carving is bold and rounded and the dress and weapons have a special interest for us because so clearly depicted. A particularly engaging detail is carved at the foot of the cross on the west face below the apprehending of Christ, where two cats are depicted licking their kittens, reminding us of the two cats in the manuscript of the *Book of Kells* (cf. p. 250 below). Most of these crosses are probably to be attributed to the early ninth century and all show the same preoccupation with narrative and figure sculpture and the same bold outline carving.

It is particularly noticeable in this group of crosses that all the scenes are subordinated with great care to the representation of Christ, generally at the crossing or occupying the arms, whether it is Christ crucified, or in glory, or as a judge. The crucifixion is very stereotyped and generally bears the figures of the sponge and the lance-bearer below the arms of the crucified figure, an early arrangement of which is found on a page of the sixth-century Syrian Gospels of Rabula. Foliage is curiously absent here as elsewhere in Irish art, but animal interlacing is much in favour and covers much of the background of the later crosses. The commonest subordinate scenes are, as we have seen, from the Old Testament, such as the expulsion of Adam and Eve from Eden; Jonah and the Whale; David as warrior and harper; the sacrifice of Isaac; and scenes from the lives of saints, notably the meeting of Paul and Antony in the desert. St Antony seems to have been a favourite saint.

When we turn from stone decoration to manuscript work we find our problem of interpretation completely reversed. We have seen that the range of tall stone crosses in particular is restricted in western Europe to the British Isles. Our problem of dating and style is therefore restricted within this compass, and is in this respect a relatively simple one. Manuscripts, however, being portable, may have travelled far, and the problem is to distinguish those manuscripts which were actually made in Ireland from those which were made on the Continent by Irish monks, or in the Irish style. The matter is made still more complicated by a claim which has recently been made for England as the home of the *Book of Durrow* and the *Lindisfarne Gospels*. For our present purpose, however, this question has little importance. The Irish style of illumination is so distinctive that it is recognizable at a glance. It matters little where it was made. Our main concern is with the distinctive style of the illumination of Irish manuscripts and its history.

We possess from the second half of the sixth century a few verses of the psalms engraved on wax tablets; but it is generally agreed that the earliest surviving Irish manuscript is the *Cathach* ('Battler') which according to tradition was written by St Columba towards the end of the sixth century. Its strange name is due to the fact that for many centuries it was handed down in the family of Conall Gulban of the northern Uí Néill and was always carried three times round the army to ensure victory before they went into battle. The book is an incomplete fragment of a psalter, originally about nine inches by six inches, and is written by a single hand in a very archaic form of Irish majuscule which may actually date from the time of St Columba. As the beginning is missing our knowledge of the illumination is confined to the large capitals at the beginning of each psalm, which are simple but confident, and often surrounded by red dots and decorated with what was probably yellow ink. The *Cathach* is not an experimental early work, but suggests earlier sixth-century Italian manuscripts, and the early Irish elements in the earliest Bobbio manuscripts. The dots are a very characteristic feature, originally found in Coptic manuscripts of the Egyptian desert, like so much else in the earliest western manuscripts.

Already in the second half of the sixth century, Irish manuscripts had developed distinctive features. Chief of these is the plan of putting in the beginning of each section of a book a decorative page on the left – sometimes a 'carpet-page', that is to say a page completely covered with decoration – and an introductory page with a large initial on the right. The ornamented page replaced the framed title page inherited from classical manuscripts. In addition to the two introductory pages mentioned above there is usually at the beginning of each Gospel a page with either a portrait or a symbol of the evangelist.

Ms. A.II.10 of the Cathedral Library of Durham is the most archaic in ornamentation of all our surviving Irish manuscripts, but it consists now of only twelve pages. The text of St Mark begins with a brilliantly coloured decorated capital on a very large scale, and the plaits of ribbon are painted yellow with an overdotting of red, while yellow, blue, red, and green are also used. This manuscript belongs to a stage later than the *Cathach* manuscript. Here we find the three staple types of the ornament of the late illumination side by side – interlacings of threads or ribbons, spirals, and zoomorphic ornament. It also shows the Irish majuscule script developing very near to that of the *Book of Durrow*, and some interesting minuscules.

The *Book of Durrow* is a truly astonishing piece of work. Despite its early date it is at the end rather than the beginning of a decorative tradition. It has caught up the elements of a simplified art and worked them into a most startling design which is calculated to arrest and impress us at a glance. Here everything is spare and reserved, as in the Ardagh chalice. The symbol of St Matthew is surrounded by a narrow simple border of interlaced edged ribbons. The figure of the Evangelist is simple and frontal, with severely stylized hair and beard, total absence of arms and sideways-moving feet. There is no perspective, no realism, but in fact their deliberate negation. The garment, all in one piece, is without a fold, but entirely covered with an angular design suggestive of a mosaic. And the symbolism is made totally impressive by the fact that this strange little figure is set against a background of plain ivory vellum. The Evangelist symbol at the beginning of St John's Gospel is equally impressive, in exactly the same way. The beginning of the script of the Gospel of St John is similarly calculated to impress at a glance rather than to distract the eye with variety. The opening page of the Gospel of St Mark is entirely surrounded with red dots, but the dots are so inconspicuous, and the whole design is so quietly and calmly proportioned, as to betoken the most fastidious, and at the same time the most practised security of taste.

This is a comparatively small manuscript, only 5½ by 6½ inches. It is chiefly a version of the Vulgate, written in a beautiful Irish majuscule. There are few colours – a deep green, a bright yellow and a glowing red – which stand out sharply on deep tones of black-brown, and sometimes the ivory colour of the vellum. The nature and the sparsity of the colouring serve to enhance the impression of maturity, like autumn leaves. There is indeed a touch of autumn about this little manuscript, and much of the design of the border, and also the colours (green, yellow and red) are used in the earliest surviving Coptic manuscripts which go back to the eighth, ninth, and tenth centuries, and are probably based on earlier models.

The book is very elaborately decorated, despite its restraint. There are several large capitals ornamented with spirals, and several pages of ornamentation. There are wide ribbons, spirals, and fantastic animals interwoven and mildly biting one another. Nearly every page is surrounded by a border of interlacings. The scheme and the whole conception, especially of the armless figure of St Matthew, recall the seventh-century cross of Fahan, and many archaic features would lead one to date it in the second half of the seventh century. Others recall the manuscripts of the eastern Mediterranean – not the Greek and Latin ones, but those of Syria, Mesopotamia, and Egypt. The idea of composition, filling pages and framed with an ornamental border, is unknown in the western illumination of those times, but some of the frames of the Syriac Gospels of Rabula of the sixth century have pages of text with frames of interlacings, which come close to Durrow. The identity of the frames in both cases includes dotted ribbons and little knots in the corners of the page, and other Syrian manuscripts, later in date, but probably archaic in tradition, have framed pages with borders of green, red, and yellow ribbons exactly like the decorated page of St Mark's Gospel; and the eighth- and ninth-century Coptic illuminations, like the Syriac, which probably incorporate older traditions, again show unmistakable affinities with the *Book of Durrow*. The Copts and Syrians almost always used green, red, and yellow for their ornaments. There can be little doubt of an eastern Mediterranean school behind all this; but how it reached Ireland, and under what circumstances remains a mystery. Incidentally, there is much in common between the *Book of Durrow* and the Great Book of the *Lindisfarne Gospels.*

The strange vicissitudes and the precarious life of the great Irish manuscripts give ample room for believing that what has come down to us is only a modicum of what has been lost. When the *Cathach*, traditionally ascribed to St Columba himself, was finally exposed to view, it was found that its pages were stuck together by damp and had to be unstuck and finally remounted. The *Book of Durrow* was kept, after the dissolution of the monastery, near Durrow by one of the MacGeoghans who used it to cure sick cattle by pouring water on it and then making them drink the water. The *Book of Kells*, the greatest of all Irish illuminated manuscripts, 'the great Gospel of Columcille' and 'the chief relic of the western world on account of its ornamental cover', was 'wickedly stolen in the night', 'out of the western sacristy of the great stone church of Kells. The same Gospel was found after twenty nights and two months, its gold having been taken off it, and a sod over it' – *A.U.*, s.a. 1006 (*recte* 1007).

The *Book of Kells* is by far the greatest of the great Irish Gospel Books, not very much later than the *Book of St Gall* with which it has much in common, though it is a much freer and a far more sophisticated piece of work. Its precise origin is unknown. Was it made in Iona in Argyll, or in Kells in Ireland; or begun in the former and completed in the latter after one or other of the sackings of Iona by the Vikings? The work is unfinished, which may be due to the flight of the community of Iona to Kells. Its date is probably between 760–70 and 815–20, and it is thought likely that the work of at least four painters is represented, and that they went on working at it for several years. But all this is mere conjecture.

The *Book of Kells* is a great Gospel Book, measuring 13 by 9½ inches, written on a thick glazed vellum, in a beautiful round half-uncial hand, which differs little from that of the Books of Durrow, Lindisfarne, Lichfield and St Gall, but in a mixed and somewhat carelessly written text. A similar haphazard appearance characterizes the illumination, which is uneven and incomplete. Yet the overall result is an amazing interplay of carpet, cruciform and architectural pages, symbols of the Evangelists, and other full page representations of Christ, as well as a continuous thread of ornamentation throughout the text. It is very possible that the original writer left blank spaces to be filled in by the artist, and independent artists have undoubtedly made their contribution; but it is difficult not to imagine a guiding mind behind the whole scheme. The impression which it makes on the reader is that it is the joint work of a barbaric but highly trained scriptorium working separately under the guidance of a single master.

Françoise Henry attributes to one artist the cruciform cover-page, known as 'the page of the eight circles', the great page of the Chi-Rho, and the initial page of each Gospel except the *Quoniam* of St Luke. These are mostly composed in two or three colours for emphasis, and inside these clearly marked frames flows an infinite variety of design consisting of every kind of typical La Tène decoration; spirals, interlocked, intertwisted, spread into a trumpet pattern; joined by a thread, yet never confused, always controlled to the end the artist has set himself. It is a world in which there is no rest. A truly remarkable feature is the realistic little figures that are included in the main design – the fully-clad little man in the top right-hand corner of the opening words of St Mark's Gospel (fol. 130 R); the tiny perfectly natural man in blue trousers and a green jacket holding a spear and round yellow shield, all surrounded with red dots in the bottom left hand corner of the Genealogy of Christ (fol. 200 R); the perfectly natural little fair-haired human head which forms the tail of the letter I in the monogram page (fol.34 R); and the quiet little insect in the same illumination of two cats watching the rats gnawing a church wafer on the great monogram page of the Generation of Christ in the beginning of St Matthew's Gospel (fol. 34 R) – see p. 236, above.

Quite a different painter is the one who painted the official portraits of the Book, the three big figures of the Evangelists and some of the symbols in square frames. He also makes use of spiral interlace, but in a more restrained fashion, whereas his main figures are superb, if conventional. The great St Matthew, with its sober colouring and monumental poise, and St Mark or St Luke (fol. 22 V) seated between two peacocks, a red book in his hand and his contrasting coloured clothes, together with the brightly coloured border – these two have been called the most impressive effigies ever designed by an Irish artist.

A great contrast is the painter of the majestic Arrest of Christ, a single figure made more impressive by the two normal but smaller human beings alongside, who are apprehending him under a simple archway with architectural rather than ornamental features. The same artist is responsible for the highly dramatic and original 'Temptation'. In this latter Christ is shown half figure surmounting a 'mountain', with guardian angels above and heads of human beings below and to the side, while an attenuated but quite unmistakable little black devil plies Him with temptations. The interest of this artist was in the dramatic possibilities of his scenes, and he brings these out in a most original manner. To him we owe also the full page Virgin and Child (fol. 7 V) with its curious eikon-like virgin under her Byzantine-like head-dress, its vivid and sharply contrasting colours of purple and green, its very human angles in the four corners, its border of interwoven animal design, and its little inconsequential inset of six tiny ordinary human beings in the margin.

There is yet another artist whose work is a source of never-ending delight to us. It was probably he who put the little realistic touches into the scene of the cats and the rats in the drawings of the first artist, for throughout the book he is responsible for many of the small capitals and other details in the text, in the borders, and in the many animals drawn between the lines. His sense of realism has left us life-like farmyard and other animals – cocks, mice, a goat, a guinea-fowl, many cats, an otter in the act of catching a fish, the whole surrounded by red dots; and all these, besides other and different figures, are twisted and twirled into unnatural shapes, passing the bounds of reality into the realms of Celtic imaginative fancy. There is even what I take to be a butterfly or moth in one of the capitals, and the capitals and important compound letters are composed of every conceivable animal and bird which twist and turn with here and there a little unnatural floral spray, or a perfectly natural little human head. His work, wherever we can isolate it, is in strong contrast to the statuesque frontal portraits of the Evangelists, or the fantastic whorls and involutions of the great pages of intricate ornament, or the great dramatic sense of the idealist or the dreamer. He introduces a lively sense of humour, a reminder that the lives of small creatures and domestic animals were going on while the great events of the world were pending. These reminders are salutary, and serve to enhance the great events by contrast. They remind us that the *Book of Kells* is not merely a collection of masterpieces but is also a miniature of the Celtic world of about 800.

CELTIC ART IN BRITAIN

The wealth and the continuity of Celtic art in Ireland have tempted us to pass by the less impressive examples of the art which has survived from Britain in the period under discussion. In fact before the Roman period Wales had been subject to artistic influences both from south-eastern Britain and from Ireland, but being a relatively poor and mountainous country she has hitherto shown less spectacular finds than the countries to the east and west. There is, however, one special art form which developed in western Britain, and which merits special attention. This is the art of grave monuments, which differ in a marked degree from those of Ireland, and which have nevertheless for the most part a certain homogeneity among themselves, especially in their type of ornamentation.

The splendid wealth and variety of design on the Irish high crosses belong to a different world, a naturalistic world, unlike the Gaulish or the British ornament. It lacks the foliage which plays so large a part in Gaulish art, and the human beings, and even the animals are generally such as we might expect to meet in our own countryside – not masks interlaced with foliage, as in Gaul. All along the western counties of Britain – Cornwall,

Wales and Galloway – on the other hand, we have a school of sculpture which is unique, and at the same time almost uniform. Animal, floral and human designs are almost absent. Instead we have the entire area of the cross below the arms – the chief part to be ornamented, in fact – filled with a pattern consisting of a geometrical design. Sometimes, as in the Cardinham cross in Cornwall, the entire surface, including the head, is ornamented with a geometrical pattern, consisting of a conventionalized vine scroll, inverted T-patterns, a chain of rings, and on the head of the cross an interlace of two strands, intertwined, and moving in opposite directions. Contemporary with the Cardinham Cross is the equally conventionalized Cross of Sancreed, also from Cornwall. Here, however, the head contains a highly conventionalized little crucifixion. These crosses are coarsely carved and probably belong to the tenth century.

The type runs right through Wales up to Galloway, though in Galloway the ornament is frequently reduced to a circle containing an early form of cross within a circle, and the stone – a rude slab – is largely devoted to an inscription in good Latin letters. In Wales there are innumerable crosses with geometrical ornamentation, and the Cornish Cardinham Cross is typical, though many of the Welsh crosses are more elaborate. The same design tends to recur frequently, as if the sculptor worked from a limited number of patterns on which he rang the changes. One of the most spectacular Welsh crosses is the well-known Carew Cross, which stands in majestic isolation to over sixteen feet in height by the roadside near Carew Castle in Pembrokeshire, and is decorated on the shaft with six panels of differing conventional design. This cross may be taken as typical of this school of sculptors, and the ornamentation is more a matter of technique than of design. The stone carver's art is hardly comparable with the realistic and varied scenes on the Irish crosses, but it might be argued that it is in fact of a higher standard of achievement. The art which could repeat the same design with an unerring hand over the entire surface argues an astonishing control over the tools. A single false step, a slip of the tool, and the entire cross would have been ruined. But we do not find false cuts. The whole is of an almost mechanical perfection, and must be the result of endless practice.

The stone crosses are not the only remains which we have of British art, though they are by far the commonest. A certain amount of manuscript illumination has survived, such as that in the manuscript of St Augustine's *De Trinitate* now preserved in the library of Corpus Christi College, Cambridge, which was written by John, son of Sulien, the bishop of St David's from 1073 to 1078 and again from 1080 to 1088. It is illuminated with vermilion, green, black and yellow, but the education of Sulien's family was of Irish tradition; and the book formerly of Llandaff, now at Lichfield, which carries a more ambitious colour scheme and Gospel entablature, is now thought to have been originally purchased from Ireland. The school of St David's, especially under Bishop Sulien, produced both good illuminated manuscripts and good penmanship, but such scriptoria are not common, and are largely of Irish inspiration. Perhaps it may be an accident that the mountains of the west should produce the most lasting results in the stone representatives of Celtic art. The length of life of the Celtic Church in Wales is more probably the real reason, for the stone crosses are a characteristic of monastic centres, which were so special a feature of the Celtic Church throughout her history. Probably, therefore, we owe it to the fact that Wales clung for so long to the ancient Celtic Church and its monastic ideals that she has left us so large a store of ancient Celtic monastic stones with their special class of ornamentation.

CHAPTER 9

Celtic Literature

IRELAND has preserved for us the oldest vernacular literature north of the Alps. Although late in acquiring the art of writing, and indeed partly because of this, she had developed an advanced body of oral tradition in which were preserved traditions dating from several centuries prior to their committal to writing. This means that although we have no written literature from ancient Gaul, certain material ritual aspects of Celtic life resemble those of Ireland, and therefore some of the traditions discernible in the very conservative Irish stories and the customs which they embody might with caution be applied to La Tène Gaul. For Britain, we have no literature which is nearly so old as that of Ireland, but in medieval literature, such as the Welsh *Mabinogion*, *The Dream of Maxen Wledig*, *Kulhwch and Olwen* and other stories, we can trace remains of similar stories and mythology.

The oldest Irish *narrative* literature is all in prose form. There is no really early Irish narrative literature in poetry. In this Irish narrative resembles that of Iceland, another island. It is commonly held that Iceland is indebted to Ireland for this, and indeed the far more conservative literature of Norway has preserved many traces of its earliest narrative in the form of poetry. On the other hand, it is not easy to see by what means Iceland could have borrowed the prose medium from Ireland in early times. There are no examples or direct evidence which indicate it, and Irish monks and slaves do not seem to have been common enough in Iceland to account for it. Moreover, we notice exactly the same thing in the Pacific Ocean, where throughout four thousand square miles the Polynesian islands have preserved their oldest traditions in prose form. Is this a characteristic of island literature as such, or is it due to their conservatism? It appears to be something quite independent of an Indo-European origin.

Taking literature as a whole, however, the earliest Irish examples to be preserved in written form are not prose but poetry. This material is largely fragmentary, and our knowledge of it is correspondingly slight; but we know something of its prosodic development, from the earliest alliterative form to the syllabic rhymed quatrains without regular rhythm, chiefly, in recent years, through the work of Gerard Murphy, Proinsias Mac Cana, and Calvert Watkins. It would seem that the earliest surviving poems are mere alliterative groups devoid of rhyme or rhythm, and dating from the sixth century. Perhaps in the eighth century the syllabic form predominated.

This early Irish poetry is not by any means always anonymous, and a number of names of early Irish poets, especially those of Munster, have come down to us. In the south the archaic form of poetry lingered long enough to be enshrined in writing. This is the old rhetorical verse with an irregular number of syllables in the line, governed by accent and making use of alliteration. This form of poetry is most often to be found in the genealogies, more especially in those of Leinster and Munster. The poet Colmán mac Lenine favoured it, and apparently copied it about 600. Colmán's poems are mostly panegyrics and satires, but though he had been a poet in early life, and some of his poetry has come down to us, he was traditionally won to repentance by St Brendan of Clonfert, and founded the cathedral church of Cloyne in Munster. Kuno Meyer has also published a number of rhythmical alliterative rhymeless strophes of the sixth and seventh centuries, which are largely concerned with prehistoric and mythical subjects. These include the death of Labraid in the saga of the *Destruction of Dinn Rig*, Finn Fili, the sons of Ros Ruid, Cathaer Mór and Cairbre of the Liffey, and poems by Senchán Torpéist in the seventh century, and an elegy by Torna Éices on the death of his teacher, Laidcenn mac Baircheda. From the eighth and ninth centuries, the order of the *filid* disappeared and their place was taken by the order of the bards, who practised their own special metres. Fragments of bardic poetry are invaluable as preserving among other themes fragmentary recollections of the early kings. We may give as an example Cathal mac Finguine, king of Munster; the Norse sea-king Olaf Cuaran; the king of the Isle of Man; Aed son of Anmire of the Déisi; the death of Fedlimmidh mac Crimthainn, king of Munster; the death of the Scots king, Kenneth mac Alpin; the little fort of Rathangan, and many others.

Where the poet has had freer play and is not confined to the service of a special patron, as the bards customarily were, there is an astonishing variety of theme and quality of poetical feeling. Kuno Meyer wrote in his *Introduction to the Ancient Irish Poetry*:

> In nature poetry the Gaelic muse may vie with that of any other nation. Indeed, these poems occupy a unique position in the literature of the world. To seek out and watch and love Nature, in its tiniest phenomena as in its grandest, was given to no people so early and so fully as to the Celt. Many hundreds of Gaelic and Welsh poems testify to this fact. It is a characteristic of these poems that in none of them do we get an elaborate or sustained description of any scene or scenery, but rather a succession of pictures and images which the poet, like an impressionist, calls up before us by light and skilful touches. Like the Japanese, the Celts were always quick to take an artistic hint; they avoid the obvious and the commonplace; the half-said thing to them is dearest.

The song of the blackbird he translates:

> The little bird:
> Has blown his whistle
> From the point of his bright yellow beak:
> He sends a song
> Over Loth Laig
> A blackbird on a branch in the well-wooded plain.

and again:

> Ah, blackbird, thou art satisfied
> Where thy nest is in the bush:
> Hermit that clingst no bell
> Sweet, soft, peaceful is thy note.

and again:

> Nimble is the yellow bee from cup to cup,
> He makes a great journey in the sun;
> Boldly he flits into the wide plain,
> Then safely joins his brethren in the hive.

The pet crane:

> My dear little crane
> Is the glory of my goodly home:
> I have not found as good a friend;
> Though he is a servant he is a gentleman.

Only fragments of these early poems remain, commonly scribbled on the margin of the book which the scribe happened to be copying. One who is copying a manuscript of Cassiodorus on the Psalms writes on the margin, 'Pleasant is the glittering of the sun today upon these margins because it flickers so.'

The longer poems have mostly been preserved from the bards' compositions of the tenth and eleventh centuries, but there is no substantial change. The song of the hermit Marban to his brother Guaire, king of Connaught, refers to the seventh century, but the poem in its present form may be of twelfth century date:

> I have a shieling in the wood,
> None knows it save my God:
> An ash-tree on the higher side, a hazel bush beyond,
> A huge old tree encompasses it . . .
>
> Swarms of bees and chafers, little musicians of the wood,
> A gentle chorus:
> Wild geese and ducks, shortly before summer's end,
> The music of the dark torrent . . .

The voice of the wind against the branchy wood
Upon the deep-blue sky:
Falls of the river, the note of the swan,
Delicious music . . .

In the eyes of Christ, the ever-young, I am no
Worse off than thou art.

We cannot wonder at Guaire's reply:

I would give my glorious kingship
With the share of my father's heritage –
To the hour of my death I would forfeit it
To be in thy company, my Marban.

It has been suggested that this love of nature is found also in our accounts of early Irish saints and hermits. Adamnán's *Life of St Columba*, written in the seventh century, contains many incidents which recall it; but the Irish poetical genius is very wide, and not always devoid of humour. How modern it all seems: this intense love of nature, this appreciation of little things, insects, birds, and their quiet secretive ways, each following its own bent, regardless of human beings and their institutions. The blackbird is a hermit that clinks no bell; the crane is a servant and yet a gentleman; the bee goes quietly about his business without measuring his distance by human span. All this is seen against a background of human effort, human striving. And for what? We are seldom told, but we are conscious of it, as were the poets themselves. Guaire implies it:

I would give my glorious kingship
To be of thy company . . .

Towards the end of the eighth century the modern note makes itself felt more unmistakably with a touch of satire in the little vignette of the monk and his pet cat.

I and my white Pangur
Have each his special art:
His mind is set on hunting mice,
Mine is upon my special craft.

I love to rest – better than any fame –
With close study at my little book;
White Pangur does not envy me:
He loves his childish play.

When in our house we two are all alone –
A tale without tedium!
We have – sport never ending!
Something to exercise our wit.

At times by feats of derring-do
A mouse sticks in his net,
While into my net there drops
A difficult problem of hard meaning.

He points his full shining eye
Against the fence of the wall:
I point my clear though feeble eye
Against the keenness of science.

He rejoices with quick leaps
When in his sharp claws sticks a mouse.
I too rejoice when I have grasped
A problem difficult and dearly loved.

Though we are thus at all times,
Neither hinders the other,
Each of us pleased with his own art
Amuses himself alone.

He is a master of the work
Which every day he does;
While I am at my own work
To bring difficulty to clearness.

By the tenth century the poetry has stepped right into the modern age with *The Flightiness of Thought*. Sophistication could scarcely go further:

Shame to my thoughts, how they stray from me.
I fear great danger from it on the day of eternal doom.

During the psalms they wander on a path that is not right:
They fash, they fret, they misbehave before the eyes of great God.
Through eager crowds, through companies of wanton women,
Through woods, through cities – swifter they are than the wind.
Now through paths of loveliness, anon of riotous shame.
Without ferry, or ever missing a step, they go across every sea:
Swiftly they leap in one bound from earth to heaven.
They run a race with folly anear and afar:
After a course of giddiness they return to their home.
Though one should try to bind them or put shackles on their feet,
They are neither constant nor mindful to take a spell of rest.
Neither sword-edge nor crack of whip will keep them down
  strongly:
As slippery as an eel's tail they glide out of my grasp . . .

It is difficult to remember that when this Irish poet was writing Alfred the Great had only just concluded his warfare with the Danes, and that less than a hundred years earlier the primitive adventures of Cú Chulainn were being written down.

It must not be supposed, however, that Old Irish poetry is all, or in fact mainly, concerned with nature or the world of the spirit, with the lives of monks and recluses. Much of it is occupied with the experiences of the common people, with everyday occurrences and objects, like the little poem on his sword by Colmán mac Lenine, who lived, it will be remembered, in the second half of the sixth century:

> As clowns to kings, as pennies to a pound,
> As kitchen wenches to princesses crowned,
> As kings to thee, to sweet songs catches roared,
> As dips to candles, all swords to my sword.

There is a touch of distinction about this little catch, and we remember that Colmán lived on in after ages as the type of a poet, and is quoted by Cormac mac Cuilennáin, king-bishop of Cashel, who was a poet himself, and also by the O'Dalys, the chief poetic family of medieval Ireland, who claim to have been his pupils. Here is the little roadside mound of Rathangan in Co. Kildare:

> The fort opposite the oak-wood –
> Once it was Bruidge's, it was Cathal's,
> It was Aed's, it was Ailill's,
> It was Conaing's, it was Cuilíne's,
> And it was Maeldúine's –
> The fort remains after each in his turn,
> And the kings asleep in the ground.

On the margin of an Irish manuscript now in the library of St Gall in Switzerland, the scribe wrote:

> Bitter is the wind tonight,
> It tosses the ocean's white hair:
> Tonight I fear not the fierce warriors from Norway
> Coursing on the Irish Sea.

And there are playful scraps too:

> When I am among my elders
> I am proof that sport is forbidden:
> When I am among the mad young folk
> They think that I am their junior.

I have discussed the poetry somewhat at length because, though the surviving portion is largely fragmentary and not great in bulk as compared with the prose, its texts are relatively old and contemporary with their composition, and give us a fair idea of the Irish mentality of the earliest period of writing. Irish prose is much more remarkable for its quantity, but the earliest written prose is largely traditional. It had a long life in oral tradition before being written down, and our manuscript versions are again largely much later still. So conservative is the tradition that it can be safely claimed that in Irish we have the oldest vernacular literature in western Europe. The earliest Irish manuscript, the Würzburg Codex, goes back to A.D. 700, although the *Amra Choluim Chille* is now believed to be a genuine sixth-century document; the rhythmical texts of the legal compilation known as the *Senchas Mór* may also belong to this early date. In this chapter, however, we shall concern ourselves only with the great prose narrative literature, the literature of the imagination. We shall exclude learned writing, law and hagiography.

This literature is preserved for the most part in great folio vellum manuscripts, of which the earliest was written at about the end of the eleventh century. Three are outstanding for their early date and the importance of the contents – the *Book of the Dun Cow* (*Lebor na h-Uidre, L.U.*), written at the beginning of the twelfth century; the *Book of Leinster* (*Lebor Laighneach, L.L.*), written before 1160; and the *Yellow Book of Lecan*, (*Y.B.L.*), a manuscript of the late fourteenth century. There is also Rawlinson B. 502 (*Rawl.*) which is in Oxford and contains twelve leaves of eleventh-century and seventy of twelfth-century date; but this manuscript contains no sagas. Most of our imaginative sagas, however, are preserved in these manuscripts, which also contain much other matter such as poetry, genealogies, and chronicle histories. In fact, they were great libraries which contained any material which the scribes wished specially to commemorate. *L.L.*, for example, contains a list of the sagas which a fully trained *filí* was expected to know. Poets of the twelfth century divided their tales into *prímscéla*, or 'main tales', and *fóscéla*, or secondary tales, and claimed to know three hundred and fifty tales, of which two hundred and fifty were main tales and a hundred subsidiary tales. Comparatively few of these tales have been preserved, but we have two lists of main tales – perhaps, as Gerard Murphy thinks, the repertoire of a tenth-century *filí* with some eleventh- and twelfth-century additions.

How, we may well ask, can these prose stories be so old since they were written down so late? This is due to the nature of the tradition. They were transmitted orally by the *filid*, at least till the middle of the seventh century, and then from the seventh till the ninth centuries by means of written manuscripts. The *filid* were the poets and the intellectuals, and a very ancient institution of which we hear first in ancient Gaul. They were responsible for the whole intellectual life of the people and for its transmission, first in rhythmical prose, later in prose and verse. Since all knowledge was transmitted in oral form the *filid* had to know and teach all acquired knowledge; and since at that time no clear distinction existed between history, as we understand it, and tradition, all narrative of the past was a part of their repertoire. Their training was long and strict, and consequently their conservatism was very great. The *filí* was trained to narrate 'the chief stories of Ireland's kings, lords and noblemen'. From an eighth-century text we learn that Mongán son of Fiachna, the east Ulster king of the early sixth century, was told a story by his *filí*, Forgall, every winter night from Samhain to Beltaine, that is to say, from the first of November to the first of May.

Turning from the poetry to the prose is like entering another world. The first thing that strikes us is a reversal of all our normal values, all our accustomed measurement of time and place, all our preconceived laws of probability, the complete ascendency of the imagination and fancy over the world of logic, and over our normal ideas of cause and effect, of the way things happen in this world. This is due to the extreme conservatism of the texts. When the sagas were written down Ireland had been Christian for many centuries, and though this did not banish the belief in magic or the traditions of the old heathen times, it shifted their emphasis. The gods were no longer all-powerful, only partially powerful. Gradually they took their places in the far past, as an ancient race, before the 'present Ireland'. But they moved about on the soil of Ireland, sometimes as a race apart, sometimes as in the strange story of the begetting of Mongán (cf. p. 281 below), having intercourse with normal human beings. The supernatural also was all-powerful. There was no spiritual opposition between the gods and the supernatural on the one hand, and the Christian Irish on the other. As we have seen (p. 170 above) the gods were not worshipped or served by sacrifice, but were simply to the story-telling *filid* a spirit-folk of the past, a human race, skilled in magic, who, at times, took a powerful part in human affairs, and who were once in possession of Ireland until they were defeated by the Goedil or Gaels. They were known as *aes side* (sing. *sid*, 'supernatural folk') or Tuatha Dé Danann ('the tribes of the goddess Danu', cf. p. 169 above).

These stories, and indeed most, if not all, old Irish sagas, are related in a form of mixed prose and verse; but the distinctive thing is that the narrative part is all in prose, the verse being restricted for the most part to speeches and commentary. Stories in which supernatural beings play the principal part we generally classify as mythological tales. Many of the chief actors are to be identified with the gods of the mythological cycles (cf. chapter 6 above). But the tales have lost all religious significance. They are related simply as tales.

The historical tradition taught that Ireland was infested by a race of giants, as well as by the Tuatha Dé Danann, before the coming of the Gael. The former, as we have seen, were known as Fomori and were enemies of the Tuatha Dé Danann, and they are represented as living on islands, at least latterly, and as coming in ships over the sea to claim tribute, especially slaves. Much of this tradition is recorded in the writings of native learning, such as the *Dinnsenchas*, or *History of Places*, in the *Cóir Anmann*, or *Fitness of Names*, and in the *Lebor Gabála*, or *Book of Invasions*. The chief saga of the mythological cycle, however, is the *Second Battle of Moytura*, which has been described already.

The *Dream of Óengus* is one of the best of the mythological tales, and is assigned to a date in the ninth or tenth century. This and the strange and beautiful tale of Étain, the wife of Manannán mac Lir, and of her rebirths, has also been already described (p. 174 above). We will therefore pass at once to the heroic tales which form the majority of the oldest stratum of stories, and which are believed to go back by a continuous oral tradition to the Irish heroic age, before the era of the Uí Néill; that is to say before the fifth century. Of these the oldest which has been preserved in anything approaching entirety is the famous *Táin Bó Cualnge*. Fragments of other heroic cycles have been preserved, notably the *Scéla Mucce Maic Da Thó* (*The Story of Mac Da Thó's Pig*), which is the most complete of the fragments surviving from a lost Leinster cycle, and which has reference to the same period and largely to the same heroes as the *Táin*. Another heroic story which has been well preserved is *Fled Bricrenn* (*Bricriu's Feast*), and yet another is the *Orgain Dinn Ríg*.

Táin Bó Cualnge is a story which relates to Ireland at the earliest period of her known history, when she was divided into the main political divisions known as *coiceda* (sing. *coiced*), 'Fifths', but it was before the development of the fifth state, and only four are recognized in the *Táin*. These, as we have seen (p. 84 above), consisted of Ulster, the whole of the north of Ireland from eastern Antrim to Donegal; Connaught in the west; Munster in the south; and Leinster in the east. Sir William Ridgeway was one of the first to recognize the relationship of the *Táin* to history, and in particular to relate its material culture with that of the La Tène period; but in attributing this to the time of Christ, or the first century, he failed to recognize the length of time that this early culture remained undisturbed in Ireland, and accordingly he is thought to have placed the *Táin* several centuries too early. Professor Kenneth Jackson has recently placed it in the fourth century A.D. Even so, much of the contents – the fighting in chariots for example – is remarkably conservative, and the *Táin* may be said to be the only European literature which gives us a picture of life in the Iron Age. The action of the story takes place in the period in which the Ulaid were predominant in Ulster and had their capital at Emain Macha, now Navan Fort, two miles from the modern Armagh; it must therefore be placed before the fifth century A.D., which is the date of the destruction of Emain Macha by the Tara dynasty.

The *Táin* is a very long saga. It has been preserved for us in a series of episodes by the *filid*, but by the time it was written down, perhaps as early as the seventh century, it had come to be represented as a continuous narrative. Even so, we can see from the various remains preserved in *L.U.*, *L.L.* and *Y.B.L.* that many versions were extant, and something of their early date can be deduced from the language. The earliest manuscript is *L.U.*, which dates from about 1100, but that has been interpolated by a later hand. In the middle of the twelfth century a writer composed a new text from the mangled version of *L.U.*, and his work is preserved in the *Book of Leinster* (*L.L.*). The Irish, who liked to have a concrete and picturesque account of the unknown, have pictured for us the discovery of the *Táin* by telling the story of its recital by Fergus mac Roich, who had taken an important part in it, and who is presented to us as rising from the dead and relating the whole narrative to the poet Senchán Torpéist (d. 659).

The *Táin*, like the heroic literature of other countries, is aristocratic in outlook, but is unique in offering its stories in a more primitive form, and has preserved something of the warrior spirit which would otherwise have been lost to Europe. Its standards of conduct are loyalty, prowess, boasting and the fulfilment of the boast. Although the supernatural plays a very distinct part, the heroes are essentially human. War is the universal profession of the men, and policy and politics are non-existent. This is an essentially individualistic society. Success in warfare is the principal standard recognized, and success or failure depends entirely on the skill or the courage of the heroes, not as a body, but as individuals, sometimes aided by magic or more frequently by other supernatural means. Details of court life, of palaces and their splendour, fine clothes, weapons and the impressive appearance of the heroes or their wives, are ever-present features which help to build up the aristocratic atmosphere in which the story moves.

The ruling king in the cycle is Conchobar mac Nessa of the House of the Red Branch at Emain Macha in Ulster, and the fighting mainly takes place on the Meath and Ulster border. The chief hero of the men of Ulster is Cú Chulainn, the son of a certain Sualtaim (or better Sualatach) according to a late tradition, or according to another a reincarnation of the god Lugh of the Long Arm. His home is in Dun Delgan (modern Dundalk), and the central part of the story tells how he holds back an army of invaders from Connaught while awaiting the arrival of Conchobar and his main army from Ulster. The Connaught army is ruled by Maeve, the wife and consort of Ailill, and the main plot of the story is that she is invading the territory of Conchobar in order to carry off a fine bull from the cantred of Cualnge which had once belonged to her, and which she covets, but which Conchobar is unwilling to relinquish to her, or even to lend to her for a year. Accordingly, she decides to take it by force and invades Ulster for the purpose. Her army is placed under the command of Fergus mac Roich, a great champion and formerly the king of Ulster, who has left and gone over to the court of Maeve because Conchobar has violated his safe-conduct for the sons of Uisneach (see below, p. 273). From this we learn that the *Táin* is not the earliest of the heroic stories, but has been preceded by *The Fate of the Children of Uisneach*.

The Ulster army is unable to go to fight on account of the strange illness or *cess*, to which they are subject, which is unidentified, but which resembles a strange form of *couvade*. The youthful Cú Chulainn and Sualtaim are exempt from this, and set out to oppose the men of Connaught. This is not the only indication that we have that Cú Chulainn was not by origin a man of Ulster. He was, in fact, foster-son both to Conchobar, king of Ulster, and also to Fergus himself. The Connaught army advance to the plains of Bregia and Muirtheimne and so into Cualnge, and reach the river Glain Cruind, but it rises against them, and they cannot cross. Cú Chulainn comes to the ford, and a large part of the narrative is occupied with the combats at the ford undertaken by Cú Chulainn, in which he is represented as performing feats of incredible valour. Finally, Maeve turns northwards to Dunseverick, and ultimately the brown bull of Cualnge is driven off, greatly to Cú Chulainn's confusion and dismay.

At this point the god Lugh comes to Cú Chulainn's help by putting him to sleep for three days and healing his wounds, while the heroes of Ulster fight in his place. When he awakes he takes vengeance for the harm suffered by the heroes of Ulster in a kind of warrior's frenzy, described at great length, in which he is said to have killed 130 kings in the great slaughter of the Plain of Muirtheimne, till at last Maeve calls upon Fer Diad, Cú Chulainn's foster-brother, to oppose him. This is the grand climax, for Fer Diad greatly laments this misfortune, but he has no honourable alternative but to consent. Despite Fergus's warning to Cú Chulainn, and despite Fer Diad's warning from his charioteer, they fight for three days, and neither has any advantage over the other. Here we have a typical touch of heroic age courtesy in that each night Cú Chulainn sends leeches and herbs to heal the wounds of Fer Diad, and Fer Diad sends Cú Chulainn a share of his food. Nevertheless on the fourth day Cú Chulainn calls for his mysterious weapon the *gae bolga*, which has been given him by Scáthach, his trainer in military arts, and which has never failed him; and at last Fer Diad is slain. Meanwhile the Ulster men, having recovered from their *cess*, march against the men of Connaught; but in the end it is Cú Chulainn who defeats the last of the Connaught men. Maeve has sent the brown bull of Cualnge to Cruachain, and he fights the white-horned bull all night, but in the morning he gallops back to Ulster with the white-horned bull on his back, and when he comes to the border of Cualnge his heart breaks and he dies.

Such is the main outline of this famous prose epic. The Old Irish version is comparatively simple and straightforward. The Middle Irish version from *L.L.* is thought to have been written *c.* 1100, and compiled in *L.L. c.* 1160. It is clear, however, that both versions are ultimately based on a compilation of notes, which from time to time has been increased by the addition of episodes, poems in various metres, sometimes given in variants, sometimes even in contradictory forms. Yet despite incredible exaggeration, despite the altogether impossible feats attributed to Cú Chulainn, which form a large part of the narrative, and the supernatural elements which take their place in the narrative from time to time, and despite the numerous episodes, all of which serve to lengthen the story, the narrative on the whole is surprisingly consistent. This consistency is, of course, due to the astonishingly conservative character of Irish oral tradition.

Another heroic story is *Fled Bricrenn* (*Bricriu's Feast*), which is preserved in *L.U.*, and dates from about the eighth century. It relates to a feud set on foot by Bricriu Nemthenga ('Poison tongue'), who has made a great feast to which he invites Conchobar and the men of Ulster. The mischief is begun by his inviting Laegaire Buadach, Conall Cernach and Cú Chulainn, each of whom claims the *curad-mír* ('the champion's portion'), that is to say the best cut of the meat at the forthcoming feast. The motif is that described by Posidonius as habitually taking place among the Gauls at their feasts. Bricriu then meets the wives of the heroes, and tells them that one of them should have precedence among all the women of Ulster forever, and the right to enter the banquet hall of Tara; whichever should go first into the banquet hall that night. Naturally, an unseemly contest follows and eventually it is decided to take the decision to Connaught, where Maeve decides in favour of Cú Chulainn and his wife Emer; but the other two champions declare that he has bribed Maeve to give this verdict, and the Ulster men decide to take the matter to Cúroi mac Dáiri of Munster, who makes the same award to Cú Chulainn, and to his wife, Emer, over the women of Ulster. Laegaire and Conall, however, deny that Cúroi has made the award to Cú Chulainn till Cúroi comes to them in the form of a giant, and imposes his verdict by a well-known beheading test. This introduces an episode well known as a folk-tale motif.

Scéla Mucce Maic Da Thó (*The Story of Mac Da Thó's Pig*) is another story like *Bricriu's Feast* which turns on the *curad-mír*, the 'champion's portion'. This is, in fact, probably the most anciently attested of all Celtic stories, and *Scéla Mucce* is a less sophisticated version of it than *Bricriu's Feast*. *Scéla Mucce* was probably composed in its present form in about 800, and except for the touch of humour it is a pure heroic story, a story about men, for men. It gives a typical picture of heroes at a feast, exactly as they are described by Athenaeus, who derived his information from Posidonius. Their cauldrons and big joints of meat are exactly such as are described by Diodorus Siculus: 'When they dine ... they have hearths with big fires and cauldrons, and spits loaded with big joints of meat... and some of the company often fall into an altercation and challenge one another to single combat – they make nothing of death.' It was probably composed by a Leinsterman, and though the contest for the champion's portion lies between the royal warriors of Ulster and Connaught through their respective heroes Conall Cernach and Cettmac Mágach, one feels that the sympathies of the story-teller really lie with Leinster. Hints, both here and in other stories, give us to understand that the story belongs to a wide circle of Leinster narratives, and that Leinster had its own cycle of heroic stories. Its heroes are identical with those of the Ulster cycle, and its heroic tradition is attached to Conchobar and the Red Branch; but there is no mention of Cú Chulainn, and the story seems to have taken shape before he had acquired prominence in the Ulster cycle.

Another fine story which is attributed to the ninth century is *Togail Bruidne Da-Derga* (*The Destruction of Da-Derga's Hostel*), but here the atmosphere is different. The story opens with a description (cf. p. 175 above) of the finding of Étain, the future wife of Eochaid Airem, from whom the hero of the tale, King Conaire, was believed to be descended. Étain is found sitting beside a well washing her hair:

> She wore a purple cloak of good fleece, held with silver brooches chased with gold, and a smock of green silk with gold embroidery. The sun shone upon her, so that the men saw the gold gleaming in the sunshine against the green silk. . . . She was undoing her hair to wash it, so that her arms were out from beneath her dress. White as the snow of the night were her hands, and her lovely cheeks were soft and even, red as the mountain foxglove.

The men of King Eochaid come upon her thus and report to the king who forthwith marries her. Then Eochaid dies, and the story passes on to tell of Conaire, a man of magic birth, born of a bird, who becomes king of Tara. But he is fated never to kill birds (i.e. he has a *geis*, or magic prohibition) and in his violation of this and many other prohibitions, one after another, he finally perishes. Although there is fighting in plenty the story really turns on magic. It is not a simple heroic story.

The Irish story-tellers grouped a number of stories loosely connected with the *Táin* under the title *remscéla* ('fore-tales'), but this is merely a matter of convenience because their substance was loosely connected with the Ulster Cycle under Conchobar mac Nessa. They are not all by any means what we should call heroic stories strictly speaking. For example, *Aislinge Óengus* (*The Dream of Óengus*) is a purely mythical tale (cf. p. 173 above). Another of them, the *Longas mac n-Usnig* (*The Fate of the Children of Uisneach*), is a love-story, the earliest in Irish literature, dating from probably the ninth century and preserved in *L.L.* and *Y.B.L.*, and it is one of the finest of the old Irish tales. It relates to the birth of a girl, Deirdre, whom Conchobar has nurtured in strict seclusion, destining her to be his bride; but she falls in love with Naisi, one of Conchobar's warriors, and escapes with him and his two brothers to Scotland. Fergus gives them his word that if they will return to Ireland Conchobar will not harm them, but on their return Naisi and all his party are killed and Deirdre is given to Conchobar, and, in consequence, Fergus retires to Connaught to the court of Ailill and Maeve. (That is why he is found leading their army against Ulster in the *Táin.*) Deirdre, however, is quite irreconcilable and dashes her head against a stone and so perishes. It will be seen that the story takes place before the *Táin*, and it contains some very ancient elements. There are some beautiful poems in the story, Deirdre's *Farewell to Alba* being one of the best of all Old Irish poems.

The astonishing richness and variety of Irish tales makes it difficult to assign them to categories. We have seen that early Irish stories exist which are purely heroic in character and which centre on an individual and his prowess, and in which the interest is primarily personal. There is another class of stories, much more extensive, and relating to princely families, in which the interest is more general and depicts rather the community and their primitive 'national' outlook. Perhaps *Cath Almain* (*The Battle of Allen*), fought in the year 718, should be classed here, since it is concerned primarily with the struggle between Leinster and Munster, but it is narrated with all the characteristics of a heroic story. Such stories relate mostly to the kings of the various provinces and their families, their battles and their history. The class of the community responsible for the transmission of these tales was, of course, the *filid*, and as these stories still have their origin in oral literature, and were intended for recitation, they have retained all its characteristics, including many of the characteristics of heroic literature from which they are not always clearly distinguished, and with which they coalesce from time to time. We notice their preoccupation with the particular rather than with the general, with individuals and their prowess and their fate rather than with wider questions and their individual tendency to depict a scene, a given situation, a dramatic episode. Being intended for recitation rather than for reading, they do not arouse reflection, but aim at impressing the imagination. Indeed it is by their loyalty to this tradition that the *filid* retained their prestige until the age of writing and well beyond.

These stories are roughly classed together into a cycle of 'King Stories' for the sake of convenience. A number of them are indeed referred to in the accounts of tribal and dynastic origins inserted into the historical tract known today as 'The Land Genealogies and Tribal Histories' and are among the earliest specimens of the 'Kings Cycle' that we possess. Their archaic language suggests that they may date from the ninth century, which in itself again suggests their originally oral character. Many of these are mere references or short anecdotes, but we can see that longer stories lie behind them, and in many cases we possess also much longer verions. It was indeed one of the responsibilities of the *filid* to know the records of the early history of Ireland, and to recite them at assemblies and royal banquets.

With these 'King Stories' is connected a number of stories of traditions of the seventh and eighth centuries. King Mongán mac Fiachna is sometimes included, with others connected with the Battle of Mag Rath (Moyra) which was fought in 637, and the Hebridean Cano mac Gartnait (d. 688). Stories from Connaught are represented by Guaire (d. 662), and from Munster by Eógan Mór, son of Ailill Aulomm, king of Munster, the brother of Mac Con, who had won the kingship of Tara by slaying Art, king of Tara, at the Battle of Mag Mucrime in Connaught. Con's son was Cormac mac Art, who was brought up in hiding by his true father's foster-father, Fiachna, till at the age of thirty years he succeeded to the throne of Tara. He is himself the hero of a whole cycle of King Stories, of which we have already narrated his journey, like that of his uncle Conn Cétchathach, to the Land of Promise. Indeed, although history is present in the background of all the 'King Stories', romance, mythology, and magic are also constantly present.

The most impressive of these stories of the kings, if indeed it can be classed among them, is *Buile Suibhne* (*The Intoxication of Sweeny*). This is one of three stories which centre on the Battle of Mag Rath (Moyra) fought in 637 between Domnall, son of Aed, king of Tara, and Domnall Brecc, king of Dálriata (cf. p. 88 above). In its present form the story belongs to the twelfth century, but it was known much earlier. In the preface to an old law tract it is stated that one of the virtues of this battle was that as a result Sweeny, something of a philosopher, mystic and poet, became *geilt* (i.e. mad or crazy), 'but the virtue is not in Sweeny's becoming *geilt*, but in all the stories and poems that he left after him in Ireland'; and indeed some of the most beautiful Irish nature poems are contained in this saga. Sweeny's is a strange story, but although unique in Irish it has points of contact with both Welsh and Norse oral literature, as we shall see.

Sweeny, son of Colman, was originally the king of Dal n' Araide on Lough Neagh, and he is shown to us at first as a vigorous ruler and a great warrior. One day he finds St Ronan, psalter in hand, marking out the boundaries of a church, and he angrily flings the psalter into the lake before going off in answer to a royal summons to the Battle of Moyra. Ronan curses him, but an otter from the lake returns his psalter to him. Meanwhile, Sweeny, during the ensuing battle, looks up to the skies and a sensation of horror comes upon him, and a longing to leave the scene and seek a new home. We are reminded of the spiritual voice heard by Merlin in battle, according to Strathclyde tradition. From this time onward Sweeny's life is that of a restless and solitary fugitive, without home or land. He seeks solitude above all things, fearing that he will be taken and forced to live among his fellows. He lives largely in the tree-tops like a bird. But his exile from both his kingdom and his home is voluntary. His poems are full of lamentations over the hardness of his lot in being restricted to a vegetable diet; but he is represented as very swift in all his movements, and he could easily have overtaken animals and birds, had he wished to do so. His is, in fact, a voluntary mortification of the flesh. Yet he does not wholly eschew human society, and he is represented as a friend of St Moling and the anchorites and also as a great poet.

On one of his journeys he comes to Britain, which may account for the name *Albannach* assigned to him in one of Moling's poems. Here he meets another *geilt*, and the two spend a year together in great seclusion. In Ireland he becomes an intimate friend of St Moling whom he often visits, and in whose vicinity he makes his chief stay. Finally, he meets his death, wounded by one of Moling's servants, but he manages to make his way to Moling's church and is buried by the saint in consecrated ground, and we are specially told that he is lamented by Moling's little community. The saint has celebrated his friendship for Sweeny in several of his own poems. The *filí* has given full rein to his humour, and this elaborate story of Sweeny is virtually a satire on the early religious communities whom the medieval writer did not understand and with whom he has little sympathy, though he has remembered the tradition and reproduced it faithfully enough, in the spirit of the writer of the *Aislinge meic Con Glinne* (cf. p. 283 below).

To the Irishman and the western Highlander of today by far the best known cycle of stories is that which centres in Finn mac Cumaill. This cycle, however, became famous only about the eleventh century. It is medieval, and the stories of Finn have undergone a transformation in accordance with medieval taste. They are mostly preserved not in prose, like the stories just considered, but in poetry. They constitute the famous cycle of Finn 'ballads', and it is for this reason that we have postponed discussion till late in the present chapter. Most of the ballads about Finn and his fellows, his *fianna* or 'war-band', are traditionally attributed to Finn and his son Oisín. The *fianna* were originally bands of professional warriors attached to local chieftains, but the most famous of them was Finn's, and it has come to be known as Finn's *fianna*, and the cycle of his poems have adopted the name *Fianaigeacht*.

Finn, however, has a long history. From the eleventh century he has been regarded as captain of King Cormac's professional soldiery in the early third century of our era, but early references represent him as a being gifted with supernatural powers. Thus, in an eighth- or ninth-century version of an early legend we have a story of how he came by his supernatural wisdom. It relates that in pursuing one Culdub into a *sidh* (supernatural mound) he trapped his finger in the door, and when he sucked it he found that he had acquired supernatural knowledge. By the tenth century, however, he was already associated with the king of Tara. We have mention of two lists of Finn tales which a *filí* was expected to be able to tell, namely *Tochmarc Ailbe* (*The Wooing of Ailbe*) and *Aithed Gráinne le Dearmait* (*The Elopement of Grania with Dermot*). The scarcity of references to Finn in tales of the twelfth-century list suggests that in the first half of the twelfth century the *Fianaigeacht* was not yet important. It is not to be supposed, however, that Finn was unknown till this date – only that he was not a well-known and popular figure.

In a 'rhetoric' which is ascribed to Senchán Torpéist, Finn is already mentioned in the seventh century, and Kuno Meyer assigns three extant stories – one in prose and two in ballad form – to the late eighth or early ninth centuries, while assigning *Finn and Culdub* in prose, and four other prose stories and two or three poetical references and quotations, to the tenth century. By the end of the twelfth century – a great period of story-telling – Finn and his *fianna* have become well-known. But their literature, as we have said, is in the form of ballads, and as Irish ballads, unlike those of the rest of Europe, are hardly ever related in the third person, the influence of the speech poems, which are commonly inserted into Irish prose sagas, may perhaps be assumed.

The Finn cycle differs considerably from the Ulster cycle. Its heroes are less exalted; not princes of provinces, but their dependants. It is romantic rather than epic, and its stories relate to small groups and are not deployed on the grand scale of the epic narratives. They are concerned more with hunting and fishing, with life in the woodland and the open air rather than that of the court. But the chief difference which we note between the two cycles is local. The Finn cycle takes place mainly in Leinster and Munster, not as in the earlier cycles in Ulster and Connaught. Thus this cycle represents southern and eastern traditions, and Myles Dillon* is doubtless right in attributing its spread to the rise of the Dalcassian clan of Munster, and its association with the growth of the kingdom of Leinster, with the decline of the ancient dynasty of the Uí Néill and the rise to prominence of Brian Boru in 1002.

Of the many stories which go to make this cycle the most popular is the *Tóraigheacht Dhiarmada agus Ghráinne* (*The Pursuit of Dermot and Grania*). The only complete narrative is not older than the fourteenth century, and may indeed not be even so old; but a version must have existed earlier because we have a variant version from *Y.B.L.*, which Meyer thought might be as early as the ninth century. The story is mentioned in both the early lists of tales which a *filí* of the twelfth century should know, together with *The Wooing of Ailbe* (cf. p. 277 above), and from a remark in the latter we know that the *Aithed Gráinné le Dearmait* (*The Elopement of Grania with Dermot*) was known already to the *filid*. There is a text in the tenth century called *Uath Beinne Étair* (*The Cave of Ben Etar*) which refers to an episode in their flight from Finn's vengeance. A reference of the tenth century in a gloss to the *Amra Choluim Chille* shows that the story was already an old one.

The story itself is a very simple one. Finn, having lost his wife, and hearing of the beauty of Grania, the daughter of Cormac mac Airt, asks him for her hand in marriage. It is granted, but when at the wedding feast Grania sees her bridegroom and realizes his age she says that his son, Oisín, would be

**Early Irish Literature*, p. 34.

a more suitable match for her, and she puts a drug in the wine which plunges most of the guests into a deep sleep. She then offers herself alternatively to Oisín and to Dermot Ua Duibhne. Both refuse, for they fear Finn, but she lays *gesa* on Dermot to take her from the hall before Finn and the kings of Ireland awaken from their sleep. Then Dermot sets out with Grania westwards from Tara to Athlone and across the Shannon until they come to a forest where Dermot has a house. The rest of the story is occupied with the pursuit by Finn, and the efforts of Dermot's friends to aid his escape, in which Aengus mac Óc takes part, for he is Dermot's divine foster-father. He eventually patches up a peace so that Dermot and Grania are able to live together, and Grania bears four sons to Dermot; but in the end Finn brings about his death. The similarity of the story of Deirdre is obvious, and the two stories have been represented as the original of the Celtic story of Tristan and Iseult.

The cycle had been Christianized, and the longest of all the stories is the *Acallam na Senórach* (*The Colloquy of the Old Men*) composed in the last quarter of the twelfth century. The story relates the meeting of the survivors of the *fianna* with St Patrick, and as they wander over Ireland together Caílte tells St Patrick the legends of the woods and hills and lakes in the manner of a *Dinnsenchas*. The poem is a great store-house of early stories, chiefly of Finn and the *fianna*, but there are also stories of kings and warriors and saints, and even of the ancient gods. We are told that Finn foretells the coming of Patrick, that Caílte is baptized, and that Heaven is promised for Caílte and for Finn and for the other warriors whom he praises. This does not prevent a complete entente between the Tuatha Dé Danann and the *fianna*, as well as St Patrick himself, the saint's hesitation being allayed by his two guardian angels who assure him that God commands him to write down the tales because it will be 'a pastime to the nobles and companies of the latter time to give ear to these stories'.

It is a part of the rich heritage of Irish literature that when it adopted fresh ideas and motifs from the outside world it did not abandon its former ways of thought, but modified and adapted them to suit the new, thus creating a fresh and unique genre. We have from the medieval period an extensive series of stories relating to the Other World. These, like the Finn 'ballads', consist of the ancient heathen lore, often combined, fantastically enough, with Christian legends, borrowed more or less directly from the Apocryphal and Christian legends of the East. The majority of them lie outside the period covered by this book, but the early ones had their beginnings in the Old Irish period, and something must be said here of this class of literature, especially as the earliest stories are, in general, the simplest and most beautiful. They consist of *echtrai* (supernatural 'adventure' stories) in which the hero visits the Other World, the 'Land of the Living', the 'Land of the Young' (Tír na n-Óc); of the *echtrai* or *imrama*, in which the interest is concentrated on the journey thither; and of the *Fís* ('Vision') of Heaven and Hell.

We have seen that the earliest of these stories relating to Conn Cétchathach was already known probably in the eighth century (cf. p. 274 above), and relates to the journey of the prehistoric 'high king' of Tara to the supernatural home of the god Lugh; and we have noted the close association of this dynasty with other journeys to this supernatural region. But the journey is not confined to the east of Ireland. The most famous of these *echtrai* is that of Bran, son of Febal, into the ocean from somewhere in the west, probably Kerry. It was probably written down originally in the seventh century.

The story relates that one day as Bran is walking alone near his dwelling he hears delightful music which lulls him to sleep, and when he awakens he finds beside him a branch with white flowers which he brings into the house, and there stands before him a woman who sings to him a long poem describing all the delights of the Other World. Then she vanishes, taking the branch with her. Next day Bran sets out over the sea with twenty-seven companions, and after two days and nights he sees a man driving in a chariot towards him over the sea. This is Manannán mac Lir who sings him a song coloured by features of the Other World. For example, he makes Bran see the sea as a flowery plain, the fish as calves and frisking lambs, and his boat as floating over an orchard of fruit trees. He tells Bran that he is on his way to beget Mongán the 'son' of Fiachna, famous among heroes, but short-lived; and he dispatches Bran to the island of women hard by. Bran eventually reaches the island of women where he is sumptuously entertained; but home-sickness seizes one of Bran's companions and they sail home to Ireland. The people on shore ask them who they are, and when Bran tells them they reply: 'We do not know such a one, though *The Voyage of Bran* is in our ancient stories (*senchas*),' and the first of the company who springs ashore on to the earth of Ireland 'became a heap of ashes as though he had been in the earth for many hundreds of years. Thereupon Bran wrote all these quatrains in *ogam*, and from that time his wanderings are not known.'

We have seen in the cycle relating to the dynasty of Conn at Tara that the voyage or the journey to the Other World is not described prominently, but only suggested, while the Other World is described in some detail. In *The Voyage of Bran* the voyage itself is given prominence, and indeed contains some of our most enchanting Irish poetry. In the second class of these supernatural adventures the *imrama* ('journey', 'voyage') is developed as the main theme, and occupies seven of the stories mentioned in the two lists of sagas already referred to. Of these the *Immram Curaig Maíle Dúin* (*The Voyage of Mael Dúin's Boat*) is the oldest and the most interesting as having immediately inspired the *Navigatio Brendani* (*The Voyage of Brendan*), so influential throughout the Middle Ages. The extant story of Mael Dúin dates from the tenth century, but is copied from an earlier original, probably of the eighth century. The setting of the text is of uncertain date, but certainly Christian, as Mael

Dúin's mother was a nun. His father is said to have come from the Aran Islands, but to have been murdered, and the voyage is ostensibly undertaken to discover the murderer; but it is in reality a long series of visits to the islands in the ocean, which are represented as wholly fantastic. Finally the voyagers are told by a hermit that they will find the slayer of Mael Dúin's father, but that they must spare him for the sake of the many dangers from which God has spared them. By following the flight of an Irish falcon they at length reach the island from which they had set out.

The second saga in the Leinster list is the *Immram Curaig Ua Corra* (*The Voyage of the O'Corra's Boat*) of uncertain date, possibly of the eleventh century. The *Immram Snédgusa ocus Maic Riagla* (*The Voyage of Snédgus and Mac Riagl*) is preserved in the original version in verse and is the narrative of the pilgrimage of two monks of Iona. The date is perhaps tenth-century for it refers to the Norse depredations. The episodes in these two stories, and the Christian allusions in these and other pieces, have led to the suggestion that the entire genre owed its beginnings to the pilgrimages and early island settlements.

Finally, it must be mentioned that out of this pilgrimage and voyage literature arose the *Fís* ('vision') literature which was largely influenced by Christian and Jewish texts, adapting their visions to one or other of the Irish saints. Examples are the *Vision of Tundale* and *St Patrick's Purgatory* (the *Purgatorium Patricii*). The earliest Irish vision tale is the Latin *Vision of Fursa*, which is incorporated in the *Vita Fursi* and was known to Bede who gives a summary of it. The earliest of the *fís* stories composed in Irish is the *Fís Adamnáin* (*The Vision of Adamnán*) dating in its present form from about the tenth century. The vision literature has obviously been influenced by the pagan tradition about the Other World. In the *Fís Adamnáin*, which was, of course, composed in much later times than those of the author of the *Life of Columba*, the soul of Adamnán leaves his body and is brought by its guardian angel first to Heaven, and afterwards to Hell, and finally beyond the Land of Torment where only demons dwell. Then Adamnán is brought back to the land of the saints, and bidden return to the body and tell in the assemblies of laity and clergy the rewards of Heaven and the pains of Hell.

Satire is too sophisticated a form of literature to have been developed in the early Irish period, but in spite of its late date we cannot close this section on literature without a reference to the *Aislinge meic Con Glinne* (*The Vision of Mac Con Glinne*), composed in its present form in the twelfth century, but thought to have been perhaps constructed on an earlier original. The saga is an extraordinarily brilliant skit on the clergy and the Church, full of malice, but so consistently funny as to disarm criticism. It opens with a great desire that comes upon the scholar Ainiér Mac Con Glinne as he is reading quietly at Roscommon to give up learning for poetry, for he is famous already for satire and eulogy. He hears that Cathal, king of Munster, is possessed by a demon of gluttony, so he sets out for Cork with his books in a satchel on his back, in the hope of good food, which he dearly loves. At the monastery of Cork, however, he is received in the most scurvy fashion, and when he satirizes his meagre fare his treatment becomes even worse. He is condemned to be crucified for the honour of the abbot Manchín, of St Finnbarr of Cork, and of the Church.

As he is stripped and tied to a pillar on the night preceding his execution an angel appears and reveals to him a vision which he relates to the monks of Cork on the following morning. It opens with the rhymed genealogy of Manchín in terms of food, and in the vision which follows he describes the voyage which he takes in a boat of lard on a lake of new milk, till he reaches a fort:

> The fort he reached was fair, with earthworks of thick custard beyond the lake. Its bridge was of butter, its wall of wheat, the palisade was of bacon.... Smooth pillars of old cheese, beams of juicy bacon in due order, fine rafters of thick cream, with laths of curds.

When Mac Con Glinne has ended his recital Manchín announces that his vision will cure the king of his disease, and that he must go to him at once. The recital before King Cathal is described with rippling humour till at length the demon of gluttony darts from his mouth, seizes one of the morsels, and hides under the cooking pot which promptly turns over and catches him; but the demon escapes and Mac Con Glinne forces him to do reverence, and makes the sign of the Cross against him with his gospel-book, and the demon flies into the air to join the hosts of Hell. The story ends with a testimony to the virtue of the angel's vision revealed to Mac Con Glinne, so the Church is duly propitiated and we feel that all is well, especially as there is a final statement of the reward due to whoever shall recite the story.

Strictly speaking we have no early British literature for the same period as that covered by the Irish literature. We have no early secular literature at all for the Cornish peninsula, or for Strathclyde, though secular themes play a subordinate, indeed a fairly prominent part in the *Lives* of the saints. In Wales, however, as in Ireland, oral tradition was highly developed, the poets being professionalized, and handing down the ancient Celtic themes for many centuries. It is however only natural that their material should have greatly changed during the course of transmission. We have relatively few themes which are recognizably Irish in origin, such as the 'Iron House'. Nevertheless, though changed, the Welsh themes are recognizably Celtic. They are not identical with the Irish, but they resemble the Irish more than any other foreign literature. They belong to the same family, and to the same old Celtic world. Neither English nor French have succeeded in changing the pattern fundamentally, however much they may have imposed themselves in details. Moreover the Welsh stories are relatively untouched by the passage of time. They are not in essence medieval.

Welsh literature, like Irish, was carried on in its earliest beginnings wholly by oral tradition, but has been preserved in its present form to a later period than Irish. On the internal evidence of metre and language a few poems are thought to be as old as the Irish, yet in general they are mostly preserved in a much later form, and only a very practised Welsh scholar can detect by close scrutiny of the text the early Welsh language which is at times incorporated in the text, revealing the early original on which it was based. Thus out of fifty-eight poems contained in the manuscript claiming to be the work of the sixth-century poet Taliesin nearly all are believed to have been composed at about 900 or 930, and not more than a dozen can be shown on textual and linguistic grounds to be of sixth-century date, or a little earlier, and therefore to represent virtually the work of Taliesin himself. On the other hand the *Gododdin*, which claims to be the work of Aneirin, has been preserved in written form from an earlier date, as a careful analysis of the manuscript shows. Aneirin is believed to have lived in the sixth century and the poem was first written down some 250 years later. The poems attributed to Llywarch Hen, another sixth-century poet, belong, not to his own day, but to a background of 850–900 or even later. They are a re-creation, a dramatic attempt at a reconstruction.

While early Welsh poetry, like Irish poetry, belongs to the world of oral tradition, we have no specimens of early texts as we have in the case of Irish, to guide us as to what the originals were like. We have however three stanzas preserved on the upper margin of the Juvencus manuscript of the metrical version of the Gospels, which are now in the University Library at Cambridge, and which were written down as early as the first half of the ninth century. Our oldest manuscript written wholly in Welsh, however – if indeed it is a single manuscript – is the *Black Book of Carmarthen* of the late twelfth century. Our other early poetical manuscripts are the *Book of Taliesin*, written *c.* 1275, the *White Book of Rhydderch*, *c.* 1325, the *Red Book of*

Hergest, *c.* 1400, and the small manuscript called the *Book of Aneirin*, *c.* 1250. As this poem existed in a written form 400 years earlier than the manuscript (see above), the core of the work may be claimed to be almost the authentic works of Aneirin, *c.* 600.

Early Welsh poetry, again like Irish, has no narrative subjects. Its favourite themes are panegyric and to a certain extent elegiac, and the panegyric poems may be regarded as a kind of official publication, for each chieftain employed a household bard whose duty it was to laud him in panegyric poetry at the feast in the evening. Narrative is present only by implications or allusions. The poet speaks not as one who narrates events of the past but as one who has been present at the events to which he alludes, or is speaking only shortly afterwards and who is himself keenly aware of all that is spoken about. The earliest poetry which has survived relates to the Men of the North, the ancient Britons, especially those between the two Walls, and we can take it back almost to the time when the Britons took over the rule of the land from the Romans. We have only allusions to Urien of Rheged, who flourished at the end of the sixth century, but Urien was a patron of Taliesin, several of whose poems are in praise of Urien himself and of his son Owain. Urien's name is mentioned by Nennius side by side with that of Aneirin as a contemporary, and twelve of Taliesin's poems deal with late sixth-century persons and events, praising Urien and the rulers of the western border.

The poet Llywarch Hen also belonged to the sixth century. He was the cousin of Urien of Rheged, who was, in fact, his patron, and he also belonged to the south-western border. But we do not possess Llywarch's poems of this period, and he was not among the poets referred to by Nennius. It was the opinion of Sir Ifor Williams, and it is now generally accepted, that the so-called poems of Llywarch are a dramatic feat, composed long afterwards in Powys, but passing under his name. Edwin is generally held to have cut off the Men of the North from the

Welsh of Wales by the Battle of Chester in about 616 and Llywarch is not himself the author of these poems, but the projected, the imaginary, speaker of them. They date, in fact, from the wars between England and Wales at about 850 on the Welsh border, especially around Shrewsbury.

Welsh prose was written down at a comparatively early period, like Irish prose, but before the time of the Laws of Hywel Dda few specimens of it have survived, and even the Laws are found at the earliest in a manuscript of about 1200, which no one now believes to represent them in their original form. We have in fact one short piece of prose which actually dates from the tenth century: the Computus Fragment preserved now in the Cambridge University Library. When these prose fragments were composed the authors were quite capable of expressing what we may call the 'literature of learning' in clear and forcible language; but this would seem to be characteristic of the prose in use for intellectual matters everywhere throughout the Middle Ages. Its more immediate origin in Wales is unknown.

There was however another somewhat different class of prose which seems to have developed more directly from the oral style of the *cyfarwyddiaid* or prose story-tellers. These appear to be a class of professional narrators who, like the bards, specialized in the traditional prose tales and the lore which they contain, and to represent more exactly the ancient Celtic tradition. They are not mentioned as frequently as the bards, doubtless because their literature for the most part died out before the literature of the Normans and continental styles which they introduced, whereas the bards continued for long as honoured officials in the houses of the Welsh nobility. But they still existed as a living tradition, for in the Mabinogi of *Math* we are told how Gwydion and his brother Gilvaethwy arrived at the court of Pryderi: 'As for Gwydion, he was the best story-teller in the world. And that night he entertained the court with pleasant talk and the telling of tales, so that he was dear to everyone that was in the court.'

As Gwydion and his brother had come to the court of Pryderi in the guise of bards the passage suggests that the *cyfarwyddiaid* were a class of bards, and that the bards were prose story-tellers as well as panegyric poets. If this is so they resembled the Irish *filid* in this also. The repertoire of the *cyfarwyddiaid* is represented for us today in a very small store, quite unlike the Irish wealth of prose tradition. Moreover it is much later than the Irish, being preserved in manuscripts which date from the beginning of the fourteenth century at the earliest. But this does not represent the date of their texts. These texts have already had a life of several centuries in oral tradition before being written down, during which they have naturally undergone many changes. Some of them are even recognizably the same as the Irish stories, but even when this is so they differ in their settings, in their combinations, in their milieux. The old Irish gods reappear here, but euphemerized or given mortal form, and they have become heroes of different stories. Of course Wales had been a Christian country for centuries. The marvel is that the Welsh retained and related these stories of the old heathen gods in a recognizable form at all.

The finest specimens of these Welsh stories are preserved in two Welsh collections: the *White Book of Rhydderch* and the *Red Book of Hergest*. In addition the MSS. Peniarth 6, 7, 14 and 16 contain portions of different stories, some of which were written down a century before the *White Book*, and some of these must be a good deal older still. Eleven stories are generally comprised under the term *Mabinogion* since Lady Charlotte Guest used this title for her translations for the *Red Book of Hergest* and the *Hanes Taliesin*. Of these the first four, generally spoken of as the 'Four Branches', comprise *Pwyll*, *Branwen*, *Manawydan* and *Math*. But there are also some short ones, *The Dream of Macsen Wledig* and *Llys and Llefelys*, the lengthy *Kulhwch and Olwen*, the briefer *Dream of Rhonabwy* and the three later Arthurian romances of the *Lady of the Fountain*, *Peredur* and *Geraint ap Erbin*.

The first four, which we may call the *Mabinogion* proper, form a unity, despite the infinite variety of their subject matter. The life history of Pryderi runs like a silken skein throughout, at times forming the underlying theme, at times slenderly linking the various episodes which may be developed as important stories in their own right. Thus we have *Pwyll* who is the hero of the *baile* (cf. p. 183 above), and the story relates his year in Annwn, the supernatural realm. In *Branwen* we have the marriage of Branwen to the King of Ireland, and her sorrows and the revenge of her brother, and the wonderful story of the magic of his severed head. In *Manawydan fab Llyr* is the marriage of Manawydan to Rhiannon, the mother of Pryderi and queen of Annwn, and the adventures of the impetuous young Pryderi in Lloegr (England), and of Pryderi himself and Rhiannon in the Waste Land, and the ultimate triumph of Manawydan over the bishop and his enchanted mice. The story of *Math* is from start to finish the story of a dynasty of magicians, and their final triumph over the hostility of Math's sister Arianrod. All these stories of the *Mabinogion* have their setting in the west coast of Wales, and the original author is believed to have been a native of Dyfed writing in the second half of the eleventh century; but this fails to explain the charm of the work which defies analysis or description. The stories are neither of the past nor the present. Perhaps of all our ancient traditional prose stories they are the most essentially Celtic – as difficult to analyse as their art motifs, which are partly human, but not men or women such as we know, existing partly in a world of fancy, and only partly in convincing reality. It is a world transformed by the magic of the imagination, only half realized by the world of reality which our more scientific age recognizes.

This magical Celtic atmosphere recurs in the other *Mabinogion* stories but more sporadically. Surprisingly enough it has transformed the known world of the Roman Emperor Macsen Wledig (Magnus Maximus) into something like a Celtic fairy tale, and a similar transformation of reality has affected *Llys and Llefelys*. The dream convention serves as a medieval transformation between these worlds of reality and fancy. In the *Dream of Rhonabwy*, the vision is encased in a typical dream convention, where King Arthur is the centre of the picture, though with him at his court, surprisingly enough, we find Owain son of Urien, a hero of north Britain, and a host of Arthur's counsellors from all parts of the heroic world – from Norway, and Denmark, and from many parts of Greece – a kind of heroic catalogue in disguise. But we find nothing artificial in the arrangement. It is a purely Celtic dream where any combination is possible and quite in place. Moreover Arthur himself is not the opponent of the Romans, nor on the other hand the hero of the romances of chivalry to whom the Normans have accustomed us, but a British king, rough, a little incomprehensible, perhaps owing something to the panegyric poetry of the bard Cadyrieith; 'but never a man was there might understand that song save Cadyrieith himself, except that it was in praise of Arthur'. But we are in the beginning of the Middle Ages, and the older literary conventions are already fading: 'And this story is called the *Dream of Rhonabwy*. And this is the reason why: no one, neither bard nor story-teller knows the Dream without a book – by reason of the number of colours that were on the horses . . . and their trappings, and on the precious mantles, and the magic stones.'

The three romances, the *Lady of the Fountain*, *Peredur ap Efrawe*, and *Geraint ap Erbin*, are all strongly transformed by Norman French influence, and though the thesis itself is native, or so it is now generally believed, it has been overlaid with the continental influence of a later age and foreign style – so much so that the rough British beginnings have been almost lost to us. Not so the *Kulhwch and Olwen*. Here the Welsh *cyfarwydd* has had a free hand, and the story is told with all the abandon and the boundless imaginative vigour of the Celtic artist. Yet there is, as always in Celtic art, a guiding spirit in its very freedom.

There are people and motifs which we recognize from folk-tale, like the giant Yspaddadyn Penkawr; the hero, Kulhwch himself, who loves his daughter but must perform well-nigh impossible tasks before obtaining her; favourite literary motifs like *Dinnsenchas*, and place-name motifs, such as the Hunting of the Twrch Trwyth. Then there is the world of Arthur, whose heroes all reappear here in an ordered framework, yet in Celtic fluidity – the form is here adapted to the theme, not the theme to the framework. The Norman fashion which has transformed the romances has left *Kulhwch and Olwen* untouched. Was the *cyfarwydd* defeated by its very wealth of imagination, by its bewildering transformations of scene and theme? Or was the story simply not known to him, or not appreciated by him? It is the most unequivocally Welsh of all the stories in the *Mabinogion*.

As we close the pages of the *Mabinogion* we leave behind the ancient Celtic world. With the Teutonic world which succeeded it we enter an ordered domain, where cause and effect follow one another with mathematical certainty and precision, where events follow one another in logical sequence, where the established time sequence can be relied on, where an established geography limits human journeys, where men and animals behave according to prescribed laws. In the earlier Celtic order all these conditions resolve themselves and are recreated by the imagination, not always by fixed laws, but by the tradition of a poet's theme or his will to reshape his subject. Memory is flexible, the spoken word more fluid than history. All this was inevitably changed with the introduction of writing. With the Roman conquest of Gaul, with the encroaching influence of the Teutonic people, the change of outlook was a radical one. The spaces of reality widened and the time limit became fixed. Time and space alike contrasted with the inevitable curtailment of the human imagination, and knowledge became synonymous with precision. We are on the threshold of the modern world.

Index

Figures in **bold type** in parentheses refer to numbered plates and *not* to pages

PENGUIN HISTORY

The Germans Gordon A. Craig

An intimate study of a complex and fascinating nation by 'one of the ablest and most distinguished American historians of modern Germany' – Hugh Trevor-Roper

Imperial Spain 1469–1716 J. H. Elliot

A brilliant modern study of the sudden rise of a barren and isolated country to the greatest power on earth, and of its equally sudden decline. 'Outstandingly good' – *Daily Telegraph*

British Society 1914–1945 John Stevenson

A major contribution to the *Penguin Social History of Britain*, which 'will undoubtedly be the standard work for students of modern Britain for many years to come' – *The Times Educational Supplement*

A History of Christianity Paul Johnson

'Masterly ... It is a huge and crowded canvas – a tremendous theme running through twenty centuries of history – a cosmic soap opera involving kings and beggars, philosophers and crackpots, scholars and illiterate *exaltés*, popes and pilgrims and wild anchorites in the wilderness' – Malcolm Muggeridge

The Penguin History of Greece A. R. Burn

Readable, erudite, enthusiastic and balanced, this one-volume history of Hellas sweeps the reader along from the days of Mycenae and the splendours of Athens to the conquests of Alexander and the final dark decades.

A History of Latin America George Pendle

'Ought to be compulsory reading in every sixth form ... this book is right on target' – *Sunday Times*. 'A beginner's guide to the continent ... lively, and full of anecdote' – *Financial Times*